Working-Class Masculini
Australian Higher Educa

CW00515020

This book takes a critical view of masculinities through an investigation of first-in-family males transitioning to higher education. Drawing on six in-depth longitudinal case studies, the focus is on how young men from working-class backgrounds engage with complex social inequalities, as well as the various capitals they draw upon to ensure their success. Through the longitudinal approach, the work problematises the rhetoric of 'poverty of aspirations' and foregrounds how class and gender influence the lives and futures of these young men. The book demonstrates how the aspirations of these young men are influenced by a complex interplay between race/ethnicity, religion, masculinity and social class. Finally, the book draws connections between the lived experiences of the participants and the implications for policy and practice in higher education.

Drawn from a larger research project, each case study compels the reader to think critically regarding masculinities in relation to social practices, institutional arrangements and cultural ideologies. This is essential reading for those interested in widening participation in higher education, gender theory/masculinities, longitudinal research and social justice.

Garth Stahl, Ph.D. (@GarthStahl) is an Associate Professor in the School of Education at the University of Queensland and Research Fellow, Australian Research Council (DECRA). His research interests lie on the nexus of neoliberalism and socio-cultural studies of education, identity, equity/inequality, and social change. Currently, his research projects and publications encompass theoretical and empirical studies of learner identities, gender and youth, sociology of schooling in a neoliberal age, gendered subjectivities, equity and difference, and educational reform.

Routledge Research in Educational Equality and Diversity

For more information about this series, please visit: www.routledge.com/ Routledge-Research-in-Educational-Equality-and-Diversity/book-series/ RREED

Working-Class Masculinities in Australian Higher Education

Policies, Pathways and Progress

Garth Stahl

Routledge
Taylor & Francis Group

LONDON AND NEW YORK

First published 2022
by Routledge
2 Park Square, Milton Park, Abingdon, Oxon OX14 4RN

and by Routledge
605 Third Avenue, New York, NY 10158

Routledge is an imprint of the Taylor & Francis Group, an informa business

© 2022 Garth Stahl

British Library Cataloguing-in-Publication Data
A catalogue record for this book is available from the British Library

Library of Congress Cataloging-in-Publication Data
A catalog record has been requested for this book

ISBN: 978-0-367-51509-6 (hbk)
ISBN: 978-0-367-51510-2 (pbk)
ISBN: 978-1-003-05418-4 (ebk)

Typeset in Galliard
by SPi Global, India

Contents

Acknowledgements

I would like to thank the Australian Research Council for funding this research.

Glossary

ATAR   In Australia, students receive an ATAR (Australian Tertiary Admission Rank) which is calculated by the state's university admissions centre and provides a 'percentile score' between 0 and 99.95 which denotes a student's ranking relative to their peers upon completion of their secondary education.

Bonus points   Also known as 'adjustment factors' which boost the ATAR to gain entry into universities and other tertiary institutions.

Centrelink   Australian government agency which delivers a range of government payments and services to those in need.

First-in-family   While there are a number of definitions, first-in-family commonly refers to students who are first in their immediate family to attend university.

HSC   Higher School Certificate which signifies successful completion of senior high school level studies in New South Wales. The comparable qualification in South Australia is the SACE.

Year 12   Final year of compulsory schooling in Australia

Youth Allowance   An income support payment available to unemployed young people aged 16–21 (aged 18–24 if a full-time student or on an apprenticeship).

Introduction

Internationally, we are experiencing an expansion of research focused on first-in-family and first-generation students in higher education. While there is no consensus regarding how first-in-family and first-generation students are defined (see Nguyen & Nguyen, 2018), evidence suggests that this population experiences a variety of class and identity barriers (Mallman, 2017). Furthermore, when compared to their middle-class counterparts, they are more likely to struggle academically, change their degrees and withdraw from their courses (Scevak et al., 2015). The study of those from first-in-family backgrounds is not new. In 1989, London interviewed 15 working-class students who experienced the challenging process of 'breaking away' from their families and examined how they attempted to reconcile their home communities with their university settings. However, more recent scholarship has extended London's work, highlighting the heterogeneity of this population (Capannola & Johnson, 2020; Jack, 2016) where there are, according to Patfield et al. (2020), 'degrees of being first' depending on 'a wide range of capital reserves' which determines their access, how they transition and what they get out of the experience.

While research has documented the ways working-class men in Australia come to university later in life (O'Shea et al., 2017; Stahl & Loeser, 2018), young men completing their final year of compulsory schooling are the least likely to go on to attend university in Australia (Lamb et al., 2015). Connell (2005a) explains that adolescence for young men may be 'understood as a period in which the embodiment of masculinity takes new forms and moves towards adult patterns' (p. 15), where adolescence should be seen 'not as a single moment in development but as a loosely-defined period of life in which certain types of encounters occur' (p. 18). However, as Wetherell and Edley (1999) demonstrate, the term 'masculinities' is rather vague and imprecise, especially at the micro level. While masculinities are always 'classed' and 'racialized' (Archer, 2003), a plethora of masculinities are enacted and experienced as young men shift from their secondary schools into university study. This is what Martino and Pallotta-Chiarolli (2003) call 'diverse masculinities' in terms of sexuality, disability, ethnicity/race and place.

However, such enactments may be constrained by what Connell (2005b) calls 'hegemonic industrial working-class masculinity' which signifies the performance of solidarity, strength and dominance. As ways of being a boy are performed (Butler, 1990), arguably, both 'softer' and more 'transgressive' options coexist alongside the dominant hegemonic forms (see Frosh et al., 2002; Pattman et al., 1998). Researching identities *in transition* longitudinally allows for an exploration of identities and masculine subjectivities that are both fluid and constrained, where individuals come to occupy different social categories often in relation to space and place. After all, masculinities are 'developed in specific institutional contexts in relation to and against each other' (Mac an Ghaill, 1994, p. 61). A change of institution – in this case from secondary school to university – involves a change in social relations, which has significant implications for the 'way masculinities are played out and validated for other men' (Westwood, 1990, p. 60).

In their research on 'matriculating masculinities', Harris and Harper (2015) call attention to how little is known about how lifeworlds inform the transition of young men from high school to postsecondary education. Such transitions require young men to draw upon personal and family resources to navigate pathways they have little familiarity with. Burke (2009, p. 84) writes: 'Masculine subjectivity as a concept helps to understand the ways that individual men construct their identities as situated subjects within complex social and cultural networks and sites, such as schools and colleges.' There is agency in how men come to construct their identities and this changes significantly as they encounter new experiences and form relationships with a wider range of masculinities. Collinson and Hearn (2005) write:

> Masculinity or masculinities can be understood as those combinations of signs that say and show someone is a man. Difference and the social construction of difference (such as that which differentiates men and masculinities according to religion, age, size, class, sexuality, ethnicity, occupation, and so on) are important bases through which gendered asymmetrical power between men, and between men and women, are often constructed and reproduced.
>
> (p. 295)

Scholars who focus on the pressure for young men to conform contend that, while a range of masculinities exist and are recognised, many boys of school age enact masculine performances aligned with both societal and institutional ideals (see Imms, 2007; Whitehead, 2003) and a disjuncture occurs when the societal and institutional ideals are not aligned (Stahl, 2015). According to Imms (2007) stereotypes regarding masculinity appear to carry significant weight: young men can and do manipulate the parameters, but only to a certain extent.

Therefore, the *First-in-Family Males Project* – which the data in this book draws from – not only considers how participants have been worked on in terms of school-based gender regimes (Frosh et al., 2002; Mac an Ghaill, 1994) but also how they disentangle themselves from such regimes in the post-school year (Alexander, 2019; Nichols & Stahl, 2017). This normative process brings forth notions of 'growth' and 'maturity'. The ways in which the participants distance themselves from their schoolboy masculinities have significant implications for how they enact and perform masculinities during this transitional time.

The transition to university can be a time of substantial identity work, especially for students from working-class backgrounds. Lehmann (2009) writes:

> Given that high levels of formal education are increasingly seen as essential in any aspect of post-industrial life and that working-class youths indeed continue to face substantial barriers to university access and completion, it is important to ask not only what contributes to the persistence of these barriers but also to overcoming them.
>
> (p. 137)

As these young men enter university, they do not leave their lifeworlds at the classroom door. For working-class young men, identifying with working-class status 'can be a source of respectability and pride' (Nixon, 2009, p. 308), though this is not always the case. All of the participants in the *First-in-Family Males Project* intended to attend university but not all were able to make university life work for them. The six case studies presented provide a glimpse into the struggles of the participants and how ultimately they did make university work for them. I am interested in their reasons for attending, their expectations of university and how these changed over time-existing in tandem with the development of their maturity, as well as their entrance into manhood. These experiences reveal the social changes influencing working-class masculinities and what it means to become upwardly mobile.

In *Guyland* (2008) Kimmel argues that college-going men need to contend with the Peter-Pan mindset in which, he writes, ' ...they party hard but are soft on studying. They slip through the academic cracks, another face in a large lecture hall, getting by with little effort and less commitment' (p. 3). This is an interesting assertion and one that contrasts with the findings from the *First-in-Family Males Project*. The boys I spoke with worked long hours on both their academics and in part-time jobs, striving to excel in multiple areas of their life while also expressing a committment to familial responsibilities and girlfriends. The participants I spoke with felt they did not have the time to engage in any sort of behaviour we would associate with Kimmel's 'Guyland'. Instead, they embraced the demands of labour and study while investing in relationships. They spent these formative years balancing a plethora of responsibilities.

The experiences of the young men discussed in this book are significantly influenced by a dramatic restructuring of university life, with what Blackmore (1997, p. 92) calls 'lean-and-mean' pedagogies of fewer contact hours with teaching staff and large class sizes. As Pötschulat et al. (2021) note, the student experience – or contemporary 'studenthood' – is framed within the neoliberalisation of higher education, which promotes a particular normative conception of what it means to be a student. Therefore, in documenting how they navigate their pathways, we are able to see some of the ways they contend with barriers that may, to varying degrees, place them in a vulnerable position. The words of first-in-family young men provide a glimpse of their fluctuating attitudes concerning 'success' and 'failure' and are also indicative of the imbrication between meritocracy as an ideological discourse and the wider social structures shaping inequality. Or, as Lehmann (2009) writes, 'working-class status and educational attainment is characterized by a preoccupation with access barriers, failure, economic and cultural deprivation, and active resistance' and, as a result, we know less about how 'working-class educational success' is realised (p. 137). Researching identities *in transition* longitudinally allows for an exploration of identities and masculine subjectivities as both fluid and constrained where individuals come to occupy different social categories.

Purpose of the research

Despite a substantial policy agenda to widen participation of students from non-traditional backgrounds, these students remain severely under-represented in the Australian higher education system. Common barriers to university participation include lack of personal connections, and social and cultural capital (Reay et al., 2005); the perception that university is boring and an extension of school (Alloway & Gilbert, 2004); parental expectations; limited course offerings; and a strong desire to pursue full-time employment immediately after compulsory schooling.

According to Gale and Parker (2013) students from low-socioeconomic-status (SES) backgrounds 'typically have diminished navigational capacities – the result of their limited archives of experience – with which to negotiate their way towards their aspirations' (p. 51). We know low-SES students often experience education with low levels of the material and cultural resources that aid educational success (Reay et al., 2005, p. 24). They are likely to leave university without their degrees and may struggle to integrate socially (Lehmann, 2007). This may limit their acquisition of social and cultural capital, which has lifelong consequences for family formation, job acquisition and network development. However, in researching how aspirations interact with SES in reference to occupational certainty, prestige, choice and justification, Gore et al. (2015) have demonstrated that students from low-SES backgrounds have stronger financial motivation, indicating aspirations for occupational futures that provide financial security. With this in mind, research continues to demonstrate that low-SES students have high aspirations but 'these aspirations cannot be realised with the lower school achievement levels and completion rates recorded for these students' (Harvey et al., 2016, p. 78). Extending this connection, Lehmann (2009) notes that working-class and first-in-family students associate their trajectory and experience 'with working-class virtues of hard work and value for money' (p. 146), often adopting the instrumental view of university as a means to an end.

First-in-family males, as an equity group, remain severely under-represented in Australian higher education (Lamb et al., 2015). The *First-in-Family Males Project* considers how first-in-family males frame their decision to attend university and how they transition, often defying considerable odds to realise their aspirations. Working-class young men have historically engaged in an uneasy relationship with their education. As traditional social and economic structures have disappeared, working-class young men have engaged in identity work within rapidly changing discourses (Nayak, 2003). Reflecting on identity, Stuart Hall (2000, p. 17) writes: 'Precisely because identities are constructed within, not outside, discourse, we need to understand them as produced in specific historical and institutional sites within specific discursive formations and practices, by specific enunciative strategies.' Or, as McLeod (2000, p. 503) writes, it is 'not simply an analysis of individual biographies, how one subjectivity is produced and formed and changed over time', but rather subjectivities should be considered in relation to institutional practices and discourses which influence biographical narratives. In considering this point in relation to the research questions, I am interested in how the masculine subjectivities of these young men are constructed in relation to changing social, economic and institutional contexts, and how they are agentic in ensuring not only their success but their sense of belonging. As Somers (1992) notes, narratives produced by people must have grand themes connected to 'the happenings of the social world' and individuals 'arrange them in some order' to make sense of their place in the world (p. 602).

The study of masculinity in Australia has also highlighted that many men suffer from poor mental health and are 'prone to protracted and serious episodes of loneliness' (Franklin et al., 2018, p. 124). Research suggests men of all ages may struggle to express their emotions and connect with others (Flood, 2005) and are less likely to seek support (Patulny, 2013). Franklin and Tranter (2008) note that, in conducting their research, it was relatively easy to access men's experiences of loneliness – duration, frequency and intensity – but it was significantly more problematic for men to identify causes.

By focusing on longitudinal case studies of six first-in-family males as they *transition to* and *experience* Australian university study in different locales and institutions, we glimpse how such a transition is mapped onto the shift from boyhood to manhood. Or, more specifically, we can see how the shift from boyhood to manhood is experienced in relation to the construction of capital, subjectivities, interaction with institutions and, of course, the tension between agency and structure. In the transition from secondary schools to university, there are high stakes for learning and often a relentless focus on academic achievement where there is the potential to depreciate 'emotional capital while simultaneously augmenting cultural capital' (Reay, 2004, p. 69). This can generate psychic costs for students from underprivileged backgrounds, particularly young men (see Stahl, 2015). In enhancing our understanding of the learner identities of working-class boys, research suggests a high-stakes environment can undermine high aspirations, leading boys to present a subjectivity of 'ordinariness' where they feel comfortable occupying a middling position, devoid of distinction (Stahl, 2013).

The six case studies presented in this monograph are focused on questions of subjectivity and the discursive construction of masculinity. The identity vectors (e.g. race, class, ethnicity, disability) are relational and situated – often, though not always, interlocking at various points in time to produce a certain construction of the self. These are not reflections of true experience but instead 'partial and discursive constructions' (Burke, 2009, p. 84). Each of the young men have limited 'exposure to the middle-class habitus and "class rules"' associated with more affluent or elite forms of masculinity (Giazitzoglu, 2014, para 8.5) which serves as a contributing factor in how they come to construct themselves within the university environment. As Connell (2005b) notes, 'The making of working-class masculinity on the factory floor has different dynamics from the making of middle-class masculinity in the air-conditioned office' (p. 36). Therefore, in presenting this longitudinal case study, I attempt to tease out how working-class masculinities interact with institutional arrangements as the young men come to exist within certain temporal spaces and what this means for the study of selfhood.

Research project overview

The *First-in-Family Males Project* was designed to document longitudinally the diversity of experiences of first-in-family males from a wide range of backgrounds, geographical locations and school sites (Stahl, 2020; Stahl & McDonald, 2019; Stahl, McDonald & Stokes, 2020; Stahl, McDonald & Young, 2021; Stahl & Young, 2019). Students at the secondary level who are high achieving can often find the transition to university problematic, resulting in deferring or dropping out, and thus a loss of talent. Two low-SES urban regions were selected for study – the northern suburbs of Adelaide and the western suburbs of Sydney – enabling the research to account for different demographic, cultural, curricular and educational histories. While there is a tendency to conflate first-generation status with low-income backgrounds, all of the young men recruited resided in two of the poorest urban neighbourhoods in Australia, though the two areas are different in terms of cultural diversity, population density and economic opportunities. Furthermore, both areas have significant percentages of new immigrant populations (e.g. Chinese, Pasifika) and those from refugee backgrounds (e.g. Sudanese, Somali, Afghani). Aligned with national trends, between 2011 and 2016 both areas have seen a steady rise in low-SES participation in higher education (Koshy, 2017) and all the participants lived within an hour from a university campus. The two areas have different economic climates. The northern suburbs of Adelaide are experiencing post-industrialisation with the closing of Holden car manufacturing. In contrast, the CBD of Sydney is an economic powerhouse and, while the participants lived on the urban fringes, they could still benefit from some of the opportunities their proximity afforded them.

Using recorded data across three different school sites in both areas (faith, independent and state), I worked closely with secondary school leadership teams to identified potential first-in-family males and to recruit volunteers from those young men aspiring to university at the end of secondary school ($n = 42$). These young men attended schools where few students went on to university. The diversity of school sites is important as students from low-SES backgrounds in Australia tend to be concentrated in state schools, which tend to have fewer resources and a greater focus on vocational studies (Kenway, 2013; Teese, 2006). Complementing research by Patfield et al. (2020), the participants were prospective first-in-family students aspiring to university. Borrowing the wording of Clark (1960), the students were *warming up* to the aspiration that an undergraduate university degree would potentially frame their future. The study primarily used semi-structured interviews to generate rich data. During the last few weeks of their final year of secondary school I conducted two or three 40-minute semi-structured initial interviews with the aim of getting to know the participants. The *First-in-Family Males Project* did not just focus on the boys' aspirations in terms of their education and future employment – instead, we spoke about their lifeworlds, their values and motivation, their interests and hobbies, as well as their peers, romantic relationships and familial responsibilities.

Follow-up interviews were then conducted every six months for the two following years regardless of whether the participants were able to make university work for them. Therefore, the study followed participants from their final year in compulsory schooling through the transition to the post-school year. Interviewing students at university allows for insights into what Mallman (2017) refers to as 'the wonder, anxiety, excitement and struggle of being in the moment' (p. 239). Before each of the follow-up interviews, I always listened to the previous interview to re-familiarise myself with the participant's biography, family life and what questions resonated with them. McLeod (2003) writes of the importance of re-reading/listening to interviews to foreground 'the constitutive effects of social processes and historical locations' as there is a risk of 'flattening out the emotional and psychological dimensions of subjectivity' (p. 209). Where possible, throughout the research, I drew on feminist methodologies to reduce power inequalities between myself and my participants in pursuit of a more collaborative and mutually constituting relationship between researcher and subject (Kenway & McLeod, 2004; Stahl, 2016).

As the research was longitudinal, I made an effort to build relationships with the participants, both to keep them invested in the study as well as to garner richer data. Furthermore, the use of longitudinal interviews meant that the students became socialised to a repetition of norms and values associated with interview protocols. Scholars have argued that 'talking' can be viewed as an act associated with the feminine and that young men can feel anxious about engaging in discussion concerning themselves and their experiences (Francis, 2000; Robb, 2007). The factors that inform one's aspirations are multifaceted and complex. The repetition of format and the general strategies of rapport building allowed me to open up spaces to speak about the nuances of the experiencing of *being* and *becoming* university students – and entering into an upwardly mobile trajectory.

Structure of the book

This monograph is divided into three parts. Part 1 is an account of widening participation in Australian higher education and provides a brief but critical account of current equity policies, programs and pathways. This is followed by an overview of some of the themes present in research on masculinities in higher education with a specific focus on working-class masculinities. I also elaborate further on the research study itself and how the research is positioned in relation to other scholarship on the study of masculinities longitudinally and how I worked to build rapport with the participants.

Part 2 presents the six in-depth case studies. I trace the boys' experiences and aspirations over three years, foregrounding the voices of the participants. As they began to become socially mobile through the pursuit of higher education, each case study compels us to think critically about masculinities, aspirations, social practices and institutional arrangements. I focus specifically on the discursive construction of masculinity as well as the participants' sense of agency. While I primarily use theories of social class and gender to explore the formation and maintenance of participants' aspirations over a three-year period, I also consider other intersectional identity vectors with a specific focus on ethnicity. In studies of masculinities in education, case studies have provided insights into how normative school practices challenge boys' conceptions of masculinities, which has implications for how these boys come to see themselves in relation to their education (Keddie, 2006; Mac an Ghaill, 1994; Reay, 2002).

Sydney, New South Wales case studies

First, I present Lucas, who identifies as Anglo-Australian and is the son of a self-employed plumber. Lucas is an adept speaker, able to articulate his opinions with a certain confidence which sets him apart from the other boys in the study. His story centres around an unwavering aspirational trajectory and strong sense of entitlement which gains him access to elite spaces where he largely feels at home, though such spaces arguably contrast with his home life. I focus on how Lucas's sense of entitlement was bolstered through his experiences as a learner in elite spaces and how he mediated the competitive university culture through a disposition towards traditional working-class values.

Second, I focus on Campbell, a Chinese-Australian young man who attended an all-boys, low-fee-paying private school in the western suburbs of Sydney. Campbell gained admittance to a respected university in Sydney's CBD which appealed to him because of its reputation and Catholic culture. However, Campbell deferred after the first semester of university because he was fortunate to secure employment in a call centre where he excelled and gained important insights into himself as well as the professional culture of Sydney. As we will see, working at the call centre did not side-track him but instead enhanced his aspirations.

Third, I discuss Rashid, a Pakistani Australian who attended a fee-paying Islamic school in the western suburbs of Sydney. Rashid primarily lived a cloistered life in a primarily Muslim community. The Islamic school he attended, which was located close to his parent's home, shares a site with the local mosque. He spoke of his uneasiness about his academic progress. His lack of self-confidence sat alongside familial and cultural pressures from his parents and grandparents to attend a prestigious university, which he achieved. Rashid's experience highlights that, in order to participate in higher education, he needed to balance a conservative Muslim upbringing with Australian mainstream values.

Adelaide, South Australia case studies

The fourth case study concerns Manny, who attended a state school in the northern suburbs of Adelaide and who is of Pacific Islander heritage and the eldest male in his family. He is very family focused and openly frames his aspirational trajectory in terms of his pride in his heritage. At the working-class university he attended, he planned to study engineering, which is highly competitive and contrasts greatly with his easy-going and casual nature. Manny, whose Australian Tertiary Admission Rank (ATAR) was bolstered by his socioeconomic and ethnic status, muddled through this program. As he confronted various barriers to his learning, he did not seek institutional forms of support, instead preferring his social networks.

The fifth case study examines Dominic, an Indigenous male, who attended a public school in the northern suburbs of Adelaide. Dominic, the eldest in his family, is tenacious and determined to succeed at university. While he likely could have enrolled at the most prestigious university in the state, he chose to attend the university closest to his home. His journey highlights the importance of real-life experience in structuring one's aspirations. In terms of his masculinity, Dominic does not identify strongly with his Indigenous heritage and instead seems fixed on an individualised discourse of choice and perseverance.

The last case study focuses on Logan who became a science student at a prestigious university. Logan presents a 'happy-go-lucky' subjectivity and he was initially unfazed by the highly competitive university environment. However, this wavered a bit as he progressed through his course, where he struggled to manage the identity negotiations that are involved with becoming a university student, his work in the service sector and the demands of academic study. While the study of marine biology was important to him and he did well, he seemed isolated at university and was largely unfulfilled by the endeavour, instead searching for other sources of inspiration.

In Part 3 I look comparatively across the six case studies, concentrating on changes in masculine subjectivities through a comparative analysis where I focus on the following overlapping themes: status identity (composed of narrative, social and future identity); how the participants became agentic; their sense of belonging; and their experiences with struggle and isolation. These I consider to be important dimensions of upwardly mobile working-class masculinities. Through this analytical approach I consider the implications for policy and practice in an effort to identify what could be done to improve the experiences of young men of first-in-family status.

There is a call for more work that counteracts the notion that first-in-family students all negotiate a similar set of 'problems' (Patfield et al., 2020). At the same time, scholars in masculinity studies (Hearn, 2018) have also asserted there needs to be more attention to documenting the various patterns of masculinities where – even when accounting for socioeconomic background – we see a wide plurality influenced by economic and social change (Alexander, 2019; Gorman Murray & Hopkins, 2014; Kenway et al., 2006; MacLeod, 2009). In the case studies I do not intend to encapsulate the first-in-family experience – rather I selected them from the wider study to illustrate the *variations in experience* of 'first-in-family' males. While certainly 'individual choices, differences, and experiences still exist' for students of first-in-family status, Wong (2018) writes, educational trajectories for the most part 'align with people from similar social upbringings and experiences' (p. 2). Academic success is not random but very much patterned in accordance with the lived experience of social class. Social mobility via an educational pathway involves a working against the grain.

The intention here that is that each case study serves as an example of an upwardly mobile masculinity in Australia today and – in assembling them together – they capture the diversity of such experiences. As this is a study of widening participation, the analytical focus is on agency, defined as the 'capacity to act intentionally, emerging between structures and aspirations as the result of a process based on reflection, compromise, negotiation and resourcefulness' (Tomanović, 2018, p. 357). Therefore, in foregrounding agency, I consider how the experiences of the participants speak to the complexity of widening participation, social mobility and the shift from boyhood to manhood. Comparing the six case studies furthers an understanding of what motivates working-class young men to become socially mobile, how they are able to make university work for them (to varying degrees) and the ways in which they draw on various resources in order to ensure their success.

References

Alexander, P. (2019). Boys from the Bronx, men from Manhattan: Gender, aspiration and imagining a (neoliberal) future after high school in New York City. In C. Beverley & P. Michele (Eds.), *Interrogating the neoliberal lifecycle: The limits of success* (pp. 39–67). Springer Nature/Palgrave Macmillan.

Alloway, N., & Gilbert, P. (2004). Shifting discourses about gender in higher education enrolments: Retrieving marginalised voices. *International Journal of Qualitative Studies in Education, 17*(1), 103–118.

Archer, L. (2003). *Race, masculinity and schooling: Muslim boys and education*. Open University Press.

Blackmore, J. (1997). Disciplining feminism: A look at gender-equity struggles in Australian higher education. In L. G. Romand & L. Eyre (Eds.), *Dangerous territories: Struggles for difference and equality in education* (pp. 75–96). Routledge.

Burke, P. J. (2009). Men accessing higher education: Theorizing continuity and change in relation to masculine subjectivities. *Higher Education Policy, 22,* 81–100.

Butler, J. (1990). *Gender trouble: Feminism and the subversion of identity,* Routledge.

Capannola, A. L., & Johnson, E. I. (2020). On being the first: The role of family in the experiences of first-generation college students. *Journal of Adolescent Research,* advance online publication. doi:10.1177/0743558420979144

Clark, B. R. 1960. The 'cooling out' function in higher education. *American Journal of Sociology, 65,* 569–576.

Collinson, D. L., & Hearn, J. (2005). Men and masculinities in work, organizations, and management. In M. Kimmel, J. Hearn, & R. W. Connell (Eds.), *Handbook of studies on men and masculinities* (pp. 289–310). Sage.

Connell, R. W. (2005a). Growing up masculine: Rethinking the significance of adolescence in the making of masculinities. *Irish Journal of Sociology, 14*(2), 11–28.

Connell, R. W. (2005b). *Masculinities* (2nd ed.). Blackwell.

Flood, M. (2005). *Mapping loneliness in Australia* (Discussion Paper 76). Australia Institute.

Francis, B. (2000). *Boys, girls and achievement: Addressing the classroom issues.* Routledge Falmer.

Franklin, A., Barbosa Neves, B., Hookway, N., Patulny, R., Tranter, B., & Jaworski, K. (2018). Towards an understanding of loneliness among Australian men: Gender cultures, embodied expression and the social bases of belonging. *Journal of Sociology, 55*(1), 124–142.

Franklin, A. S., & Tranter, B. (2008). *Loneliness in Australia* (Occasional Paper 13). Housing and Community Research Unit, University of Tasmania.

Frosh, S., Phoenix, A., & Pattman, R. (2002). *Young masculinities: Understanding boys in contemporary society.* Palgrave.

Gale, T., & Parker, S. (2013). *Widening participation in Australian higher education: Report to the Higher Education Funding Council for England (HEFCE) and the Office of Fair Access (OFFA), England.* CFE (Research and Consulting) and Edge Hill University.

Giazitzoglu, A. (2014). Qualitative upward mobility, the mass-media and 'posh' masculinity in contemporary north-east Britain: A micro sociological case-study. *Sociological Research Online, 19*(2), 1–11.

Gore, J., Holmes, K., Smith, M., Southgate, E., & Albright, J. (2015). Socioeconomic status and the career aspirations of Australian school students: Testing enduring assumptions. *Australian Educational Researcher, 42*(2), 155–177.

Gorman Murray, A., & Hopkins, P. (2014). *Masculinities and place.* Ashgate.

Hall, S. (2000). Who needs 'identity'? In P. du Gay & P. Redman (Eds.), *Identity: A reader* (pp. 15–30). Sage.

Harris, F., & Harper, S. R. (2015). Matriculating masculinity: Understanding undergraduate men's precollege gender socialization. *Journal of the First-Year Experience & Students in Transition, 27*(2), 49–65.

Harvey, A., Andrewartha, L., & Burnheim, C. (2016). Out of reach? University for people from low socio-economic status backgrounds. In A. Harvey, C. Burnheim, & M. Brett (Eds.), *Student equity in Australian higher education: Twenty-five years of a fair chance for all* (pp. 69–87). Springer.

Hearn, J. (2018). Moving men, changing men, othering men: On politics, care and representation. *Quaderns de l'Institut Català d'Antropologia, 34,* 30–53.

Imms, W. (2007). Boys engaging masculinities. *Journal of Interdisciplinary Gender Studies, 10*(2), 30–45.

Jack, A. A. (2016). (No) harm in asking: Class, acquired cultural capital, and academic engagement at an elite university. *Sociology of Education, 89*(1), 1–19.

Keddie, A. (2006). Fighting, anger, frustration and tears: Matthew's story of hegemonic masculinity. *Oxford Review of Education, 32*(4), 521–534.

Kenway, J. (2013). Challenging inequality in Australian schools: Gonski and beyond. *Discourse: Studies in the Cultural Politics of Education, 34*(2), 286–308.

Kenway, J., Kraack, A., & Hickey-Moody, A. (2006). *Masculinity beyond the metropolis.* Palgrave.

Kenway, J., & McLeod, J. (2004). Bourdieu's reflexive sociology and 'spaces of points of view': Whose reflexivity, which perspective? *British Journal of Sociology of Education, 25*(4), 525–544.

Kimmel, M. (2008). *Guyland: The perilous world where boys become men.* HarperCollins.

Koshy, P. (2017). *Equity student participation in Australian higher education: 2011 to 2016.* National Centre for Student Equity in Higher Education, Curtin University.

Lamb, S., Jackson, J., Walstab, A., & Huo, S. (2015). *Educational opportunity in Australia 2015: Who succeeds and who misses out.* Mitchell Institute.

Lehmann, W. (2007). 'I just didn't feel like I fit in': The role of habitus in university drop-out decisions. *Canadian Journal of Higher Education, 37*, 89–110.

Lehmann, W. (2009). University as vocational education: Working-class students' expectations for university. *British Journal of Sociology of Education, 30*(2), 137–149.

London, H. B. (1989). Breaking away: A study of first-generation college students and their families. *American Journal of Education, 97*, 144–170.

Mac an Ghaill, M. (1994). *The making of men: Masculinities, sexualities and schooling.* Open University Press.

MacLeod, J. (2009). *Ain't no makin' it: Aspirations and attainment in a low-income neighborhood* (3rd ed.). Westview Press.

Mallman, M. (2017). The perceived inherent vice of working-class university students. *Sociological Review, 65*(2), 235–250.

Martino, W., & Pallotta-Chiarolli, M. (2003). *So what's a boy?* Open University Press.

McLeod, J. (2000). Subjectivity and schooling in a longitudinal study of secondary students. *British Journal of Sociology of Education, 21*(4), 501–521.

McLeod, J. (2003). Why we interview now – Reflexivity and perspective in longitudinal studies. *International Journal of Research Methodology, 6*(3), 201–211.

Nayak, A. (2003). 'Boyz to men': Masculinities, schooling and labour transitions in de-industrial times. *Educational Review, 55*(2), 147–159.

Nguyen, T.-H., & Nguyen, B. M. D. (2018). Is the 'first-generation student' term useful for understanding inequality? The role of intersectionality in illuminating the implications of an accepted – yet unchallenged – term. *Review of Research in Education, 42*(1), 146–176.

Nichols, S., & Stahl, G. (2017). 'Gotta get that laziness out of me': Negotiating masculine aspirational subjectivities in the transition from school to university in Australia. In G. Stahl, J. Nelson, & D. O. Wallace (Eds.), *Masculinity and aspiration in the era of neoliberal education: International perspectives* (pp. 166–184). Routledge.

Nixon, D. (2009). 'I can't put a smiley face on': Working-class masculinity, emotional labour and service work in the 'New Economy'. *Gender, Work & Organization, 16*(3), 300–322.

O'Shea, S., May, J., Stone, C., & Delahunty, J. (2017). *First-in-family students, university experience and family life motivations, transitions and participation.* Palgrave Macmillan.

Patfield, S., Gore, J., & Fray, L. (2020). Degrees of 'being first': Toward a nuanced understanding of first-generation entrants to higher education. *Educational Review*, advance online publication. doi:10.1080/00131911.2020.1740172

Pattman, R., Frosh, S., & Phoenix, A. (1998). Lads, machos and others: Developing 'boy-centred' research. *Journal of Youth Studies, 1*(2), 125–142.

Patulny, R. (2013, July 11). Don't be fooled, loneliness affects men too. *The Conversation.*

Pötschulat, M., Moran, M., & Jones, P. (2021). 'The student experience' and the remaking of contemporary studenthood: A critical intervention. *Sociological Review, 69*(1), 3–20. doi:10.1177/0038026120946677

Reay, D. (2002). Shaun's story: Troubling discourses on white working-class masculinities. *Gender and Education, 14*(3), 221–234.

Reay, D. (2004). Gendering Bourdieu's concepts of capitals? Emotional capital, women and social class. *Theory, Culture & Society, 20*(6), 57–74.

Reay, D., David, M. E., & Ball, S. (2005). *Degrees of choice: Social class, race and gender in higher education.* Institute of Education.

Robb, M. (2007). Gender. In M. J. Kehily (Ed.), *Understanding youth: Perspectives, identities and practices* (pp. 109–145). Sage.

Scevak, J., Southgate, E., Rubin, M., Macqueen, S., Douglas, H., & Williams, P. (2015). *Equity groups and predictors of academic success in higher education: A 2014 Student Equity in Higher Education Research Grants project.* National Centre for Student Equity in Higher Education, Curtin University. http://bit.ly/1FU4pgj

Somers, M. (1992). Narrativity, narrative identity, and social action: Rethinking English working-class formation. *Social Science History, 16*(4), 591–630.

Stahl, G. (2013). Habitus disjunctures, reflexivity and white working-class boys' conceptions of status in learner and social identities. *Sociological Research Online, 18*(3), 1–12. http://www.socresonline.org.uk/18/3/2.html

Stahl, G. (2015). *Aspiration, identity and neoliberalism: Educating white working-class boys.* Routledge.

Stahl, G. (2016). Relationship-building in research: Gendered identity construction in researcher–participant interaction. In M. R. M. Ward (Ed.), *Gendered identity construction in researcher–participant interaction* (pp. 145–164). Emerald.

Stahl, G. (2020). 'My little beautiful mess': A longitudinal study of working-class masculinity in transition. *NORMA: International Journal for Masculinity Studies, 15*(2), 145–161.

Stahl, G. D., & Loeser, C. (2018). 'My choice was not to become a tradesman, my choice was to go to uni': Australian working-class masculinities, widening participation and lifelong learning. *Education and Training, 60*(6), 608–619.

Stahl, G., & McDonald, S. (2019). Social capital and self-crafting: Comparing two case studies of first-in-family males navigating elite Australian universities. *International Journal of Inclusive Education*, advance online publication. doi:10.1 080/13603116.2019.1632945

Stahl, G., McDonald, S., & Stokes, J. (2020). 'I see myself as undeveloped': Supporting Indigenous first-in-family males in the transition to higher education. *Higher Education Research & Development, 39*(7), 1488–1501.

Stahl, G., McDonald, S., & Young, J. (2021). Possible selves in a transforming economy: Upwardly mobile working- class masculinities, service work and negotiated aspirations in Australia. *Work, Employment and Society, 35*(1), 97–115.

Stahl, G., & Young, J. (2019). 'ACE boys': Gender discourses and school effects in how first-in-family males aspire to Australian university life. In H. Cuervo & A. Miranda (Eds.), *Youth, inequality and social change in the Global South* (pp. 67–81). Springer.

Teese, R. (2006). Condemned to innovate. *Griffith Review, 11.* https://www.griffithreview.com/articles/condemned-to-innovate/

Tomanović, S. (2018). Reconstructing changes in agency in the young people's social biographies through longitudinal qualitative research. *Young, 27*(4), 355–372.

Westwood, S. (1990). Racism, black masculinity and the politics of space. In J. Headen & D. Morgan (Eds.), *Men, masculinities and social theory* (pp. 55–71). Unwin Hyman.

Wetherell, M., & Edley, N. (1999). Negotiating hegemonic masculinity: Imaginary positions and psycho-discursive practices. *Feminism & Psychology, 9*(3), 335–356.

Whitehead, J. M. (2003). Masculinity, motivation and academic success: A paradox. *Teacher Development, 7*(2), 287–310.

Wong, B. (2018). By chance or by plan? The academic success of nontraditional students in higher education. *AERA Open, 4*(2), 1–14.

Part 1

Overview

.

1 Australian higher education

Policies, pathways and progress

Concerted recent efforts in OECD countries to widen university options have been – and continue to be – largely driven by a global need to boost economic and global competitiveness (see Bradley et al., 2008; OECD, 2015). It would appear that access to higher education for all is a matter of global importance. Or, adopting a more cynical approach, Marginson (2016, p. 420) argues: 'Expanding higher education is also consistent with state political agendas. It is easier to create educational opportunities than jobs. It transfers responsibility for social outcomes from the state to educational institutions and families.' Despite substantial investment, higher education is not as diverse as it could be as institutions struggle to become more inclusive (Murray & Klinger, 2013). Wong (2018) writes that higher education 'is often projected as an opportunity for upward social mobility, especially for nontraditional students' (p. 5) though the challenges associated with entry into and success within university are often glossed over.

Policies in higher education define low-socioeconomic-status (low-SES) students based on the ABS estimates of Socio-Economic Index for Areas which uses 2011 Census data. Low-SES students come from the bottom 25% of Australian SA1s in a national ranking (ABS, 2015; Koshy, 2017). Socioeconomic background continues to be a strong predictor of academic success, from readiness for school to entry to university (Lamb et al., 2015). In an opinion piece in an Australian newspaper, Geoff Maslen (2009) writes: 'Students who have been to the top private schools and whose fathers hold degrees are five times more likely to win a place at university than those from working class backgrounds' (p. 12).

While there exists a global policy remit to 'increase access' and 'widen participation', most universities remain beholden to the middle and upper classes. Schooling in Australia is highly segregated along social, ethnic and racial lines (Gale & Parker, 2013; Lamb et al., 2015) and, according to the Gonski Review on school funding, the quality of schooling available is distorted by severely inequitable funding structures (Kenway, 2013). A recent analysis of Longitudinal Surveys of Australian Youth data indicated that school attributes (e.g. school type and student population) are responsible for almost 20% of the Australian Tertiary Admission Rank (ATAR) variation between students (Gemici et al., 2013). This significantly impacts their potential university participation (Harvey, 2014; Tranter, 2011). The National Centre for Student Equity in Higher Education has shown that low-SES students are disadvantaged by a university application process, which is dependent on appropriate school guidance and resourcing (Cardak et al., 2015). However, evidence suggests that low-SES students with similar ATARs often outperform high-SES students once enrolled at university (Harvey & Burnheim, 2013). With these disparities in mind, this research could be considered what Lumb et al. (2020, p. 9) call 'aspiration-eliciting' research which can inform evaluation and future planning in higher education.

Recent equity polices in Australian higher education

In 1990, *A fair chance for all* was published within the broader Dawkins recommendations which aimed to radically change the student population; it was 'focused explicitly on access and representation, advocating the need for composition of the student population to reflect the broader population' (Harvey, Burnheim, & Brett, 2016b, p. 6). *A fair chance for all* advocated more enabling and bridging programs, and university outreach programs, and called attention to the expansion of sub-degree level study (Harvey, Andrewartha, & Burnheim, 2016a). This framework was followed by the Bradley Review of Higher Education (Bradley et al., 2008), which contended that it was economically imperative to widen the participation of under-represented groups. Pledging that by 2020 20% of undergraduate students should be from low-SES backgrounds, this review asserted that students from such backgrounds required higher levels of support, including financial assistance and greater academic support, mentoring and counselling services.

While not belittling the importance of such pledges or disputing, there have been significant changes in undergraduate composition; it is important to note that policies to support a more diverse student intake have not been well-conceived. Interventions to address the socioeconomic gaps have been hampered by what Lynch et al. (2015) call a 'bums on seats' approach to widening participation as well as 'a tendency for knee-jerk reactions by institutions … [and] add-on remedial or needs-based support, rather than integrated evidence-based programs which are sustainable across increasingly diverse cohorts' (O'Shea et al., 2017, p. 36). Furthermore, within the fragmented widening participation in Australia, there exists 'differential levels of access and participation by the type of institution (first tier/elite versus other) and degree (prestigious degrees such as medicine versus lower status/social mobility degrees such as nursing or teaching)' (Bennett & Southgate, 2014, p. 23). Therefore, while there has undeniably been a growth in students from low-SES backgrounds, it has primarily been in second-tier universities.

Research into equity and widening participation indicates that, despite efforts to widen higher education participation, not only is inequality not easily erased but, more specifically, the classed, gendered and racialised experiences of university students remain particularly salient in shaping what is possible. The reasons for this remain complex and varied. Students from low-SES backgrounds are less likely to have access to knowledge about what strategies are needed to map a pathway through higher education and beyond. Such students are less likely to have the resources, opportunities or networks of people to support their aspirations and navigational capacity (Gale & Parker, 2013). Furthermore, in considering another dimension of stratification, Harvey, Andrewartha and Burnheim (2016a) note few strategies have addressed 'disparities by course, institution and level of study' (p. 71).

Discourses of higher education are often shaped around access, and various 'factors, including academic preparation, aspirations for further study, and ability to actually enrol and attend higher education, contribute to whether students are successful in terms of their access' (Naylor et al., 2016, p. 265). To gain entry to university, students receive an ATAR which is calculated by each state's university admissions centre and provides a 'percentile score' between 0 and 99.95 which denotes a student's ranking relative to their peers upon completion of their secondary education. Those who receive high ATARs are more likely to be offered their first preference of university courses. In short, one's ATAR determines one's eligibility for university education and their subject of study. The sport and academic scholarships that have expanded opportunities in the United States (Alexander, 2019) do not exist in Australia. Students can pay their university fees up front or take out a HECS-HELP loan, which defers their payments until they start earning above a compulsory repayment threshold. The price of a university course depends on the 'band' that the course sits within, which is determined by the federal government. For example, a medicine degree sits in Band 3 and in 2018 could cost up to $10,266 a year, whereas an education degree sits in Band 1 and can cost up to $6,152 a year.

In Australia, universities in urban centres typically fall into three categories which differ significantly in symbolic capital and student intakes: the Australian Technology Network which includes institutions that gained university status in the late 1980s/early 1990s; 'greenfield' universities developed in the 1960s and 1970s; and the 'Group of Eight' which includes the oldest and most research-intensive institutions. There are also the Innovative Research Universities, Regional Universities Network and Unaligned Universities (see Koshy, 2017).

The discursive construction of the university student

We know there exists in Australia today great disparities in terms of wealth for those entering higher education, which both highlight pervasive, entrenched inequality and show the power of class to influence opportunity and life chances. Yet, in Australian society more of the Australian population are attending university than ever before. Researching how aspirations interact with SES, Gore et al. (2015) have demonstrated that many students from low-SES backgrounds have high aspirations and do see university as part of their future. On the other hand, as Hattam and Smyth (2003) write, it is not 'possible to understand the complex process of youth identity formation without understanding the interplay between young people's desire for economic independence and their struggles to establish, confirm, and in many cases endure, a socio-cultural identity' (p. 383). While aspirations may be high, and university may be seen as achievable, many working-class students will find the transition to university study a confronting experience.

Universities are future-oriented spaces where students are expected to self-craft in order to become employment ready (Stahl & McDonald, 2019). Though they differ substantially, universities often privilege the formation of the 'entrepreneurial self', a neoliberal subjectivity where the self must commit to an existence focused on capitalisation through calculated acts and investments combined with the shrugging off of collective responsibility for the vulnerable and marginalised. In their Foucauldian analysis of Australian widening participation higher education policy, Bennett and Southgate (2014) assert there are two subject positions within the policies – 'the cap(able) individual and the proper aspirant' (p. 22) – which has implications for how widening participation is understood and experienced. Highlighting the contradictory nature of widening participation policy, Bennett and Southgate (2014) note that it continues to exclude because the *imagined student already possesses* cap(ability)' (p. 29, italics in the original) and privileges a narrow conception of an aspirational subject that strongly echoes neoliberal prerogatives.

An investigation of student subjectivity and subject positions requires a consideration of 'the production of the subject position "university student"' which 'is inextricably tied to complex classed, gendered and racialized relations of power and inequality' (Burke, 2009, pp. 83–84). This is a continual process of meaning-making closely aligned with the social order of things – the university student is discursively constructed and *comes into being* through language practices and rituals, which structure what is normative. Pötschulat et al. (2021) problematise the terminology of 'the student experience', contending that such terminology 'has implications for how we come to understand a complex set of practices' (p. 4). They assert students enter into a negotiation with the norms and expectations attached to contemporary 'studenthood' and they judge their everyday practices in relation to such conceptualisations.

Loveday (2015) notes that working-class students in universities struggle to 'pass' as middle class. Calling attention to the discourse which contributes to the construction of the university student, Loveday (2015, p. 573) foregrounds an argument that doxic notions of success involve working-class students engaging in the careful self-management of their identities in the university space to guard against feeling of shame and guilt (Reay, 2005). This working-class management of identity is aligned closely with a middle-class construction of personhood, one of legitimacy and entitlement (Lehmann, 2009a; Mallman, 2017). Furthermore, this identity management is what Skeggs (2004) refers to as the 'techniques of selfhood' required by the dominant symbolic. Such self-management has significant implications for how working-class students become agentic and their sense of belonging, as well as how they may come to counteract struggles with isolation.

To conclude, on the one hand, Australian society appears committed to a 'university for all' with the expectation that a university degree will secure future employment. This is bound up in institutions of higher education actively promoting an idealised version of selfhood/'studenthood' (e.g. the capable worker, the proficient student). Arguably, such a notion of the 'ideal student' positions people in a permanent state of meritocratic competition with each other. Littler (2018) writes that 'Meritocracy offers a ladder system of social mobility, promoting a socially corrosive ethic of competitive self-interest which both legitimises inequality and damages community' (p. 3). On the other hand, efforts to widen participation can often undermine the very inequalities they seek to remedy. Students from lower socioeconomic backgrounds who often have limited academic resources can struggle with academic standards and require not only support but the confidence and belonging to seek such support when it is required.

Social class, social mobility and higher education

Theories of social class and social mobility have evolved considerably since the structural approaches represented in the early seminal texts of Marx, Weber and Durkheim. Influenced by these seminal scholars, the last half of the twentieth century was witness to a move towards quantitative and positivist methodologies to explore class. These approaches, which primarily concerned the development of class schemas, mainly defined class in terms of employment (Goldthorpe, 1996). Within these studies, which were typically large scale – education was often in the background – economics was often emphasised and there was a great interest in developing rational-choice models (Goldthorpe, 1998) and studying intra-class differences (Bernstein, 1962).

Contemporary research on social class and mobility takes a much broader theoretical stance in order to incorporate the study of a wider range of practices. Many of these approaches, which gained popularity over the late twentieth and early twenty-first centuries, were strongly influenced by Bourdieusian concepts, specifically the acquiring (and maintaining) of capitals, symbolic violence and the internalisation of class (habitus). Bourdieu conceived of education as an institutional structuring of social separation, an 'ideological and cultural site of socialization that ... was often more likely to reproduce, rather than challenge, social inequality in the state' (Dillabough, 2004, p. 490). Rendered simply, Bourdieu argues that, within educational contexts, the cultural capital of the middle and upper classes is rewarded, while the capitals of the lower classes are systematically devalued. Within the social sciences, the ongoing 'structure–agency' debate heavily influenced Bourdieu's development of both his theory of practices and his theoretical tools in his study of class-based power.

For many sociologists, Bourdieu's theoretical contribution led to a deeper theorising of class which emphasised the importance of emotions, stigma, history and lived experience. Class is now theorised as formed *in* and *through* identities, agentic practices and historic discourses, rather than a simple reflection of present financial capital and occupations. In understanding the role social class plays in identity formation, a range of theorists have documented how family socialisation practices reproduce social class differences across generations (Lareau, 2003; Vincent et al., 2013). For example, in contrast to working-class parents, middle-class parents have been documented as describing their children as 'bright', and fostering certain dispositions towards academic attainment (Reay et al., 2011), while putting 'a tremendous amount of effort into cultivating particular identities [and] stacking the deck in their child's favor' (Weis & Cipollone, 2013, p. 710).

Feminist research has highlighted that researching social class requires sensitivity as language may give rise to emotions of 'shame and the fear of shame' (Reay, 2005, p. 923) as well as feelings of self-worth, injustice and moral evaluation (Skeggs, 2002). As a clear departure from early class theories, contemporary theorising of class identities concerns how forms of cultural capital are worked upon and inhabited (Skeggs, 2004). Capitals, when activated, allow individuals easier movement between various social spaces. However, these hierarchical social spaces are shaped by unequal recognition and various degrees of exploitation which, in turn, can lead to 'psychic costs' (Reay, 2005). Class difference, therefore, is often explored in reference to the affective dimension where such identity practices can involve ignoring or rejecting wider repertoires of classed hierarchies in order to construct oneself as a person of value (Skeggs, 2014).

The *First-in-Family Males Project* is positioned in scholarship which shows the differentiation of class strategies to navigate unequal education systems – strategies that exist alongside a spectrum of privilege (Thomsen et al., 2011; Thomsen, 2013). It also speaks to research on *class travellers* as the boys move away from their cultural and social origins (Lee & Kramer, 2013) and are compelled to construct themselves in different ways. I build on theories of class as formed *in* and *through* identities, closely tied to capital and opportunities/constraints. Contemporary theorising of class identities focuses on how such identities are worked on and embodied and how subjects come to inhabit them, often in relation to feelings of self-worth, injustice and moral evaluation. Lehmann (2009b) writes:

> Working-class youths at university have already embarked on a transition pathway that suggests a move away from their social background. It is important to realize, however, that their decisions to attend university are still profoundly rooted in class habitus. The pragmatism of their choice to attend university is in the hope for upward mobility.
>
> (p. 141)

This speaks to sociological research on the managing of 'cleft habitus', the difficulty in balancing new experiences with the dispositions ascribed in one's social origin (see Bourdieu et al., 1993).

Class differences, inequalities, access and social mobility remain areas of fascination for sociologists working in education. As Egerton and Halsey (1993) write, three significant aspects shaped conversations regarding access to higher education over the twentieth century. These were, first, a period of significant expansion, second, a reduction in gender inequality and, third, little to no reduction in social class inequality. In analysing global trends in higher education including increasing participation rates, Marginson (2016) proposes that families often find themselves in contexts that 'either intensify competition and tightly limit educational and social success or within HPS [high participation systems] that are organised on the basis of equal rights and the common good, and enhance the scope for social mobility' (p. 415). In documenting how first-in-family and working-class young people negotiate the university space, Lehmann (2009b) writes: 'Labor market conditions, a pervasive public discourse about the benefits of higher education, and parental hopes push them to university. The institutional culture and demands of university, however, often remain elusive and fraught with uncertainty' (p. 138). Debates concerning how class is realised in education, specifically higher education, have focused on many different areas including the effects of poverty, first-in-family/first-generation status, government efforts to widen participation, resilience, competition and intergenerational histories. However, as Miles et al. (2011) write, 'we know little about how the upwardly mobile understand their life trajectories' (p. 419).

Individuals' ability to navigate the education system successfully is often dependent on the material and psychological resources available to them (Reay, 2005). Snowden and Lewis (2015) write of 'mixed messages' regarding what higher education has come to mean and call attention to how a

> public discourse of university access continually speaks of 'history,' being 'born into' circumstances, a 'culture' of low aspiration, positioning individuals from non-traditional backgrounds as captive to external forces, and yet creating and subjecting themselves to 'a culture' of 'low hope' and 'dropping out'.
>
> (p. 593)

This discourse has many dimensions. Reay and Lucey (2000) describe working-class ambivalence to social mobility as a form of resilience, where working-class young people view their locality as 'good enough', expressed through refusal and reclassification. The research of Browman et al. (2017) captures how academic persistence among lower-SES students is contingent on their beliefs about whether socioeconomic mobility is achievable. Other research from Capannola and Johnson (2020) emphasises familial support as integral to academic success. First-generation students in their study came to see themselves as role models but also able to positively access both what the university had to offer and their working-class home lives. Social mobility is always a process of separating oneself from one's embodied class habitus (Reay, 2005) as well as the normative practices of one's gender identity (Adkins, 2003); consequently, social mobility is a process of constraints and opportunities for agency as well as subjectivity. As a result, socially mobile individuals may not feel a sense of belonging among the middle class or upwardly mobile sectors of the working class.

In framing the experiences of working-class students, Thomsen et al. (2011) also note that such students are more liked to 'choose programs with instrumental aims', reaffirming that education is considered a means to an end. They note that, in their comparative data set of middle-class and working-class students, working-class students were four times more likely to be risk averse and 'avoid educational pathways perceived to be too risky in terms of future work and income' (pp. 476–477). Therefore, working-class students tend to be more risk averse and transactional in their perspective of education (Thomsen et al., 2011). Rubin and Wright (2015) have found that working-class students have less desire and concern about making new friends than middle-class students in the university context. Furthermore, working-class young people's decision to attend university is often based on personal experiences and advice from others. Lehmann (2009b) argues decision-making associated with university and careers is 'pragmatic, rather than rational' in that it is 'based on incomplete and filtered information, because of the social context in which the information is obtained and processed' (p. 139).

Rubin et al. (2019) highlight the importance of working-class students' social integration at university, where a 'relatively low degree of social integration at university is associated with their poorer academic outcomes and their poorer mental health' (p. 89). Furthermore, constraints on both time and money serve as a powerful barrier to working-class young people fully embracing the social experience at university, contributing to a persistent feeling of being out of place, an outsider. Such experiences can lead to what psychologists call 'John Henryism', a predisposition to cope regardless of circumstance which can lead to negative consequences for long-term health. In their research on high-SES African-American men, Bonham et al. (2004) document that they 'believe that just about any obstacle can be overcome through hard work and a strong determination to succeed' (p. 737), although their participants also suffered from hypertension and other prolonged health issues related to long-term stress. This raises significant questions concerning whether maintaining a positive outlook – and performing an identity associated with strength and tenacity – can actually have negative effects.

Class differences, intersectionality and higher education

There exist substantial differences in the higher education participation of people from low-SES backgrounds and those from different ethnic and cultural backgrounds. The equity-oriented ambition of both institutions and nation-states in the twentieth century to diversify the university student population has resulted in more students from non-traditional backgrounds entering university. As a result, sociologists have sought to broaden their approach and adopt new theoretical tools in order to compose more nuanced understandings of social class disadvantage. In revising theoretical approaches to class, theorists have embraced intersectional axes of difference such as gender, ethnicity, disability and sexuality (Crenshaw, 1991).

Studies of intersectionality stem from wider shifts in identity analyses where new research presents identity as fragmented, discursive and hybridised under the banners of post-structuralism, postmodernism, performativity and queer theory (Wetherell & Mohanty, 2010). Since its inception, intersectionality research has focused on multiple axes of inequality and how these axes of inequality speak to one another. Omi and Winant (1994) posit that 'race, class, and gender are not fixed and discrete categories'; instead they 'overlap, intersect, and infuse with others in countless ways' (p. 68). Conjuring an image of a nesting doll, Prins (2006) writes that 'gender is always lived in the modalities of ethnicity and class, nationality in the modalities of gender and race, and class in the modalities of gender and nationality' (p. 278). Born out of feminist theory, specifically Crenshaw's (1991) and Collins' (2000) scholarship investigating societal oppression and women of colour, intersectionality has sought to address how theorists identify *categories of difference* and to demonstrate the ways in which these categories interact or become entangled.

Another dimension of intersectionality is how it is used to theorise multiple forms of identity and multiple strategies of (dis)identification where it is useful in accounting for the processes by which identities are flexible, shifting, multiply located and continually (re)combined. Analysing disadvantage with reference to only one identity vector – what Crenshaw (1991) termed 'single axis analysis' – runs the risk of distorting our understanding of those impacted by more than one system of discrimination. The intersectional analysis of social divisions has come to occupy central spaces in theorising identities but there has been a gradual recognition of the inadequacy of analysing various social divisions separately. Furthermore, adding to the complexity, the theoretical approach to each identity vector may have different logics, making cross-comparative analysis impossible, as, for example, gender identities and practices change alongside conceptions of class.

In research on higher education, intersectional identity categories have been considered as 'mediating factors' in reference to social class (Reay et al., 2005, p. 85). Reay et al. (2005, p. 11) show that students from ethnic backgrounds often have different 'choice making processes' for the pursuit of higher education, although class differences are more apparent and significant than ethnic identity differences. Boliver (2015) explored the various reasons why ethnic minority applicants to elite Russell Group universities in the UK were less likely to receive offers of admission than comparably qualified white applicants. In *The diversity bargain: And other dilemmas of race, admissions, and meritocracy at elite universities*, Warikoo (2016) demonstrates that white students in the US support race-based affirmative action to the extent that such programs afford them opportunities to learn about, and profit from, diversity. However, Warikoo draws a contrast with students in the UK of more diverse backgrounds who reject race and class-based admission measures, thus legitimating their investments in a meritocratic system and their identities of privilege. In Australia, Naylor et al. (2016) have called for a consideration of 'hyper-intersectionality' in widening participation; they feel a shift is warranted from 'viewing disadvantage through the structure of crude sociological groups, to instead looking through prisms that give life to each person' (p. 268). Intersectionality, as a theoretical approach, has highlighted new axes of difference while emphasising the utility of comparative studies in higher education that illustrate patterns of racism and exclusion (Nichols & Stahl, 2019).

Intersectionality has also naturally informed widening participation initiatives for men from non-traditional backgrounds with a specific focus on the resources they draw upon to ensure their success. For example, Harper (2006) found that African-American men's academic success in primarily White institutions in the United States was affirmed through African-American peer circles. This form of support worked to counteract feelings of isolation or dropout. In Australia, Indigenous males have reasonable rates of participation in vocational education and training, but they are far less likely to engage in university than Indigenous females (Harvey, Burnheim, & Brett, 2016b; Shalley et al., 2019). To counter these challenges, many Australian universities now operate alternative pathways and enabling programs to increase the participation and retention of Indigenous students (Pitman et al., 2017). Asmar et al. (2015) write that more needs to be known about whom Indigenous students interact with at university and where they turn for support. There is definitely a need to widen how we consider intersectionality and its role in contributing to students becoming successful in higher education. The research presented in this book is concerned with the discursive construction of masculinity, which requires attention to identity vectors such as ethnicity.

Working-class masculinities in education

There exists a complex relationship between social class, masculinities and the motivation for academic achievement (Stahl, 2015; Whitehead, 2003). This has resulted in a longstanding fascination with working-class masculinities, specifically how they value themselves in relation to their education. Many scholars have cited the massive societal transformation in economic and gender relations (Fine et al., 1997; Mac an Ghaill, 1994; Nayak, 2003, 2006; Weis, 2004) which have framed the twentieth and twenty-first centuries. Within these shifts and fragmentation, many scholars have focused on working-class masculinities and the renouncing of the 'mental' for the 'manual' (see Swain, 2005 for a listing of this research). Documenting the rise in globalisation and post-industrialisation, Kenway et al. (2006) present an argument that 'melancholic masculinities' are infused with a sense of nostalgia for a bygone era which directly impacts the next generation of young men. After all, as Kenway et al. (2006) argue, all conceptions of 'worthwhile work and the admirable worker remain from the past and are carried across the generations' (p. 69), which gives rise to an over-embellishment of working-class masculine norms (see Nayak, 2003). In considering how working-class men become upwardly mobile, Goldthorpe (1987 [1980]) noted that many of his participants were disinclined to embrace notions of luck and instead they attributed their upwardly mobility to their own efforts. Goldthorpe writes: 'the dominant reality for these upwardly mobile men ... is that of the careers that they had "made for themselves", in their present professional, administrative and managerial occupations' where their personal qualities – their sense of their own agency – are foregrounded (p. 234). One could argue working-class masculinity is now often enmeshed with notions of what it means to be educated or, specifically, what it means to reconcile working-class masculinity with educational success (Archer & Leathwood, 2003; Reay, 2002).

This section provides a brief overview of some of the main themes present in the study of masculinities in higher education internationally, with a focus on working-class masculinities. Before I outline these themes, I draw the reader's attention briefly to the struggles of working-class boyhood. In providing a focus on what precedes higher education my aim is to capture how many working-class boys contend with both school-based and societal conceptions of working-class masculinity that significantly influence their opportunity to be successful in their education.

The struggle of working-class boyhood

In a consideration of masculinities in higher education, it is important to think critically about their journeys as learners prior to entering university. Whitehead's (2003) research calls attention to how both working-class and middle-class boys struggle with being perceived as intelligent, and reveals that the reasons for this could lie in wider societal discourses as well as school cultures. Swain (2005) describes schools as sites 'where boys learn that there are a number of different, and often competing, ways of being a boy and that some of these are more cherished and prestigious, and therefore more powerful, than others' (p. 214). Epstein et al. (1998) identify separate discourses used in the popular and academic press to explain the educational underperformance of boys, ranging from 'poor boys', 'boys will be boys', 'at risk boys', to 'problem boys'. These discourses have framed key debates in gender theory concerning boys; furthermore, neoliberal policy drivers ensure that working-class boys are individualised and held accountable for their failure (Francis, 2006, p. 191). Such neoliberal discourses, while denying the existence of any real class distinctions, limit the discursive space in which various forms of working-class masculinity are acceptable.

For working-class boys, the interconnectedness between behaviour, identity and attainment starts very early as does the reductive educational processes of categorisation and labelling. From the moment a boy, specifically a working-class boy, enters a school, he is shaped according to his gender, as many 'teachers consistently rate girls higher than boys in deportment, and much of their contact with boys tends to be negative and disciplinary' (Entwisle et al., 2007, p. 115). It has been documented that primary school boys are significantly more likely to be identified as having special educational needs than their female counterparts (Bleach, 2000). However, there is evidence working-class boys do 'move away from the classic "macho" mode of working-class masculinity towards a more middle-class notion of masculinity centred on competitive achievement' and it is entirely possible schooling may 'modify working-class "anti-intellectual" notions of masculinity' (Whitehead, 2003, pp. 290, 304). Mac an Ghaill (1994) identified groups of working-class boys, including the 'Academic Achievers' who engaged positively with their education in an effort to ensure their upward mobility and the 'New Entrepreneurs' who identified strongly with technology developments as a route to advancement (p. 290). In this work Mac an Ghaill (1994) notes 'Academic Achievers' were not consistent in being 'unambiguously pro-school' and instead 'their appropriation of the curriculum involves complex social practices, informed by varied cultural investments' (p. 59). In contrast, 'New Entrepreneurs', who were more focused on the high-status capital of technology work, invested more heavily in 'a new mode of school student masculinity with its values of rationality, instrumentalism, forward planning and careerism' (p. 63).

There exists longstanding research in Australia on the conflation between effeminacy, masculinity and academic achievement. As Kenway and Fitzclarence (1997, p. 122) note, the figure of 'academically-oriented masculinity' is denigrated. More recently, Lusher (2011) contends that boys' social status and peer validation is not necessarily at odds with academic achievement and boys may often choose to associate themselves with friends 'of similar levels of academic application to themselves' (p. 670).

Boys in Australia who are from low-SES backgrounds often fail to meet the milestones for school readiness, continually underperform throughout their schooling and are less likely to complete school than girls – 78.5% compared to 69.5% (Lamb et al., 2015). In Australia, there have been a plethora of policy responses to improve the academic outcomes of boys but very few take into account the 'very significant ways in which the social construction of gender impacts significantly on curriculum, pedagogical practices and relations with and between students in schools' (Lingard et al., 2009, pp. 9–10). Furthermore, in the policy discourses surrounding boys and schooling, there are 'constant slippages' that reaffirm what are '*natural* predispositions or learning behaviours and orientations for both boys and girls' [emphasis in original] (Mills et al., 2007, p. 15). Drawing on biological essentialist notions and Gardner's multiple intelligences, certain common tropes dominate these discourses such as kinaesthetic learning, devaluing inter/intrapersonal skills, preferring explicit/relevant teaching, and requiring male role models to learn. Such strategies fail to acknowledge the culture of masculinity as well as environments and discourses from which boys draw their identity. Such a policy initiative risks homogenising working-class boys into one cohesive group when we must recognise heterogeneity and their diversity in values, attitudes and behaviours, and the influence on these of their school and social contexts.

Working-class masculinities in higher education

The shift to post-industrialisation is arguably felt more harshly by the working-class male whose 'reproduction of working-class masculinity has been ruptured' given the employment of his fathers and grandfathers is in short supply (Kenway & Kraack, 2004, p. 107). Today, working-class youth have to contend with a rise in credentialisation alongside a hazy economic future where stable forms of employment are less common (Brown, 2013). As traditional economic structures are reshaped, young men, particularly those from lower and working-class backgrounds, have to invest in new forms of subjectivity (Nayak, 2003). Arguably, the impact of post-industrialism on working-class masculine identity is now increasingly framed by efforts of young men to preserve tradition and engage in new searches for 'respectability' and 'authenticity' (Dolby & Dimitriadis, 2004; McDowell, 2003; Nayak, 2003). This search sits alongside normative practices concerning the transition from boyhood to adulthood as young men come to pursue 'adult status and masculine prestige among their peers' (Connell, 2005, p. 15).

While the Australian higher education system has experienced decades of reform focused on widening participation, young men from low-SES backgrounds remain severely under-represented (Lamb et al., 2015). As young men complete their secondary schooling in Australia, they have a variety of options available: job, apprenticeship, defence force, private college, TAFE, a university entry pathway or enabling program and, finally, university. The reasons why working-class men do not enter higher education are varied and may include: the pervasive pressure to be a breadwinner as well as the lure of full-time employment typically in trade work (O'Shea et al., 2017); the lack of generational history and betrayal of one's class background (Sennett & Cobb, 1972; Stahl, 2015); the shame and stigma associated with academic success (Harris & Harper, 2015); and the role of 'macho capital', which can serve as powerful social currency, but become an impediment to learning at the secondary level (Duckworth, 2013; Willis, 1977).

Research suggests many men are unable to identify with university students, seeing 'participation as incompatible with notions of working-class masculinity' and as 'entailing numerous costs and risks to masculine identities' (Archer & Leathwood, 2003, p. 179). The men in Burke's (2009) study perceived higher education as 'a form of self-improvement and subjective transformation' (p. 91), a process through which they actively distanced themselves from normative working-class masculinity practices. Burke (2009) writes that the working-class men she studied were positioned 'across different and competing formations of identity' and they constructed themselves in relation to an 'imagined hegemonic masculinity in their struggle towards success and respectability' (p. 91). This work echoes arguments in studies of social mobility that describe the process of separating oneself from the embodied class habitus (Reay, 2005) as well as the normative practices of gender identity (Adkins, 2003). In studies of upward mobility, class and gender practices are often informed by an imagined ideal. This is also noted by Alexander (2019), who contends there exists a 'future neoliberal masculinity' grounded in the accrual of financial and symbolic capital which speaks to boys from low-SES backgrounds. Research by Iwamoto et al. (2018) focused on how, in the transition to university, men feel pressure to 'prove' their masculinity by engaging in what they imagine to be traditional masculine behaviours (gender conformity), resulting in detrimental effects on their overall well-being.

Complementing extensive research on the problematic behaviour of boys in primary and secondary schools, there exists a wide spectrum of studies focused on the behaviour of men in university (Davis & Laker, 2004; Harper & Harris, 2010). Researching in the United States, Harris and Harper (2015) document that many male students arrive at university 'having learned to prioritize traditional, and in some cases patriarchal, conceptualizations and expressions of masculinity' (p. 59), which directly influences both their academic and social engagement, though they are clear that this is not true for all men. They highlight the need for effective strategies which counteract poor help-seeking behaviours and social isolation.

Conversations about working-class masculinities often focus on change, whether it be in behaviour, values or lifestyle. Entry into and movement within the university space also involves prolonged interaction with middle-class masculinities. Universities have always been the domain of middle-to-upper-class men who, in their governance and participation, produce an 'idealised' form of personhood (Lund et al., 2018). Working-class masculinities are established in relation to a middle-class masculinity where middle-class men conflate masculinity and personal achievement in order to secure a high-status career where the traits required are leadership and competition (Whitehead, 2003). In his work on class and masculinity Morgan (2004) highlights that middle-class hegemonic masculinity is imbued with rationality, independence, individualism and competition. The university is a space of capital accrual and can often involve fierce competition as students find ways to make themselves distinctive and thus attractive to employers.

In research on the tension between working-class and middle-class masculinities, Giazitzoglu (2014) and Giazitzoglu and Muzio (2020) researched over a five-year period the experiences of ten white male participants from non-privileged socioeconomic backgrounds as they entered into prestigious white-collar employment, capturing how working-class masculine norms and dispositions lead to exclusion, marginalisation and discrimination in organisations. Longitudinally, Giazitzoglu (2014) described these men as 'the Changers', who actively found ways to construct themselves through othering their working-class community of origin, which they considered to be populated by people who were ignorant or lacking ambition. The

Changers exercised strategies to disassociate themselves from their disadvantaged backgrounds (often through pathologisation) as they invested heavily in the search for 'acceptance, belonging and legitimacy', which had implications for their well-being (para 2.5). Furthermore, as the participants undertook identity work while becoming socially mobile, they became boastful about what they had accomplished, and rationalised what they had attained through their hard work (Giazitzoglu, 2014, para 4.9). Education and class are important here: the Changers did well academically despite their low-performing secondary schools, though all except one attended post-1992 universities.

Addressing working-class masculinities and social mobility requires careful attention to how individuals understand themselves within a falsely meritocratic system. As Littler (2018, p. 3) notes, meritocracy 'offers a ladder system of social mobility, promoting a socially corrosive ethic of competitive self-interest which both legitimises inequality and damages community' where the meritocratic illusions position people in a permanent state of competition with each other. The research presented in this book examines how boys from working-class backgrounds who become the first in family to attend university understand themselves as meritocratic subjects, how they *come to be* socially mobile; such a process can be significantly informed by negotiating a disjuncture with traditional working-class cultures and communities. Such an investigation necessitates a negotiation with what McLeod (2000) calls the 'subjectivity–social dilemma' (p. 502) which informs the subjectivity–schooling relationship (p. 504). Males, especially young men from lower SES backgrounds, invest time and energy in resisting the neoliberal 'four Cs – change, choice, chances, and competition' (Phoenix, 2004, p. 229) as they struggle to find discursive space in which various forms of working-class masculinity are acceptable and validated (Burke, 2009; Stahl, 2015).

Longitudinal research on masculinities

Harris and Harper (2015) argue that there is a pressing need for the 'longitudinal study of masculine conceptions' in order to 'further enhance understanding of masculinities and men's development during and after college' (p. 62). In focusing on the transitional experiences of first-in-family males, the study presented in this book documents how aspirations are challenged over time and how aspirations intersect with class, gender and ethnicity. Holmegaard (2020) highlights the strengths of qualitative longitudinal research, specifically revealing 'through repeated interviews the transitions taking place over time and making room for the complexity of the life being lived' (p. 112). Adopting a narrative approach does not necessarily equate to an understanding of a truer self. Instead Holmegaard (2020) argues such an approach fosters a deeper understanding of the complexity of agency, subjectivities and institutional arrangements which are 'being negotiated, are disconnected, and part of an ongoing process being played out over time'

(p. 112). McLeod (2000) writes that 'gender and class subjectivity is worked out in the lives of young people during their secondary schooling and adolescent years' (p. 501), a period noted for its transformational aspects.

Despite the importance of longitudinal research, it remains rather limited in studies of masculinities and widening participation, where the primary focus has been on psychology and health sciences. Longitudinal research periods can range from six months (Iwamoto et al., 2018) to one year (Alexander, 2019; Nichols & Stahl, 2017) to 18 months (Dasgupta, 2013). The seminal ethnographic study in the canon of working-class masculinities – *Learning to labour: How working-class kids get working-class jobs* (Willis, 1977) – documented changes in masculinities over the course of a year. In MacLeod's (2009) *Ain't no makin' it: Aspirations and attainment in a low-income neighborhood* he returned to Clarendon Heights eight years after his first study to revisit the Brothers and the Hallway hangers. These studies capture the gendered patterns present in the social practices of working-class and working-poor young men to expand our understanding of how identities are formed. In considering the gendering of social mobility, I draw on the words of Connell (2000):

> Social practice is creative and inventive, but not inchoate. Practice that relates to the structure of gender, generated as people and groups grapple with their historical situations, does not consist of isolated acts. Actions are configured in larger units, and when we speak of masculinity and femininity we are naming configurations of gender practice.
>
> (pp. 27–28)

Both Willis (1977) and MacLeod (2009) speak to how gender practices are configured within specific classed locales, structured by the economic circumstances of a particular time. They recognise that young men are agentic, albeit within structural constraints. The analysis in these works foregrounds gender as a collective activity and – to borrow Connell's (2000) words – something to be 'grappled' with.

In recent longitudinal research on masculinities, we have seen a wide array of topics. Recent work commissioned by the Australian Longitudinal Study on Male Health led to the *Ten to Men* project, which surveyed a national sample of men between age 10 and 55 (Milner et al., 2019; Pirkis et al., 2017). The aim of this study was to examine key determinants of the health of male Australians including social, economic, environmental and behavioural factors. In other longitudinal research, Pachankis et al. (2018) documented how gay and bisexual men experienced stigma and mental health over the course of eight years. Way (2013) documents a longitudinal study of boys' friendships across a variety of spaces (e.g. their neighbourhood, school, peer group) from early to late adolescence. She argues that boys are experiencing a 'crisis of connection' because they live in a culture where human needs and capacities are ascribed to femininity and a sexuality (e.g. gay). This sets up robust barriers for young men as they navigate adolescence.

Over the course of one year in the Bronx, Alexander (2019) ethnographi-cally documented 'partial and multiple narratives of future selves' (p. 40) in relation to an imagined, hegemonic, neoliberal masculine self as young men sought to untangle themselves from their disadvantaged backgrounds. In the United States, the *Black and Latino Male School Intervention Study* con-ducted between 2006 and 2011 sought to explore the merits of single-sex schools through a study of seven public all-male schools, documenting their effectiveness in meeting the academic and social needs of predominately Black and Latino males (Torres, 2017).

McDowell (2003, 2020; Hardgrove et al., 2015) conducted research with three cohorts of young working-class men experiencing extreme dis-advantage in English towns between 2001 and 2017, thus covering the first 17 years of the new millennium. These men lived in Cambridge, Swin-don and Hastings, each of which was experiencing significant youth unem-ployment. The research totalled semi-structured qualitative interviews with 65 un(der)employed young men between the ages of 16 and 25. While the work is wide-ranging and seeks to make connections between economic/social change and the lived experience of the participants, the words of the participants demonstrate how experiences with long-stand-ing unemployment 'reduce young men's ability to construct an alternative identity through consumption and through the development of a form of street-based social capital that confers a degree of status among their peers' (McDowell, 2020, p. 979).

Returning to the *First-in-Family Males Project*, while a duration of three years seems quite short for longitudinal research which considers identities in relation to social change, though between 2017 and 2019 Australia experi-enced considerable political and cultural changes, specifically multiple prime ministers and a controversial marriage equality plebiscite. Furthermore, in terms of what Mac an Ghaill (1994) calls the 'school–waged labour couplet', the Australian public has seen a steady rise in marketisation around universi-ties, TAFE and various forms of micro-credentialing. This attention to social change is important when one considers how we, as researchers, come to interpret agency as '"embedded" in the changing contexts' (Tomanović, 2018, p. 367).

Gaining from a longitudinal approach

Longitudinal qualitative research allows for the study of individuals' chang-ing agency in reference to local and global shifts. In the *First-in-Family Males Project*, the research allowed the documentation of the participants' identities as both boys and men as they navigated the various dimensions of adolescence. In *Guyland*, Kimmel (2008) writes: 'The passage between adolescence and adulthood has morphed from a transitional moment to a separate life stage' (p. 25). Highlighting all the paradoxes involved with this liminal time, Kimmel considers the performativities associated with the 'lost boy,' a topsy-turvy, Peter-Pan mindset [where] young men shirk the responsibilities of adulthood and remain fixated on the trappings of boyhood, while the boys they still are struggle heroically to prove that they are real men despite all evidence to the contrary.

(p. 4)

While the argument is more than a bit reductive, defining 'Guyland' as both careless and carefree, ultimately Kimmel gives due attention to the shifting paradigms of masculinity that not only accompany wider social change but also adapt to different behaviours depending on the immediate social contexts. After all, as Swain (2005, p. 225) writes: 'The journey from boy to man is unpredictable, disorderly, and frequently hazardous, with multiple pathways shaped by social class, ethnicity, and sexuality.' While one could argue all adolescence is subject to this, boys – specifically working-class boys – do contend with powerful societal discourses which both pathologise and police their conduct. These discourses significantly inform how they navigate their lifeworlds.

Clearly, longitudinal qualitative research opens up spaces to explore the shift from boyhood to manhood but also how such shifts are formed relationally. Loeser (2014), in her exploration of masculinity, disability and identity work, highlights how, for young men, friendship is a form of 'affective sociality involving an active engagement with the care of the self at the same time as caring for others' (p. 194). Calling attention to the construction of masculinities as collective endeavours, Loeser (2014) focuses on subject positions which are policed and regulated (p. 195), where identity 'is built on the interpretation of their male friends where there is always a disjuncture between how one evaluates the self and how the other evaluates one' (p. 211). Furthermore, studying the shift from boyhood to adulthood also allows for an exploration of changing masculinities in relation to family life as a site of feminine nurture, specifically in reference to what Adams and Coltrane (2005) call 'the virtues of nurturing, caring, service, and emotional involvement that provide the underpinnings for successful family functioning' (p. 243).

Furthermore, longitudinal research also opens up space to consider men as participants within 'a system that is neither of their choosing nor of their design' (Karioris, 2014, p. 220); a system which can be quite uncomfortable and problematic. Karioris (2014) draws our attention to the importance of considering identities in relation to the wider social, specifically homosocial, relations, which foregrounds 'gender as performative and each person as both complicit in and bounded by social structures' (p. 220). However, these social structures are ever changing and post-structuralist efforts seek to position masculinities as relational constructions and away from notions of masculinity as 'static and solid' (Hølter, 2005, p. 18). Structure, in this instance, refers to the social organisation where

gender is seen as a way in which social practice is organized, whether in personal life, interpersonal interaction, or on the larger scale. It is common to refer to the patterning in social relations as 'structure', so the relational approach is sometimes summarized by describing gender as a social structure.

(Connell, 2000, p. 24)

Longitudinal research can provide particular insights into the personal changes of individuals and the social changes of wider society. McLeod (2003) writes the 'interpretive challenge is actively and methodically to listen for both "immanent structures" and emotional investments, to play them back against each other' (p. 209).

While I am generally in favour of adopting the role of 'naive' interviewer, where the participant assumes the role of the expert in his/her own life (Barnes, 2013), this becomes less possible in longitudinal research. In fact, there becomes an in-built expectation that the interviewer is aware of the particular details of each participant (e.g. home life, employment, etc.) as this knowledge functions as a currency integral to building the relationship. Holmegaard (2020) described how, despite using

> insights from the previous waves of interviews to ask, challenge, and invite in other ways, the interviewer refrained from bringing her own versions of the past and previous interviews into the actual interview setting. This was crucial for the knowledge produced during the interviews.
>
> (p. 126)

McLeod (2003) writes: 'One of the specific strengths of longitudinal interviews is the accumulation of responses that could be read against each other. A picture could be built up of orientations and beliefs across different times, ages and moods' (p. 205). A longitudinal study of the experiences of young men allows for a consideration of how their aspirations are 'cooling out, warming up, and holding steady' (Alexander et al., 2008, p. 375) as they navigate the university space. Alexander et al. (2008) here extend the wording of Clark (1960), who documented how post-secondary experiences dampen the unrealistic optimistic expectations of those from disadvantaged backgrounds. With this in mind, according to Moller (2007), research on masculinity should not focus on the hegemonic but instead men's weakness, vulnerability and disempowerment, thus challenging models of masculinity that are read through the lens of domination and subordination. However, weaknesses ebb and flow as do notions of domination and subordination. Longitudinal research, therefore, provides an opportunity to discover the nuances of where young men are vulnerable and how they negotiate these vulnerabilities.

The centrality of participant voice

In presenting the case studies, I foreground participant voice wherever possible in an effort to illustrate subjectivities in terms of *being* and *becoming*. It could be argued I attempt to sidestep the role of my own interpretative authority (Egeberg Holmgren, 2013). I acknowledge the subject is always constituted as 'in process' not fixed, a 'discursive category' (McLeod, 2000, pp. 504–505) where the interview – as a snapshot – involves the interviewer being able to 'zoom in on the interview subject's language, attributions of meaning, experiences, perceptions, resources, defense mechanisms, and other aspects' (Holmegaard, 2020, p. 112). By drawing heavily on the words of the young men, I do not feel this means I took the interviewees at face value. Their words are re-presentations of their realities and work as subjectivities, developed over time. Tomanović (2018) writes of 'biographization', where in research young people 'relate their agency to their identity and subjectivity, thereby giving meaning to their actions' (p. 356).

In a special issue on 'Youth Voices in Educational Research' in the *Harvard Educational Review*, editors Spindel Bassett and Geron (2020) write: 'Too often in our work, the voices of youth live inside the confines of quotation marks; their outrage is edited, preoccupations condensed through ellipses, and vivid vernacular obfuscated through academic jargon' (p. 166). Educational researchers have a responsibility to listen to young people and draw upon their words to foster better conditions. Certainly, academic scholarship requires an adeptness in terms of how young people are (re) presented and how their voices are heard. Presenting an argument for a consideration of the state of empirical sociology, Savage and Burrows (2007, p. 893) propose that the 'in-depth interview remains a useful device for allowing respondents to reflect on their practices, histories and identities'. After all, Foucault (1976) once spoke of the interview as 'confessional technology' where people present an account of themselves in a way they may find therapeutic.

It may be useful to consider the interview as a co-constructed meaning-making practice where both interviewer and interviewee work collaboratively to produce text – as well as textual analysis – that captures both experience and change in identity over time. Scholarship continues to document the reciprocal relationship where both researcher and researched learn from one another and have a voice in the study (Pini & Pease, 2013; Powell & Takayoshi, 2003; Stahl, 2013). Disclosures are always subject to relationship building which, in turn, is always framed within a power dynamic. However, prior to this the participant needs to have experienced a reflexive process focused on the self and their own sense of progress. Powell and Takayoshi (2003, p. 406) note:

> we as researchers would be wise to do more than 'invite' our participants to share with us; in order to build truly reciprocal relationships, we must be equally willing to share with them, to give them control over the spaces and forms in which they see us.

However, such an analysis disassociates the research process from the power, privilege and positionality embedded in *doing gender* (Egeberg Holmgren, 2013). This will be explored further in the next section.

Building rapport

Many studies focused on the experiences of students from disadvantaged backgrounds have engaged actively with the participants over many hours and sometimes by building relationships and trust throughout a period of years (Holmegaard, 2020; Carreón et al., 2005). Understanding how certain facets of gender (i.e. embodiment, physicality and performance) are valued and devalued depending on context is integral to how research actively works to promote trust and an ethos of care (Stahl, 2016). Interviews open up spaces to build rapport and interviews conducted longitudinally open up multiple spaces for this to occur. Similar to qualitative research by Egeberg Holmgren (2013), in the *First-in-Family Males Project* a set of protocols naturally developed over the course of the three years. The interview participants themselves chose where they wanted to be interviewed (e.g. dormitory rooms, local libraries, cafés). Also, I was willing to meet them at any time, even after shift work late at night or on their lunch breaks. Given their sometimes frantic schedules balancing employment and university study, the aim was always to make things as easy as possible for them to ensure I could keep as many participants in the study for as long as possible.

Scholars have raised concerns about the connections that can form between male researcher and participant (Skelton, 1998), which could have implications for confronting sexist views or hegemonic versions of masculinity (Mac an Ghaill, 1994). Hearn (2013) writes: 'For men to critically interview men is likely to be a contradictory process – necessitating politeness and respect, avoidance of collusion, and even use of control, firmness and authority in the interview' (p. 27). While not discounting this critique, or the power differences in research interviews, there is a need for increased reflexivity at every stage of the research (Vanderbeck, 2005) given that both the masculinity of the participants and the masculinity of the researcher are subject to change in terms of routines and performances realised through ongoing interactions. Reflexivity, as an approach for interrogating researcher subjectivity, fosters a continual awareness of the influence of the interviewer's gender on the interpretation of data (see Hearn, 2013; Pini & Pease, 2013). I was consciously aware I served as an audience to the participants and certain identities were performed. Clearly, the interview in itself can work as an important setting for *doing gender* (Egeberg Holmgren, 2013) and good research keeps a critical eye on power, privilege and positionality.

Research is always framed by uneven complexities and dilemmas surrounding relationship building – often termed 'rapport development' (Pitts & Miller-Day, 2007; Stahl, 2016). Pini and Pease (2013) assert that '[w]hen men interview men, they need to be reflexive about the impact of gender sameness on the construction of interviewee narratives and the analysis and interpretation of the interview material' (p. 8). Such a consideration has implications for how the voices of the participants are treated. As a researcher, my understanding of power relations in research settings is crucially informed by previous experiences with gendered, classed and ethnic identity practices. Masculinities are constructed in relation to space and time and there is exactly 20 years' age difference between the participants and me. While Schwalbe and Wolkomir (2001) recognise the diversity of men's identities, they contend that there are certain cultural ascriptions associated with masculinity that influence the interview process. Building on their work, Mac an Ghaill et al. (2013) assert the interview 'operates as an opportunity to display masculinity, but also a space where masculinities are under threat' (p. 78). Of course, one could make the argument that our gender identity is always under some sort of duress consciously or unconsciously.

The interviews (and subsequent data analysis) required a balance between an equal and empathic relationship while keeping some form of critical distance. These were not interviews as sites 'for reproducing, or challenging, men and masculinities' (Hearn, 2013, p. 28). This was partly because the interviews were so wide ranging in scope, rather than focusing on gender in particular, though gender, as we will see, was discussed. Masculinity was discussed but largely the connections I make to gender are inferred. I chose not to follow the participants on social media aside from what was publicly available, and I was willing to share some of my experiences at university. I did not have access to their academic grades unless they disclosed this information themselves nor did I know their immediate peer groups. The students were aware I was affiliated with a university and the general purpose of the research but they rarely probed deeper. I actively resisted making recommendations regarding their pathway or when they stumbled. Overall, I was not friends with the participants (cf. Dasgupta, 2013), though the interaction was always cordial and friendly.

According to Connolly and Reilly (2007), the research relationship does not just manifest naturally; it requires not simply the recognition of power differentials but an active engagement in building – often moment by moment – a relationship between the researcher and the researched. I employed strategies to develop and maintain the participants' trust in an effort to motivate the participants to stay in the study for its duration. What is most important to note here is that, in echoing McDowell's (2001) words, young men are typically not reflexive about their gender and class experiences and certain strategies need to be adopted in order to foster critical thinking. Chief among these strategies was humour, which worked to distil anxieties, and adopting a non-judgemental approach. Over the three years, I developed close relationships with the majority of the participants and, while a certain distance was always maintained, I did feel invested in seeing them do well. Observing them transition to university and experience the pitfalls of adolescence was a privilege. As they navigated various transitions (secondary school, part-time/full-time work, university) and relationships (partners, parents) I needed a certain adaptability and sensitivity as the participants evolved and changed.

Throughout the case studies which form Part 2, I make connections to my own reflexivity, accounting for the complex nature of identities, lifestyles and perspectives present in researcher–participant interaction. Intersectional identity vectors – along with embodiment, physicality and performance – all shape participant–researcher interaction. Pini and Pease (2013) note that when the men being interviewed 'are working class and non-white and the researcher is a white professional, issues of unequal power are intensified' (p. 9). As Dasgupta (2013) notes, in conducting research certain binaries foundational to fieldwork methodology 'such as outsider/insider, researcher/ informant and "objective" ethnography/"subjective" autobiography' (p. 104) shift and change and are, therefore, subject to continual negotiation. Power relations are innate to all relationships and I capitalised on my outsider status in terms of foreign nationality to neutralise certain elements such as social class that were normative to my participants, but, simultaneously, I drew upon my insider status in terms of gender and knowledge of Australian masculinities (Stahl, 2016). Similar to Dasgupta's (2013) research on men in Japan from a non-Japanese perspective, my outsider status which existed on a variety of levels (e.g. nationality, class, age and, depending on circumstance, ethnicity) directly contributed to the gender relations that were realised through embodiment, physicality and performance (see Stahl, 2016).

Learning from comparative case studies

Case studies include as many variables as possible and accommodate in-depth data and multiple examples of thick information (Creswell, 2007). Creswell (2007, p. 73), describing case studies in more detail, asserts that they can be a single 'case' or multiple 'cases' involving 'detailed, in-depth data collection'. Indeed, according to Eidlin (2010, p. 65), case studies are at times undertaken 'for the uniqueness of the case'. There are many definitions of case studies, but for the most part there seems to be consensus that a case study is 'an in-depth description and analysis of a bounded system' where the term *bounded system* is here understood as a single entity, a unit around which there are boundaries (Merriam, 2009, p. 40). Furthermore, according to Merriam (2009), there are three primary characteristics of *case study* research, namely particularistic, descriptive and heuristic. A case study is considered *particularistic* because it focuses on a particular phenomenon or situation and what that phenomenon might represent. A case study is *descriptive* in the sense that a case study has the capacity to create a thick description of the studied phenomenon, with different angles or dimensions (Gobo & Marciniak, 2016). Lastly, a case study is *heuristic* in the way that it intends to illuminate the readers' understanding of the phenomenon under study (Merriam, 2009). Case study research can bring about the discovery of new meaning, extend the reader's experience, or confirm what is known, drawn from 'highly pertinent' characteristics of the phenomenon under research (Yin, 2003, p. 13). The specific rationale for adopting a *comparative case study* design is that it allows for comparison and contrast of multiple dimensions of the phenomenon under scrutiny.

Saldaña (2011, p. 9) classifies three methods of selecting a case to study: *deliberately* because of its unique character, thus presenting itself as a rich opportunity and exemplar for focused study; *strategically* because it is deemed to represent the most typical example of its kind; or simply and purposively for *convenience*. This raises some important questions regarding how I selected the case studies which serve as illustrative examples. Collinson and Hearn (2005) refer to the 'unresolved tension' in critical studies on men and masculinities between 'multiplicity and diversity' and 'men's structured domination, their shared economic and symbolic vested interests and sense of unity' (p. 300). In selecting these case studies I foreground this tension and consider how each case speaks to the study of upwardly mobile working-class masculinities. The young men – Lucas, Campbell, Rashid, Manny, Dominic and Logan – all come from different ethnic backgrounds. Furthermore, they provide a glimpse of what Davies (1993) calls 'processes of subjectification' which are intertwined with the gendered construction of learner identities – where gender is relational, multiple and becoming.

Lastly, it should be noted I did not have a perfect flow of conversation with each of the participants and there were examples of awkwardness and confusion at various moments. However, over time the rapport shifted, as sometimes when I met up with the participants they were more forthcoming and sometimes they were more taciturn (McDowell, 2000). Five of the six were the eldest in their family and thus their family were new to the university application process. Studies on prospective first-in-family students often draw attention to the importance of having access to older siblings or extended family members who had already entered university (Gofen, 2009; Patfield et al., 2020; Wong, 2018). First-in-family students, it is assumed, benefit from such networks. None of my case study participants voiced an attraction to alternative pathways such as apprenticeships or trade work, which was dissimilar from others in the study. All six of the boys ended up in competitive programs. All experienced different issues at university but were ultimately able to make university work for them. Three were located in Sydney while the other three were located in Adelaide. Therefore, the cases in the current study were selected for at least two reasons: *deliberately* and *strategically*.

Conclusion

Working across the disciplines of widening participation, social mobility and working-class masculinities, this chapter has provided an overview of the main themes which correspond to the case studies presented in Part 2. I have addressed the research study itself and how the research is positioned in relation to other scholarship on the longitudinal study of masculinities as well as studies of masculinities in education. In the following part, I explore the identity and changing lifeworlds of six young men over a three-year period, foregrounding how class and gender work to structure their journey as learners.

References

Adams, M., & Coltrane, S. (2005). Boys and men in families: The domestic production of gender, power, and privilege. In M. Kimmel, J. Hearn, & R. W. Connell (Eds.), *Handbook of studies on men and masculinities* (pp. 230–248). Sage.

Adkins, L. (2003). Reflexivity: Freedom or habit of gender? *Theory, Culture & Society, 20*(6), 21–42.

Alexander, K., Bozick, R., & Entwisle, D. (2008). Warming up, cooling out, or holding steady? Persistence and change in educational expectations after high school. *Sociology of Education, 81*, 371–396.

Alexander, P. (2019). Boys from the Bronx, men from Manhattan: Gender, aspiration and imagining a (neoliberal) future after high school in New York City. In C. Beverley & P. Michele (Eds.), *Interrogating the neoliberal lifecycle: The limits of success* (pp. 39–67). Springer Nature/Palgrave Macmillan.

Archer, L., & Leathwood, C. (2003). Identities, inequalities and higher education. In L. Archer, M. Hutchings, & A. Ross (Eds.), *Higher education and social class: Issues of exclusion and inclusion* (pp. 175–192). Routledge Falmer.

Asmar, C., Page, S., & Radloff, A. (2015). Exploring anomalies in Indigenous student engagement: Findings from a national Australian survey of undergraduates. *Higher Education Research and Development, 34*(1), 15–29.

Australian Bureau of Statistics (ABS). (2015). Socio-economic indexes for areas. *ABS.* http://www.abs.gov.au/websitedbs/censushome.nsf/home/seifa?opendocument&navpos=260

Barnes, C. (2013). Using visual methods to hear young men's voices: Discussion and analysis of participant-led photographic research in the field. In B. Pini & B. Pease (Eds.), *Men, masculinities and methodologies* (pp. 236–249). Palgrave Macmillan.

Bennett, A., & Southgate, E. (2014). Excavating widening participation policy in Australian higher education: Subject positions, representational effects, emotion. *Creative Approaches to Research, 7*(1), 21–45.

Bernstein, B. (1962). Social class, linguistic codes and grammatical elements. *Language and Speech, 5*(4), 221–240.

Bleach, K. (Ed.). (2000). *Raising boys' achievement in schools.* Trentham Books.

Boliver, V. (2015). Exploring ethnic inequalities in admission to Russell Group universities. *Sociology, 50*(2), 247–266.

Bonham V. L., Sellers, S. L., & Neighbors, H. W. (2004). John Henryism and self-reported physical health among high-socioeconomic status African American men. *American Journal of Public Health, 94*, 737–738.

Bourdieu, P., et al. (1993). *The weight of the world: Social suffering in contemporary society.* Stanford University Press.

Bradley, D., Noonan, P., Nugent, H., & Scales, B. (2008). *Review of Australian higher education: Final report.* Commonwealth of Australia.

Browman, A., Destin, M., Carswell, K. L., & Svoboda, R. C. (2017). Perceptions of socioeconomic mobility influence academic persistence among low socioeconomic status students. *Journal of Experimental Social Psychology, 72*, 45–52.

Brown, P. (2013). Education, opportunity and the prospects for social mobility. *British Journal of Sociology of Education, 34*(5–6), 678–700.

Burke, P. J. (2009). Men accessing higher education: Theorizing continuity and change in relation to masculine subjectivities. *Higher Education Policy, 22*, 81–100.

Capannola, A. L., & Johnson, E. I. (2020). On being the first: The role of family in the experiences of first-generation college students. *Journal of Adolescent Research*, advance online publication. doi:10.1177/0743558420979144

Cardak, B., Bowden, M., & Bahtsevanoglou, J. (2015). *Are low SES students disadvantaged in the university application process?* National Centre for Student Equity in Higher Education, Curtin University.

Carreón, G. P., Drake, C., & Barton, A. C. (2005). The importance of presence: Immigrant parents' school engagement experiences. *American Educational Research Journal, 42*(3), 465–498.

Clark, B. R. (1960). The 'cooling out' function in higher education. *American Journal of Sociology, 65,* 569–576.

Collins, P. H. (2000). *Black feminist thought: Knowledge, consciousness, and the politics of empowerment* (2nd ed.). Routledge.

Collinson, D. L., & Hearn, J. (2005). Men and masculinities in work, organizations, and management. In M. Kimmel, J. Hearn, & R. W. Connell (Eds.), *Handbook of studies on men and masculinities* (pp. 289–310). Sage.

Connell, R. W. (2000). *The men and the boys.* Polity Press.

Connell, R. W. (2005). Growing up masculine: Rethinking the significance of adolescence in the making of masculinities. *Irish Journal of Sociology, 14*(2), 11–28.

Connolly, K., & Reilly, R. C. (2007). Emergent issues when researching trauma: A confessional tale. *Qualitative Inquiry, 13,* 522–540.

Crenshaw, K. (1991). Mapping the margins: Intersectionality, identity politics, and violence against women of color. *Stanford Law Review, 43*(6), 1241–1299.

Creswell, J. W. (2007). *Qualitative inquiry & research design: Choosing among five approaches* (2nd ed.). Sage.

Dasgupta, R. (2013). Conversations about otokorashisa (masculinity/'manliness'): Insider/outsider dynamics in masculinities research in Japan. In B. Pini & B. Pease (Eds.), *Men, masculinities and methodologies* (pp. 103–115). Palgrave Macmillan.

Davies, B. (1993). Beyond dualism and towards multiple subjectivities. In L. K. Christian-Smith (Ed.), *Texts of desire: Essays on fiction, femininity and schooling.* Falmer Press.

Davis, T., & Laker, J. A. (2004). Connecting men to academic and student affairs programs and services. In G. E. Kellom (Ed.), *Developing effective programs and services for college men* (pp. 47–57). Jossey-Bass.

Dillabough, J.-A. (2004). Class, culture and the 'predicaments of masculine domination': Encountering Pierre Bourdieu. *British Journal of Sociology of Education, 25*(4), 489–506.

Dolby, N., & Dimitriadis, G. with Willis, P. (Eds.). (2004). *Learning to labor in new times.* Routledge Falmer.

Duckworth, V. (2013). *Learning trajectories: Violence and empowerment among adult basic skills learners.* Routledge.

Egeberg Holmgren, L. E. (2013). Gendered selves, gendered subjects: Interview performances and situational contexts in critical interview studies of men and masculinities. In B. Pini & B. Pease (Eds.), *Men, masculinities and methodologies* (pp. 90–103). Palgrave Macmillan.

Egerton, M., & Halsey, A. H. (1993). Trends by social class and gender in access to higher education in Britain. *Oxford Review of Education, 19*(2), 183–196.

Eidlin, F. (2010) 'Case Study and Theoretical Science' in Mills, A. J., Durepos, G., & Wiebe, E. (Eds.). (*Encyclopedia of case study research* (pp. 65–66). Sage.

Entwisle, D. R., Alexander, K. L., & Olson, L. S. (2007). Early schooling: The handicap of being poor and male. *Sociology of Education, 80,* 114–138.

Epstein, D., Elwood, J., Hey, V., & Maw, J. (Eds.). (1998) Schoolboy frictions: Feminisms and 'failing boys'. In Epstein, D., Elwood, J., Hey, V., & Maw, J. (Eds.). *Failing boys? Issues in gender and achievement* (pp. 3–19). Open University Press.

Fine, M., Weis, L., Addelston, J., & Marusza, J. (1997). Secure times: Constructing white working-class masculinities in the late 20th century. *Gender & Society, 11*(1), 52–68.

Foucault, M. (1976). *A history of sexuality*, Vol. 1. Penguin.

Francis, B. (2006). Heroes or zeroes? The discursive positioning of 'underachieving boys' in English neo-liberal education policy. *Journal of Education Policy*, *21*(2), 187–200.

Gale, T., & Parker, S. (2013). *Widening participation in Australian higher education: Report to the Higher Education Funding Council for England (HEFCE) and the Office of Fair Access (OFFA), England*. CFE (Research and Consulting) and Edge Hill University.

Gemici, S., Lim, P., & Karmel, T. (2013). *The impact of schools on young people's transition to university*. NCVER.

Giazitzoglu, A. (2014). Qualitative upward mobility, the mass-media and 'posh' masculinity in contemporary north-east Britain: A micro sociological case-study. *Sociological Research Online*, *19*(2), 1–11.

Giazitzoglu, A., & Muzio, D. (2020). Learning the rules of the game: How is corporate masculinity learned and enacted by male professionals from nonprivileged backgrounds? *Gender, Work and Organization*, advance online publication. doi:10.1111/gwao.12561

Gobo, G., & Marciniak, L. T. (2016). What is ethnography? In D. Silverman (Ed.), *Qualitative research* (pp. 103–120). Sage.

Gofen, A. (2009). Family capital: How first-generation higher education students break the inter-generational cycle. *Family Relations*, *58*(1), 104–120.

Goldthorpe, J. H. (1987) *Social mobility and the class structure in modern Britain*. Clarendon. First published in 1980.

Goldthorpe, J. H. (1996). Class analysis and the reorientation of class theory: The case of persisting differentials in educational attainment. *British Journal of Sociology*, *47*(3), 481–505.

Goldthorpe, J. H. (1998). Rational action theory for sociology. *British Journal of Sociology*, *49*(2), 167–192.

Gore, J., Holmes, K., Smith, M., Southgate, E., & Albright, J. (2015). Socioeconomic status and the career aspirations of Australian school students: Testing enduring assumptions. *Australian Educational Researcher*, *42*(2), 155–177.

Hardgrove, A., Rootham, E., & McDowell, L. (2015). Precarious lives, precarious labour: Family support and young men's transitions to work in the UK. *Journal of Youth Studies*, *18*(8), 1057–1076.

Harper, S. (2006). Peer support for African American men: Racial identity, male role norms, gender role conflict, and prejudicial attitudes. *Journal of Men's Studies*, *3*, 107–118.

Harper, S. R., & Harris, F., III. (2010). Beyond the model gender majority myth: Responding equitably to the developmental needs and challenges of college men. In S. R. Harper & F. Harris III (Eds.), *College men and masculinities: Theory, research, and implications for practice* (pp. 1–16). Jossey-Bass.

Harris, F., & Harper, S. R. (2015). Matriculating masculinity: Understanding undergraduate men's precollege gender socialization. *Journal of the First-Year Experience & Students in Transition*, *27*(2), 49–65.

Harvey, A. (2014). Early and delayed offers to under-represented university students. *Australian Journal of Education*, *58*(2), 167–181.

Harvey, A., Andrewartha, L., & Burnheim, C. (2016a). Out of reach? University for people from low socio-economic status backgrounds. In A. Harvey, C. Burnheim, & M. Brett (Eds.), *Student equity in Australian higher education: Twenty-five years of a fair chance for all* (pp. 69–87). Springer.

Harvey, A., & Burnheim, C. (2013). Loosening old school ties: Understanding university achievement and attrition by school type. *Professional Voice*, *9*(2), 29–36.

Harvey, A., Burnheim, C., & Brett, M. (2016b). Towards a fairer chance for all: Revising the Australian student equity framework. In A. Harvey, C. Burnheim, & M. Brett (Eds.), *Student equity in Australian higher education: Twenty-five years of a fair chance for all* (pp. 3–20). Springer.

Hattam, R., & Smyth, J. (2003). 'Not everyone has a perfect life': Becoming somebody without school. *Pedagogy, Culture and Society*, *11*(3), 379–398.

Hearn, J. (2013). Methods and methodologies in critical studies on men and masculinities. In B. Pini & B. Pease (Eds.), *Men, masculinities and methodologies* (pp. 26–39). Palgrave Macmillan.

Holmegaard, H. T. (2020). Complexity, negotiations, and processes: A longitudinal qualitative, narrative approach to young people's transition to and from university. In N. E. Fenton & W. Ross (Eds.), *Critical reflection on research in teaching and learning* (pp. 107–130). Brill.

Hølter, Ø. G. (2005). Social theories for researching men and masculinities: Direct gender hierarchy and structural inequality. In M. Kimmel, J. Hearn, & R. W. Connell (Eds.), *Handbook of studies on men & masculinities* (pp. 15–34). Thousand Oaks, CA: SAGE Publications.

Iwamoto, D. K., Brady, J., Kaya, A., & Park, A. (2018). Masculinity and depression: A longitudinal investigation of multidimensional masculine norms among college men. *Journal of Men's Health*, *12*(6), 1873–1881.

Karioris, F. G. (2014). Amicus et sodalitas, sicut: The figure of homosocial relations in men's lives. In F. G. Karioris & C. Loeser (Eds.), *Reimagining masculinities: Beyond masculinist epistemology* (pp. 219–237). Inter-Disciplinary Press.

Kenway, J. (2013). Challenging inequality in Australian schools: Gonski and beyond. *Discourse: Studies in the Cultural Politics of Education*, *34*(2), 286–308.

Kenway, J., & Fitzclarence, L. (1997). Masculinity, violence and schooling: Challenging 'poisonous pedagogies'. *Gender and Education*, *9*, 117–133.

Kenway, J., & Kraack, A. (2004). Reordering work and destabilizing masculinity. In N. Dolby, G. Dimitriadis, & P. Willis (Eds.), *Learning to labor in new times* (pp. 95–109). Routledge Falmer.

Kenway, J., Kraack, A., & Hickey-Moody, A. (2006). *Masculinity beyond the metropolis.* Palgrave.

Kimmel, M. (2008). *Guyland: The perilous world where boys become men.* HarperCollins.

Koshy, P. (2017). *Equity student participation in Australian higher education: 2011 to 2016.* National Centre for Student Equity in Higher Education, Curtin University.

Lamb, S., Jackson, J., Walstab, A., & Huo, S. (2015). *Educational opportunity in Australia 2015: Who succeeds and who misses out.* Mitchell Institute.

Lareau, A. (2003). *Unequal childhoods.* University of California Press.

Lee, E. M., & Kramer, R. (2013). Out with the old, in with the new? Habitus and social mobility at selective colleges. *Sociology of Education*, *86*(1), 18–35.

Lehmann, W. (2009a). Becoming middle class: How working-class university students draw and transgress moral class boundaries. *Sociology*, *43*, 631–647.

Lehmann, W. (2009b). University as vocational education: Working-class students' expectations for university. *British Journal of Sociology of Education*, *30*(2), 137–149.

Lingard, B., Martino, W., & Mills, M. (2009). *Boys and schooling: Beyond structural reform.* Palgrave Macmillan.

Littler, J. (2018). *Against meritocracy: Culture, power and myths of mobility.* Routledge.

Loeser, C. (2014). The potentialities of post-essentialism for hearing (dis)abled masculinities in friendship. In F. G. Karioris & C. Loeser (Eds.), *Reimagining masculinities: Beyond masculinist epistemology* (pp. 193–219). Inter-Disciplinary Press.

Loveday, V. (2015). Working-class participation, middle-class aspiration? Value, upward mobility and symbolic indebtedness in higher education. *Sociological Review, 63*, 570–588.

Lumb, M., Burke, P. J., & Bennett, A. (2020). Obscenity and fabrication in equity and widening participation methodologies. *British Educational Research Journal,* advance online publication. doi:10.1002/berj.3663

Lund, R., Meriläinen, S., & Tienari, J. (2018). New masculinities in universities? Discourses, ambivalence and potential change. *Gender, Work and Organization, 26*(10), 1376–1397.

Lusher, D. (2011). Masculinity, educational achievement and social status: A social network analysis. *Gender and Education, 23*(6), 655–675.

Lynch, J., Walker-Gibbs, B., & Herbert, S. (2015). Moving beyond a 'bums-on-seats' analysis of progress towards widening participation: Reflections on the context, design and evaluation of an Australian government-funded mentoring programme. *Journal of Higher Education Policy and Management, 37*(2), 144–158.

Mac an Ghaill, M. (1994). *The making of men: Masculinities, sexualities and schooling.* Open University Press.

Mac an Ghaill, M., Haywood, C., & Bright, Z. (2013). Making connections: Speed dating, masculinity and interviewing. In B. Pini & B. Pease (Eds.), *Men, masculinities and methodologies* (pp. 77–90). Palgrave Macmillan.

MacLeod, J. (2009). *Ain't no makin' it: Aspirations and attainment in a low-income neighborhood* (3rd ed.). Westview Press.

Mallman, M. (2017). The perceived inherent vice of working-class university students. *Sociological Review, 65*(2), 235–250.

Marginson, S. (2016). The worldwide trend to high participation higher education: Dynamics of social stratification in inclusive systems. *Higher Education, 72*, 413–434.

Maslen, G. (2009, March 9). Facing a higher issue: All things aren't equal. *The Age,* Education Section, p. 12.

McDowell, L. (2000). The trouble with men? Young people, gender transformations and the crisis of masculinity. *International Journal of Urban and Regional Research, 24*(1), 201–209.

McDowell, L. (2001). 'It's that Linda again': Ethical, practical and political issues involved in longitudinal research with young men. *Ethics, Place and Environment, 4*, 87–100.

McDowell, L. (2003). *Redundant masculinities? Employment change and white working class youth.* Blackwell.

McDowell, L. (2020). Looking for work: Youth, masculine disadvantage and precarious employment in post-millennium England. *Journal of Youth Studies, 23*(8), 974–988.

McLeod, J. (2000). Subjectivity and schooling in a longitudinal study of secondary students. *British Journal of Sociology of Education, 21*(4), 501–521.

McLeod, J. (2003). Why we interview now – Reflexivity and perspective in longitudinal studies. *International Journal of Research Methodology, 6*(3), 201–211.

Merriam, S. B. (2009). *Qualitative research: A guide to design and implementation.* Jossey-Bass.

Miles, A., Savage, M., & Bühlmann, F. (2011). Telling a modest story: Accounts of men's upward mobility from the National Child Development Study. *British Journal of Sociology, 62*(3), 418–441.

Mills, M., Martino, W., & Lingard, B. (2007). Getting boys' education 'right': The Australian government's parliamentary inquiry report as an exemplary instance of recuperative masculinity politics. *British Journal of Sociology of Education, 28*(1), 5–21.

Milner, A., Shields, M., & King, T. (2019). The influence of masculine norms and mental health on health literacy among men: Evidence from the ten to men study. *American Journal of Men's Health, 13*(5), 1–9.

Moller, M. (2007). Exploiting patterns: A critique of hegemonic masculinity. *Journal of Gender Studies, 16*, 263–276.

Morgan, M. (2004). Class and masculinity. In M. Kimmel, J. Hearn, & R. W. Connell (Eds.), *Handbook of studies on men and masculinities* (pp. 165–177). Sage.

Murray, N., & Klinger, C. M. (Eds.). (2013). *Aspirations, access and attainment: International perspectives on widening participation and an agenda for change.* Routledge.

Nayak, A. (2003). 'Boyz to men': Masculinities, schooling and labour transitions in de-industrial times. *Educational Review, 55*(2), 147–159.

Nayak, A. (2006). Displaced masculinities: Chavs, youth and class in the post-industrial city. *Sociology, 40*(5), 813–831.

Naylor, R., Coates, H., & Kelly, P. (2016). From equity to excellence: Reforming Australia's national framework to create new forms of success. In A. Harvey, C. Burnheim, & M. Brett (Eds.), *Student equity in Australian higher education: Twenty-five years of a fair chance for all* (pp. 257–275). Springer.

Nichols, S., & Stahl, G. (2017). 'Gotta get that laziness out of me': Negotiating masculine aspirational subjectivities in the transition from school to university in Australia. In G. Stahl, J. Nelson, & D. O. Wallace (Eds.), *Masculinity and aspiration in the era of neoliberal education: International perspectives* (pp. 166–184). Routledge.

Nichols, S., & Stahl, G. (2019). Intersectionality in higher education research: A systematic literature review. *Higher Education Research & Development, 38*(6), 1255–1268.

OECD. (2015). *Education at a glance 2015: OECD indicators. OECD Publishing.* doi:10.1787/eag-2015-en

Omi, M., & Winant, H. (1994). *Racial formation in the United States.* Routledge.

O'Shea, S., May, J., Stone, C., Delahunty, J. (2017). *First-in-family students, university experience and family life motivations, transitions and participation.* Palgrave Macmillan.

Pachankis, J. E., Sullivan, T. J., Feinstein, B. A., & Newcomb, M. E. (2018). Young adult gay and bisexual men's stigma experiences and mental health: An 8-year longitudinal study. *Developmental Psychology, 54*(7), 1381–1393.

Patfield, S., Gore, J., & Fray, L. (2020). Degrees of 'being first': Toward a nuanced understanding of first-generation entrants to higher education. *Educational Review*, advance online publication. doi:10.1080/00131911.2020.1740172

Pini, B., & Pease, B. (2013). 'Gendering Methodologies in the Study of Men and Masculinities.' In Pini, B., & Pease, B. (Eds.). *Men, masculinities and methodologies.* (pp. 1–26). Palgrave Macmillan.

Pirkis, J., Currier, D., Carlin, J., Degenhardt, L., Dharmage, S. C., Giles-Corti, B., Gordon, I. R., Gurrin, L. C., Hocking, J. S., Kavanagh, A., Keogh, L., Koelmeyer,

R., LaMontagne, A. D., Patton, G., Sanci, L., Spittal, M. J., Schlichthorst, M., Studdert, D., Williams, J., & English, D. R. (2017). Cohort profile: *Ten to Men* (the Australian Longitudinal Study on Male Health). *International Journal of Epidemiology, 46*(3), 793–794.

Pitman, T., Harvey, A., McKay, J., Devlin, M., Trinidad, S., & Brett, M. (2017). The impact of enabling programs on Indigenous participation, success and retention in Australian higher education. In J. Frawley, S. Larkin, & J. Smith (Eds.), *Indigenous pathways, transitions and participation in higher education* (pp. 235–249). Springer.

Pitts, M. J., & Miller-Day, M. (2007). Upward turning points and positive rapport development across time in researcher–participant relationships. *Qualitative Research, 7*(2), 177–201.

Pötschulat, M., Moran, M., & Jones, P. (2021). 'The student experience' and the remaking of contemporary studenthood: A critical intervention. *Sociological Review, 69*(1), 3–20. doi:10.1177/0038026120946677

Powell, K. M., & Takayoshi, P. (2003). Accepting roles created for us: The ethics of reciprocity. *College Composition and Communication, 54*(3), 394–422.

Prins, B. (2006). Narrative accounts of origins: A blind spot in the intersectional approach? *European Journal of Women's Studies, 13*(3), 277–290.

Reay, D. (2002). Shaun's story: Troubling discourses on white working-class masculinities. *Gender and Education, 14*(3), 221–234.

Reay, D. (2005). Beyond consciousness: The psychic landscape of class. *Sociology, 39*(5), 911–928.

Reay, D., Crozier, G., & James, D. (2011). *White middle-class identities and urban schooling*. Palgrave Macmillan.

Reay, D., David, M. E., & Ball, S. (2005). *Degrees of choice: Social class, race and gender in higher education*. Institute of Education.

Reay, D., & Lucey, H. (2000). 'I don't really like it here but I don't want to be anywhere else': Children and inner-city council estates. *Antipode, 34*, 410–425.

Rubin, M., Evans, O., & McGuffog, R. (2019). Social class differences in social integration at university: Implications for academic outcomes and mental health. In J. Jetten & K. Peters (Eds.), *The social psychology of inequality* (pp. 87–102). Springer.

Rubin, M., & Wright, C. L. (2015). Age differences explain social class differences in students' friendship at university: Implications for transition and retention. *Higher Education, 70*, 427–439.

Saldaña, J. (2011). *Fundamentals of qualitative research*. Oxford University Press.

Savage, M., & Burrows, R. (2007). The coming crisis of empirical sociology. *Sociology, 41*(5), 885–899.

Schwalbe, M., & Wolkomir, M. (2001). The masculine self as a problem and resource in interview studies of men. *Men and Masculinities, 4*, 90–103.

Sennett, R., & Cobb, J. (1972). *The hidden injuries of class*. Cambridge University Press.

Shalley, F., Smith, J., Wood, D., Fredericks, B., & Robertson, K. (2019). *Understanding completion rates of Indigenous higher education students from two regional universities: A cohort analysis*. National Centre for Student Equity in Higher Education, Charles Darwin University.

Skeggs, B. (2002). *Formations of class and gender*. Sage.

Skeggs, B. (2004). Exchange, value and affect: Bourdieu and 'the self'. *Sociological Review, 52*(S2), 75–95.

Skeggs, B. (2014). Values beyond value? Is anything beyond the logic of capital? *British Journal of Sociology, 65*(1), 1–20.

Skelton, C. (1998). Feminism and research into masculinities and schooling. *Gender and Education, 10*, 217–227.

Snowden, C., & Lewis, S. (2015). Mixed messages: Public communication about higher education and non-traditional students in Australia. *Higher Education: The International Journal of Higher Education Research, 70*(3), 585–599.

Spindel Bassett, B., & Geron, T. (2020). Youth voices in education research. *Harvard Educational Review, 90*(2), 165–171.

Stahl, G. (2013). Habitus disjunctures, reflexivity and white working-class boys' conceptions of status in learner and social identities. *Sociological Research Online, 18*(3), 1–12. http://www.socresonline.org.uk/18/3/2.html

Stahl, G. (2015). *Aspiration, identity and neoliberalism: Educating white working-class boys.* Routledge.

Stahl, G. (2016). Relationship-building in research: Gendered identity construction in researcher–participant interaction. In M. R. M. Ward (Ed.), *Gendered identity construction in researcher–participant interaction* (pp. 145–164). Emerald.

Stahl, G., & McDonald, S. (2019). Social capital and self-crafting: Comparing two case studies of first-in-family males navigating elite Australian universities. *International Journal of Inclusive Education*, advance online publication. doi:10.1 080/13603116.2019.1632945

Swain, J. (2005). Masculinities in education. In M. Kimmel, J. Hearn, & R. W. Connell (Eds.), *Handbook of studies on men and masculinities* (pp. 213–229). Sage.

Thomsen, J. P. (2013). Exploring the heterogeneity of class in higher education: Social and cultural differentiation in Danish university programmes. *British Journal of Sociology of Education, 33*(4), 565–585.

Thomsen, J. P., Munk, M. D., Eiberg-Madsen, M., & Hansen, G. I. (2011). The educational strategies of Danish university students from professional and working-class backgrounds. *Comparative Education Review, 57*(3), 457–480.

Tomanović, S. (2018). Reconstructing changes in agency in the young people's social biographies through longitudinal qualitative research. *Young, 27*(4), 355–372.

Torres, M. (2017). An exploratory study of the academic engagement and beliefs of Latino male high school students. *Race, Ethnicity and Education, 20*(4), 546–560.

Tranter, D. (2011). Unequal schooling: How the school curriculum keeps students from low socio-economic backgrounds out of university. *International Journal of Inclusive Education, 16*(9), 901–916.

Vanderbeck, R. M. (2005). Masculinities and fieldwork: Widening the discussion. *Gender, Place and Culture, 12*, 387–402.

Vincent, C., Ball, S., Rollock, N., & Gillborn, D. (2013). Three generations of racism: Black middle-class children and schooling. *British Journal of Sociology of Education, 34*(5–6), 929–946.

Warikoo, N. K. (2016). *The diversity bargain: And other dilemmas of race, admissions, and meritocracy at elite universities.* University of Chicago Press.

Way, N. (2013). *Deep secrets: Boys' friendships and the crisis of connection.* Harvard University Press.

Wetherell, M., & Mohanty, C. T. (Eds.). (2010). *The Sage handbook of identities.* Sage.

Weis, L. (2004). Revisiting a 1980s 'moment of critique': Class, gender and the new economy. In N. Dolby, G. Dimitriadis, & P. Willis (Eds.), *Learning to labor in new times* (pp. 111–132). Routledge Falmer.

Weis, L., & Cipollone, K. (2013). 'Class work': Producing privilege and social mobility in elite US secondary schools. *British Journal of Sociology of Education, 34*, 701–722.

Whitehead, J. M. (2003). Masculinity, motivation and academic success: A paradox. *Teacher Development, 7*(2), 287–310.

Willis, P. (1977). *Learning to labour: How working class kids get working class jobs.* Columbia University Press.

Wong, B. (2018). By chance or by plan? The academic success of nontraditional students in higher education. *AERA Open, 4*(2), 1–14.

Yin, R. K. (2003). *Case study research: Design and methods* (3rd ed.). Sage.

Part 2

Longitudinal case studies

2 Lucas

Year 1: last year of compulsory schooling

Lucas lives in the western suburbs of Sydney where he attended an all-boys Catholic school, the same one his older brother attended. His father works as a self-employed plumber, and his mother supports the family business as a part-time secretary. Lucas's older brother attempted university but did not complete the first year, securing full-time employment instead. Lucas is a confident and adept speaker, able to articulate his opinions, which sets him apart from the other boys in the study. As a school prefect, he took on many leadership responsibilities at school which worked to extend this skill, though many teachers I spoke with were worried that he did not behave like other students his age. When I spoke with his mother, I got the sense that she and Lucas's father supported him in whatever choices he made but did not pressure him towards a particular aspiration. Lucas's self-assured nature set him apart from the rest of the participants in the study:

> I'm very – I'm very different to other people … I'll grab this textbook and I'll just start reading it and then, I don't know if I have partial photographic memory or if it's just something, I can memorise, like, whether legal studies cases, legislation, media, I can pick it up *very* fast.

Lucas's transition to university followed an aspirational trajectory that brought him into contact with elite spaces. How he came to adapt to these circumstances and position himself advantageously conflicts with a lot of the research about working-class students in elite spaces.

Having been heavily involved in Australia's Youth Parliament, the Australian Catholic Youth Festival as well as a community youth advocacy group for several years prior to Year 12, Lucas had been exposed to a variety of mentors. Thomsen et al. (2011) note that working-class students 'are more dependent on contingent encounters with role models outside of their family' (p. 470) who contribute to the structuring of their aspirations. Such opportunities gave Lucas, the 'exposure to the middle-class habitus and "class rules" associated with affluent males' (Giazitzoglu, 2014, para 8.5). He was serious about his political values: 'I mean I tend to lean more to the right side of politics', citing inspiring historical figures such as Abraham Lincoln, Winston Churchill and Robert Menzies. However, Lucas was clear to note:

> I mean I don't – I haven't looked up to them and said I want to inspire to be like them because I think it's about charting your own course and charting who you are and that's why I sort of stumbled in the sense of popular culture, like oh, I want to be like this sporting person or that or I want to be like this.

His involvement in youth-focused politics provided Lucas with his greatest sense of belonging and it served as a major social outlet. I got the impression that, while Lucas was accepted and generally well liked, he did not have many close friends at school. At secondary school, he seemed much closer to the teachers, whom he spoke of as supportive. Describing what he looked for in friends, he said:

> It's that sort of I don't mind the exchange of ideas but someone who is kind-hearted, who's down to earth, who sort of doesn't just think about their immediate self but also looks out for other people, because I think that's, as a friend, that's what you're supposed to do.

While other participants vacillated between various aspirations in their final year of compulsory schooling, Lucas made it clear that he aspired to attend the prestigious University of Sydney:

> I've always wanted to – whether it be pursue law and become a barrister and then make … into become a judge in High Court hopefully of justice or pursue public life and go into politics and do something like that.

Mac an Ghaill (1994) describes how the masculine identities of his 'Academic Achievers' were focused on 'the projected future of a professional career' (p. 63). When I asked him why he did not want to attend the university closest to where he lived, Lucas called attention to the stigma associated with working-class universities in Australia and how this could serve as a barrier for someone wishes to enter law:

> I mean there's always a stigma … I guess to an extent a stigma, or it's like a prestige of going to, like, a law school in … even though UNSW [University of New South Wales] technically has a higher ATAR cut off – USYD [University of Sydney] has this glamour about it being Australia's oldest university.

Lucas was extremely knowledgeable both about the degree program and the grades he would have to get in his HSC (Higher School Certificate in NSW), the weighting of certain subjects and how his ATAR (Australian Tertiary Admission Rank) would be aggregated (see Stahl & McDonald, 2019). It was clear he had invested extensive time in researching his potential future. While other students were clearly experiencing anxiety in the weeks leading up to exams, Lucas remained positive: 'I haven't felt overly pressured or overly stressed, which I think has been a really positive thing.'

While Lucas was aspirational and set high standards for himself, he also took the time to note repeatedly that he was grounded and had a good sense of self. When speaking about his achievements and how completing Year 12 and gaining an ATAR was widely considered an accomplishment, Lucas was clear that academics were only one facet of his life:

> I mean an award doesn't define who you are, similar to how a mark doesn't define who you are. You're more remembered for the relationships and that that you create and how people perceive you and it's also how you perceive yourself that defines success.
>
> I guess I'm taking more pride in sort of the intrinsic stuff, like being a good person, doing a good deed, all that. That's like, being just a compassionate and caring person, is more so than like the physical success, as much as I want to succeed in life and that, and whatnot, like it's not like a, it's not like marks are what define me and my success. It's actually how I present myself as a person and my ability as a person rather than my ability in academic study.

In a further interview, Lucas spoke about looking forward to the social aspect of university and joining the right clubs and societies. It was clear that Lucas was aware of how to both operationalise and gain social capital to his advantage, describing law as 'it's not necessarily what you know, it's who you know – it's one of those industries'. He proceeded to highlight how competitive the job market would be and how he would need to network:

> So like, I think it's like, only 15 to 25% of jobs are actually listed, are like properly listed, it's like 75% of them, it's basically you've just got to know the people and just be in that industry and really develop it.

The next time I encountered Lucas was on the day the ATARs were released in December when his school held an 'ATAR BBQ' for students and their families. This was an emotionally charged day for many students and the event took on a strange ambiance. When I spoke with Lucas and his parents, it was clear their emotions were running very high. Lucas was crying. His mother was holding back tears. While entry into a law degree at the University of Sydney required an ATAR of 98.1, Lucas's ATAR was 97.8. Thus, his aspiration was in jeopardy. Visibly upset and turning to his parents for comfort, they told him they wanted him to focus on 'what he had achieved' and to 'take a few deep breaths'.

There are three things to note here. First, Lucas's subjectivity was being realised through routine institutional practices – the doling out of academic ranking – which significantly influenced his biographical narrative (McLeod, 2000, p. 503). Second, Adams (2006, p. 525) writes of 'painful awareness' where 'the delimitations of field enclosures uncoupled from resource realization amount to frustrated isolation'. Through this painful process of not achieving the required ATAR, Lucas felt denied. This experience became engrained on his habitus. Third, this moment became important for relationship building in the years to come because it allowed me to make a deeper connection to Lucas and to understand why he became fixed on a certain trajectory. Given the small gathering of people and my affiliation with a university context, Lucas spoke with me and sought my advice. This highlights that trust is not straightforward and has to be built over time from moment to moment (Stahl, 2016).

In a later interview, Lucas tactfully described the moment as a 'period of uncertainty', and he was open about feeling his hard work was not recognised. This resonates with the research of Browman et al. (2017), which focused on how academic persistence is viewed among lower-SES students and how such beliefs are contingent on whether socioeconomic mobility is achievable. At the same time, Lucas was quick to note that he was in the top '2.2 per cent' and the university would potentially be able to make compromises once they knew the numbers of applicants. As the school year concluded, it looked likely that the University of Sydney would accept Lucas and he would take a significant first step towards fulfilling his ambition. As Lehmann (2009) eloquently writes: 'Lacking the social capital that guarantees (or at least eases) access to lucrative middle-class careers, working-class students have only human capital – in this case a professional, applied degree – to break into middle-class career paths' (p. 144). As Lucas suffered on the day of the ATAR BBQ, not only was his perception of socioeconomic advancement called into question but we can assume he came to reflect on what capitals would be most advantageous in his future.

Year 2: the post-school year

Ultimately, Lucas was accepted into the University of Sydney to do a double degree in law and economics. Lucas was crafting his learner identity as a university student at an elite university by continuing his leadership work, where he described himself as 'networking my way'. Increasingly, Lucas seemed to view education as primarily a game of social capital accrual where, according to him, 'university is just really about capitalising on as many things – whenever you get given something you've got to take it or if something comes up you've got to pursue it'. In just the first few weeks at the University of Sydney, Lucas arguably became more fully engaged with becoming an 'active entrepreneur of the self' imbued with 'a reactivation of liberal values of self-reliance, autonomy and independence as the necessary conditions for self-respect, self-esteem, self-worth, and self-advancement' (Davies & Bansel, 2007, p. 252). In rationalising this approach to his time at university, Lucas said: 'because it's like, you miss a hundred percent of the shots you don't take, sort of thing, you never know what one conversation might lead to'. Lucas was always aware of his own positionality in relation to others as well as the meagre social capital he entered University of Sydney with, as he explained:

everyone gets their economics degree in the end let's say and everyone's wanting to apply for Treasury or RBA or whatever, maybe one of the big four accounting firms in Australia. But if you know someone in there then they can vouch for you. They can literally go and be like, yes, this person has qualifications, I know who he is. And now instead of being with that three hundred, you might be only with ten but no people. So it's that whole idea of you need both the knowledge and the drive and the actual foundation and the degree, but you need now the networking and that as well.

As Lucas began to settle into the elite space of the University of Sydney, he seemed comfortable and, according to him, found it easy to make friends. There exists a wide remit of studies spanning approximately 40 years regarding how working-class students struggle in elite spaces (Corrigan & Frith, 1976; Jin & Ball, 2019). In his work on upwardly mobile working-class masculinities in a secondary school, specifically the 'Academic Achievers', Mac an Ghaill (1994) describes how the 'process of equipping themselves for social mobility' drew largely on working-class resources and practices. However, Lucas's experience with leadership in Youth Parliament and various other clubs and organisations appeared to have strengthened his confidence to navigate this elite world. I asked him directly to describe the university culture and he stated:

> Yeah, it's very pompous, very over the top, very glamour, but then there's also the reality of it. So it's like, most schools, they present themselves as the beacon of education. The O-Week stuff that they do, like the grand welcoming, they had the whole entrance procession, they had a huge organ playing in the grand hall and we have a – there was the, it's called the DL scholars, it's almost like the Rhodes Scholars program that they have – it's a similar thing for that. And we had the opening night this Tuesday and it was – everyone had to get dressed up and it was in the oldest hall, and all the academics came, all the heads of the executive, all the boards and that; so it was they really pump it up to be this really elitist place. But in reality most kids don't really care about that. In reality most people are just easy-going people; you can walk up to anyone really and talk to them.

Lucas remained for the most part confident and bold. However, further along in the interview he seemed to become a bit more confessional:

> meeting new friends and that, and I've tried to take a really positive approach versus it's very daunting, it's very scary. I've sort of tried to jump into it as open as I can and with as much enthusiasm and I think it's paid off and that.

He clearly felt nervous but what he described was counteracting such nervousness. From his perspective, performing an outgoing and sociable identity had worked to reaffirm his aspirations.

Programs of study such as politics, philosophy and economics are associated with privilege. They are inhabited by the 'career-oriented, ambitious, politically conservative student – coming from a well-off home – enrolled in a relatively prestigious program' (Thomsen et al., 2011, p. 467). Many of these students will enter the corporate world. In documenting a corporatised masculinity, Giazitzo-glu and Muzio (2020) speak of the habitus of middle-class and upper-middle-class masculinity that is focused on the unspoken rules of the game. While Lucas, as the son of a plumber, would seem unlikely to be in possession of such knowl-edge, the subjectivity he presents seems adaptable. A habitus disjuncture, noted in other studies of extreme social mobility, does not appear present. Instead, Lucas over-identifies with a middle-class hegemonic masculinity, imbued with rationality, individualism and the spirit of competition (Morgan, 2005).

Furthermore, Lucas did not seem to suffer academically and continued to perform well. The long commute – nearly an hour by train – did drag him down a bit but he used the time productively. He often spoke about how students must have a balance between 'breadth and depth' of knowledge. We spoke about law and economics both being degrees that are commonly conceived to be very competitive. Reaffirming his right-wing political beliefs, Lucas said:

> See I don't mind friendly competition, like competition where it's – you're trying to better each other but not in a malicious way. Because when it happens in a way that it's like, oh yeah, I won, it's not nice, it's not a nice – but the competition/competitive environment within uni I think is good because it drives you to continue to be on top and to find the best that you can be.

In concluding the interview, I mentioned that Lucas's family must be proud of him. He described them as 'over the moon, they're very excited, they're very happy to see how I go and how far I progress'. It is important for young men to feel a sense of choice in the pursuit of their aspirations. Lucas's par-ents' supportive and non-pressuring approach resonated with him.

> I was blessed and I'm very lucky that my parents never pressured me to go anywhere. They were very much: we'll let you do whatever you want to do and we'll support you in whatever way shape or form, and that really was critical. And I think it will be very much so because you can't – they were always there for me and that's the thing. I know if I ever need anything I can go back to them.

As Lucas's first year of university concluded, he was very much on track. He asserted: 'I've had a blast, I'm not going to lie. It's been pretty fun.' Rather than feel weighed down by the long hours in a hyper-competitive atmos-phere, Lucas seemed energised:

> you know, big fish in a little pond, to a small fish in a big pond, sort of thing. But that in itself, I think, is exciting, like it's not – like, I mean,

it can be daunting at first, but like, you know, it means there's more – there's more experiences to be had than just your own small little funnel of things and that.

As the year concluded Lucas had picked up part-time work one day a week working for an upper house Member of Parliament. This was an opportunity afforded to undergraduate students in elite spaces and had the potential to be a powerful experience in terms of his upward trajectory. Where many studies have focused on working-class disadvantage in elite educational spaces there has been less attention to the working-class experience in elite workplaces (Giazitzoglu & Muzio, 2020). Through this opportunity, Lucas was able to do a variety of tasks from social media and speech writing to liaising with the wider constituency, and he enjoyed the variety:

> No two days are the same, sort of thing, because I mean, you're dealing with new legislation, new issues, new constituents. It's all just a very interesting cycle and it keeps you on your feet, but it's rewarding at the same time.

While the work itself was satisfying, it also reaffirmed that Lucas was on the right track: 'Yeah, no, I don't think, you know, twelve months ago I thought I'd be at the position I'm in.' Also, not only was it a confidence boost, Lucas felt ahead of the curve compared to others in his cohort.

Studies of widening participation internationally continue to document how collegiate extracurricular activities are where students gain access to social and cultural resources which are typically valued by privileged classes (Stuber, 2009; Thomsen, 2013). Despite his time being stretched between part-time work and his university studies, Lucas was devoted to his extra-curricular activities (e.g. the student council), seeing them as essential to building his social capital:

> I don't think people understand that, like, you know, you never know where someone's going to end up in life. Like you know, the fact that like, that friend of mine that I met, you know, through another friend, like you know, twelve months ago, you know, went to my eighteenth birthday and that, now deals with, like, executive clients at Westpac [Australian bank]. Like I didn't realise, like someone like that, like he was just doing a commerce degree at Macquarie and that, and just, you know, trudging along. But now he's on there and that, so that's like, you know, both on a friendship level, like obviously, it's still very strong, but then on a professional level, like you know, that's someone that you can, you know, whether you need to write a reference or that, or what not, it's very – I don't think people understand that, you know, just being friends with people and helping people along the way, you know, people remember that, and you know, it will help in whatever way, shape or form, whether it be personal or professional, emotional or mental.

Lucas's words here provide a glimpse into how he sees networking. Defining his own subject position as someone who does understand and is 'in the know', he mentioned twice that people do not understand the importance of networks. Whereas Lucas correctly associated the University of Sydney with a high degree of symbolic capital, we see that he was almost surprised by his acquaintance at Macquarie succeeding in the banking sector. This knowledge seemed to lead Lucas to see this person in a new light. Where previously he was a friend, now the possibility of professional advancement structured Lucas's perception, though this appeared to be in tension with his sense of self and how he conducts his friendships.

As the interview concluded, I spoke to Lucas about how he saw himself changing over his first year of university. He felt he had gained both confidence and maturity but these had always been a part of his character:

> And I've, sort of tried to keep a balance and that, I mean my life naturally tilts towards the side of, you know, doing things that are very much adult and very much mature, which you know, is just the way that I like to do things.

Also, he called attention to some significant sacrifices he had made:

> Have I sort of re-evaluated things – I guess, yeah, that's sort of, maybe a big thing, is like re-evaluating things that are important and that, and what not, like you know, like the time – you know, I don't get to see like, my family, really throughout the whole day, like I'll see them in the mornings and see them at night, whereas, you know, you'd have a lot more time to spend with them. So, like the time you do have with them, you really, I've really learned to cherish that a lot more, which I think is a very nice thing.

Spending less time together due to long hours at university, part-time employment or commuting has altered the family dynamic. Lucas seemed to be in an intense period of re-evaluation and, interestingly, this seemed to be quite gendered. Discussing his views on gender, Lucas acknowledged:

> I think society has openly tried to shift [views on gender], and realised that, you know, men, like women, are emotional and have emotions and are trying to – you know, not everything goes the way that you always want it to, and just trying to promote a more, you know, active way of promoting men as being people who are able to share who they are as a person, and it's alright to, you know, ask for help, that sort of thing.

As Lucas spoke of changes in the expectations around masculinity ('I don't think people expect every man to be six foot four, you know') his views, by his own admission, remained muddled. For example, Lucas spoke about not drinking alcohol and the societal pressures that associate drinking with masculinity. He insisted he attends events and still has a good time: 'I don't drink and that, as a person, so like, it doesn't – you know, I'm not the kind of person to have a very, you know, rowdy night and that.' He also further noted:

> I don't know, like you'd still say, like men traditionally are breadwinners but, I mean, not really in the economic sense, anymore, just due to the fact that, like, you know, need two people working to sustain or to buy a house to live in in Sydney, so.

Year 3: new beginnings

When I reached out to Lucas mid-way through his second year of university I was interested to see how his extended time at university – and his strategic application to expanding his networks – had affected him. When we met he was formally dressed, having just come from work. This echoes research on upwardly mobile working-class masculinity where participants were able to 'enact corporate masculinity with increasing naturalness, using symbolic cultural capital to "play the game"' (Giazitzoglu & Muzio, 2020, p. 13). Lucas seemed very settled at university and comfortable with all his various leadership positions and spoke several times of not wanting to leave the university environment and staying around after class to speak with other students. Furthermore, his experiences at the University of Sydney had reaffirmed his aspirations. We spoke about his experience running for student council where he 'developed a team' of people to implement his campaign and ensure his success:

> Sydney Uni is renowned for that sort of political environment. It's – some people say it's a teething ground for a lot of competitions and whatnot because of, it's been, it's had such – it has such a unique political vibe, I guess, and it's interesting because it gives you that experience of sort of being in the real thing and that, whether it be having to campaign and whatnot, so yeah, it's very – it was very interesting.

He was able to connect his learning to his anticipated role as a future leader in society:

> some stuff I have learnt or some electives that I have learnt obviously have been – dealt with real serious social issues or periods of time in human history where there has been confronting things or whatnot, obviously that charges a lot of emotion …

In Lucas's view, his work as a leader requires diligent attention to responsibility. This is best seen in how he positions himself in relation to his experience working in parliament part-time, which he described as working in a place where day-to-day, people's lives are getting affected, it's like, I make the conscious decision to make sure that I always go through the front door, for example, when I go and work because it's like, it's a sobering fact that where I'm mentoring, even though I'm not a representative or whatnot, but the things that I'm doing and helping have effectively changed how things happen in society and that. And that's in the same way of going to university and that, I'm studying to become – starting with economics and eventually law, and studying to eventually hopefully beneficially contribute to society. That sort of experience happens because maybe I try and foster an ... approach to life, it's not about me, it's about us, it's about everyone else.

Lucas sees his work as 'sobering' as there are real-world consequences and he is contributing to the well-being of society. Unlike many of the first-in-family boys I spoke with, Lucas's overlap between the political and personal was apparent in every interview. From our first interview, this has always been an important part of Lucas's character. He asserted:

I mean, I guess I'm a very ideological person, so perhaps it's that idea of justice and idea of right and wrong and morality are something that I obviously hold very close, to facilitate not just in my own life but in the wider society.

He spoke about being one of the few students in his cohort from the western suburbs of Sydney, but his previous biography did not seem to play much of a role. The extended time at university networking and showing his abilities had allowed a certain freedom to explore new aspects of himself. When I asked Lucas what he was most proud of, he preferred to see his success not in terms of numbers but in terms of experience as a whole:

All my uni results obviously, that's obviously a thing that you celebrate or whatnot, but even just celebrating the little things and that in life, I guess I find great elation and happiness in knowing that I've been able to meet so many new people and discover so many new different thoughts, different experiences of, through peoples' past, through people's past – every person lives an entirely different story to what you do and so it's nice to expand that and understand that.

As the year concluded I spoke with Lucas one last time and he expressed excitement about joining the Rural Fire Brigade as a volunteer firefighter and the local Rotary club. The commitment to both will mean he will spend more time in his local community and less time at university and in Parliament. He seemed energised by this new endeavour: 'So actually after this [interview] I'm going to head up to my brigade and do maintenance training and that.' When I asked him what brought this about, Lucas supplied an interesting rationale:

So it was more like re-orientating after having that transition period from university. The one thing that I kept, I think a lot of teachers and that also warned me about is, that you lose that, unless you jump on it, you kind of lose that community engagement outside of high school. And it continued on for a bit, but then they kind of just dropped off the radar because new people would obviously rise up and take that, so I was like, 'Okay …'

Where previously Lucas spoke adeptly about the accrual and operationalisation of social capital, which was arguably quite superficial, he now presented a different picture. While Lucas never pathologised his community, he now spoke of it with a robust pride:

I definitely would say I do have pride for my community, in the positive sense in that respect. That I love where I live, I love the people that I interact with and being able to help people around me … To be able to be part of that and help people, I think it just gives your life so much more purpose and meaning, for me personally.

This highlights several interesting tensions. Not only do his words suggest a recognition of 'community cultural wealth' (O'Shea et al., 2017), Lucas is keen to eventually run for an elected political office and the experience working as a volunteer firefighter and for the local Rotary will certainly enhance his prospects. Such a move also complements Lucas's sense of self: he considers himself adaptable, able to hobnob with the Sydney elite but also the working class of Western Sydney.

Given that Lucas has had more exposure than most to a wide spectrum of people from different social classes, we spoke a bit about social class in Australian society, specifically egalitarianism and the reality television show *Cashed Up Bogans*. Still ascribing to his right-wing principles, Lucas explained:

I think class warfare doesn't really lead to significant … [The rhetoric] doesn't really achieve much. It kind of just says, 'Oh, this particular group of people should have to change in ways of …' It sectionalises society when we should really be looking at more collaborative efforts on how do we unilaterally work as a group.

Seeing class warfare as more a part of the media landscape than of actual consequence is interesting given not only Lucas's experience at an elite institution but the fact that the interview was conducted in one of the poorest urban areas in all of Australia, about twenty minutes from where Lucas grew up.

Conclusion

Holmegaard (2020) posits that a strength of qualitative longitudinal research is that it creates a deeper understanding of complexity – 'where they make room for narratives that are being negotiated, are disconnected, and part of an ongoing process being played out over time' (p. 112). In the interview the interviewer and interviewee are both active subjects contributing to complex meaning-making processes (Holstein & Gubrium, 2004). While Lucas did undergo transformative experiences over the course of three years, he was noticeably consistent in the subjectivity he presented to me. Probably more than the other students in the *First-in-Family Males Project*, Lucas, as a gifted speaker, was more confident in expressing his opinions and disagreeing with the nature of the questions. While his opinions on issues fluctuated from time to time, his core values did not seem to change. Arguably, Lucas presents a somewhat unique case of upwardly mobile working-class masculinities. Only a select few ever end up in an elite institution – what Southgate et al. (2017) call 'extreme social mobility'. Whereas an abundance of research has highlighted the cultural mismatch between working-class values and university values which leads to a detrimental effect on working-class students' motivations and accrual of social capital (Soria & Stebleton, 2013; Stephens et al., 2012), Lucas's story is very different. He is an informed consumer who knows both what he wants and how to get it; furthermore, he is very open about both his rationale and his strategies for doing so. Where other young men struggle, Lucas's words suggest that feels not only that he belongs but that he is entitled to be there.

References

Adams, M. (2006). Hybridizing habitus and reflexivity: Towards an understanding of contemporary identity. *Sociology, 40*(3), 511–528.

Browman, A., Destin, M., Carswell, K. L., & Svoboda, R. C. (2017). Perceptions of socioeconomic mobility influence academic persistence among low socioeconomic status students. *Journal of Experimental Social Psychology, 72*, 45–52.

Corrigan, P., & Frith, S. (1976). The politics of youth culture. In S. Hall & T. Jefferson (Eds.), *Resistance through rituals: Youth subcultures in post-war Britain* (pp. 195–205). Hutchinson.

Davies, B., & Bansel, P. (2007). Neoliberalism and education. *International Journal of Qualitative Studies in Education, 20*(3), 247–256.

Giazitzoglu, A. (2014). Qualitative upward mobility, the mass-media and 'posh' masculinity in contemporary north-east Britain: A micro sociological case-study. *Sociological Research Online, 19*(2), 1–11.

Giazitzoglu, A., & Muzio, D. (2020). Learning the rules of the game: How is corporate masculinity learned and enacted by male professionals from nonprivileged backgrounds? *Gender, Work and Organization*, advance online publication. doi:10.1111/gwao.12561

Holmegaard, H. T. (2020). Complexity, negotiations, and processes: A longitudinal qualitative, narrative approach to young people's transition to and from university. In N. E. Fenton & W. Ross (Eds.), *Critical reflection on research in teaching and learning* (pp. 107–130). Brill.

Holstein, J. A., & Gubrium, J. F. (2004). The active interview. In D. Silverman (Ed.), *Qualitative research: Theory, method and practice* (2nd ed., pp. 113–129). Sage.

Jin, J., & Ball, S. (2019). Precarious success and the conspiracy of reflexivity: Questioning the 'habitus transformation' of working-class students at elite universities. *Critical Studies in Education*, advance online publication. doi:10.1080/17 508487.2019.1593869

Lehmann, W. (2009). University as vocational education: Working-class students' expectations for university. *British Journal of Sociology of Education, 30*(2), 137–149.

Mac an Ghaill, M. (1994). *The making of men: Masculinities, sexualities and schooling.* Open University Press.

McLeod, J. (2000). Subjectivity and schooling in a longitudinal study of secondary students. *British Journal of Sociology of Education, 21*(4), 501–521.

Morgan, M. (2005). Class and masculinity. In M. Kimmel, J. Hearn, & R. W. Connell (Eds.), *Handbook of studies on men and masculinities* (pp. 165–177). Sage.

O'Shea, S., May, J., Stone, C., & Delahunty, J. (2017). *First-in-family students, university experience and family life motivations, transitions and participation.* Palgrave Macmillan.

Soria, K., & Stebleton, M. (2013). Social capital, academic engagement, and sense of belonging among working-class college students. *College Student Affairs Journal, 31*, 139–153.

Southgate, E., Brosnan, C., Lempp, H., Kelly, B., Wright, S., Outram, S., & Bennett, A. (2017). Travels in extreme social mobility: How first-in-family students find their way into and through medical education. *Critical Studies in Education, 58*(2), 242–260.

Stahl, G. (2016). Relationship-building in research: Gendered identity construction in researcher–participant interaction. In M. R. M. Ward (Ed.), *Gendered identity construction in researcher–participant interaction* (pp. 145–164). Emerald.

Stahl, G., & McDonald, S. (2019). Social capital and self-crafting: Comparing two case studies of first-in-family males navigating elite Australian universities. *International Journal of Inclusive Education*, advance online publication. doi:10.1 080/13603116.2019.1632945

Stephens, N. M., Fryberg, S. A., Markus, H. R., Johnson, C. S., & Covarrubias, R. (2012). Unseen disadvantage: How American universities' focus on independence undermines the academic performance of first-generation college students. *Journal of Personality and Social Psychology, 102*, 1178–1197.

Stuber, J. M. (2009). Class, culture, and participation in the collegiate extra-curriculum. *Sociological Forum, 24*(4), 877–900.

Thomsen, J. P. (2013). Exploring the heterogeneity of class in higher education: Social and cultural differentiation in Danish university programmes. *British Journal of Sociology of Education, 33*(4), 565–585.

Thomsen, J. P., Munk, M. D., Eiberg-Madsen, M., & Hansen, G. I. (2011). The educational strategies of Danish university students from professional and working-class backgrounds. *Comparative Education Review, 57*(3), 457–480.

3   Campbell

Year 1: last year of compulsory schooling

Campbell is of Mauritian/Chinese heritage and is extremely hard working and self-sufficient. He attended a low fee-paying private all-boys Catholic school. With limited education, his parents have been fortunate. His mother works as a team leader at a superannuation company where she has worked for 20 years. His father worked in insurance. He has two younger brothers. A significant source of inspiration for Campbell's aspirations is his grandfather whom he spoke of with admiration, 'He's been through so much, so much hardships.' Adams and Coltrane (2005) note that 'It is not just birth parents and step-parents who socialize children with gendered expectations, but also grandparents, extended family members, fictive kin, teachers, and other adults who are part of children's lives' (p. 234). As Campbell transitioned to university he was prompted to carefully consider what a university degree actually means as he encountered labour opportunities that could potentially position him well for his future. How he processed the opportunities he gained demonstrates that aspirations – as future projects – often involve negotiation on a daily basis.

During the last two years of secondary school Campbell described to me that he was working approximately 25 hours in addition to his studies and it was clear he took employment seriously, mentioning numerous times that he wanted to 'make his own way'. Similar to some of the other boys in the *First-in-Family Males Project*, Campbell pushed himself very hard, maximising the use of his time. Campbell enjoyed pushing himself – or what he called 'pumping' it out.

> So I usually get – I usually work all Sunday so that's about 10 hours. I usually work Friday, Saturday night which is 20 and then my boss will give me one shift during the week at night which is 4 hours – 4 to 5 hours depending. I balance that out by studying after school, on – during the week so pump that out during the week and then on the weekend after work because I'm – I don't – I go to sleep really late and I wake up really early. It's kind of weird. I – after work I usually just get a bit of revising done and it's what I did during that day, especially on Fridays and then, yeah that's how I study.

When I asked him if he planned to slow down as his exams were quickly approaching, Campbell answered affirmatively, 'Yeah I've told my boss that I'm going to – if you can roster me less because – especially during the HSC and now because yeah I really want to do well.' Campbell also highlighted that his friendship with his boss – who was in charge of the rostering – allowed him that flexibility. Campbell's work ethic has been shaped over the course of his life, tied very closely to his grandfather who used to own a small business where Campbell worked from a young age. This business eventually failed ('He used to have a successful business but then it all just fell down and yeah, he's just been through heaps'), but it provided Campbell with an opportunity to be able to save money, purchasing a car as soon as he secured his permit. Having his own car was what allowed him to keep his tight schedule.

Campbell's story is one of sacrifice and strategy, and negotiating the tension between labour/financial capital and securing valuable academic capital (his ATAR). He spoke about not getting the necessary time with family and friends as his work and school schedule limited his availability (although his mother and him made a point of watching *Game of Thrones* and *The Walking Dead*). Once this tension was resolved as Campbell's Year 12 exams finished, he promptly picked up a second job working in a restaurant where he desired to attain a better position: 'so I'm taking a lot of pride in my work right now. I'm presenting myself and working a lot harder.' While Campbell exudes a strong work ethic, his interviews suggested a strong disposition to explore himself and the world around him:

> I want to experience things. I want to travel the world. I want to – I want to give back. I want to become – I want to become successful but not to the point where I'm ignorant and I ignore people. I want to give back because so much has been given to me and so much opportunity has been provided to me … I define success by happiness, satisfaction with your life. Everyone has their own goals and everyone has their aspirations but if you achieve them that's your own success. Because there's no generic form of success because someone could value love over money and vice versa, so yeah.

Campbell described applying for a degree in finance and business at a private Catholic university because, according to his calculations, 'my ATAR's not going to be very good, so yeah'. When probed further he disclosed that, based on his trial exams, 'I'm looking at maybe 65 to 70 ATAR, so it's really just like, I don't know, we'll see'. He drew my attention to how '[the university] will take other stuff like my social justice activities and whatnot, so yeah, that's how I'm seeing it.' Whereas at the beginning of the year he wanted a high Australian Tertiary Admission Rank (ATAR), Campbell said this changed over the course of the year. He summarised the experience of his final year of compulsory schooling as: 'I haven't achieved all my goals but I've achieved a few and I've let a few go admittedly, so … to a degree … very successful.' He described his learner identity:

I'm not the smartest but I try my best – and yeah that sums it up. Yeah I try but naturally – you know there's people who are just naturally smart and gifted and can just ace a test without studying. I always ask support from my teachers, support from my friends that are like that and try to maximise my marks. But yeah, I'm not the best student admittedly.

However, Campbell – perhaps paradoxically – described himself as motivated to do well with a strong desire to impress his family: 'I'm self-motivated because I know I want to do well because I want – my motivation is to make people proud, my family proud and whatnot. So that's what motivates – that's what gets me through the days, so yeah.' He drew attention to the money his parents had spent on his education: 'It's more just pressure from my family to do well because they've forked out so much money for a … private education and I just don't want that to go to waste'. Therefore, he asserted, 'I want to impress them and I don't want to let them down. That's probably my biggest pressure.' Campbell also expressed an awareness of his first-in-family status and what this meant for his family, particularly his grandfather:

Yeah, not only that but I'm the very first person in my whole family to go to uni, not just my brother and sisters, my mum and dad didn't go to university, none of their brothers went to university, so yeah, it's a pretty big steppingstone because Gramps wants to see me go.

When I asked him how his life would be different from his parent's lives, Campbell marked his progress with his father and grandfather in mind:

My life's pretty similar to my dad's, where he was just pretty kicked back [relaxed], he didn't really care about school, but I've changed a bit from that. He was just like, he didn't really care. He was just – he met my mum pretty early so that's where his time was all invested in, while my grandfather was really, really hardworking and always on the grind and always wanting the best for his family. So in a way, my grandfather is what I aspire to be where my dad is what I am now. That's what I'm seeing.

Campbell spoke of pride in his local area and how attending university would require him to spend significantly less time in what he described as an 'inclusive community'. Campbell's journey as a learner is also faith-based. We spoke at length about his studies and what resonated with him in terms of his learning. During these discussions, Campbell continually referred to his teacher for Religious Studies and the influence this teacher–student relationship had on him:

He's definitely turned me into a more religious person, if that makes sense? I was baptised Catholic and everything but I was more luke-warm. I didn't really go to mass; I didn't really pay attention to what's happening. But he's influenced me to be more aware and defend the faith because there's a lot of people that are – yeah, but at the same time I – I'm – I won't go out of my way to say, oh gay marriage is wrong. If they want to do that, that's fine. That's none my business. I stick to myself. But yeah, if someone challenges me, I'll defend the faith.

When I commented that he was vacillating between different influences (e.g. education, parents, peers) that may contribute to his value formation, Campbell said:

Yeah, kind of. I used to be 'Oh, gay marriage is wrong' because my parents always said it was wrong and this and that and this and that, but it's just their business. If they want to do it, that's fine, they can do it … Yeah, I am – I'm just trying to – I'm still trying to find what I – I'm still trying to find my values at the same time as well. I'm still trying to determine what's right and wrong in a sense in some areas, so yeah. Yeah, so I'll base – I'll determine a situation, I'll see what the Catholic church says, I'll see what everyone else says and I'll just try and find a middle ground to – and to see what's right, what should be right, what's the most ethically right?

When asked what he looked forward to at university, Campbell revealed a mixture of emotions. Given his heavy investment in his employment he already did not get to see his friends as much as he liked and he was concerned university, as well as the commute to university, would only make this more challenging. According to Campbell:

I mean at the end of the day if it's a really strong friendship you'll always find time to get along and whatnot. So I don't know this is like – this is kind of like a test of the friendship, this whole shift of life. Life, yeah, yeah. Shift of life. That's – it's just all a test on a friendship in my opinion. I can tell who I'm going to stay in contact with, who I'm going to meet up with every weekend and who I'm just going to treat as a stranger.

Still, he was excited by the prospect of the new experience and looked forward to

Getting to know a lot more people, that seems like a lot of fun at uni. Learning – business genuinely interests me, that's why I put a lot of effort into it. So, I don't know, I'm really keen on learning. I don't know, this sounds a bit nerdy, but I am keen on learning the subject.

Similar to other participants, Campbell expressed a perception that university was more high stakes. Whereas few students in the *First-in-Family Males Project* considered the financial implications of university study, Campbell consistently drew attention to it:

Yeah, it's difficult because at university, if you don't do well then no-one cares, right? Because here [at secondary school], if you don't do well, people care, we're on your back and telling you to do better and then at university it's just like, well, you're out of $700, tough luck, that sort of thing.

Similar to his relationship with religion, Campbell's interest in business was furthered by an inspiring business teacher. Campbell weighed up various post-school opportunities, and he mentioned that when he applied for university he also applied for several government and non-profit internships, one in Canberra, the nation's capital:

Applied for that yesterday, so yeah – but [if I get it] I have to move to ACT which is far from everyone and my one core value is to stay close to family. So yeah, that's moving very far away. So that is my plan B if I don't get into university and then – because that's a full-time job, at nights and stuff I can do online courses, so yeah, and then do business through there. And then hopefully after that get – get into university through – what's it called – late entry or something, so yeah.

Extending this point, when discussing future plans, Campbell spoke about his mother's work as a team leader in superannuation, 'She said to me that she can get me a job there. So after my degree I'm going to do that and hopefully work my way up like she did, so yeah.' When I asked him if his interest in finance and business was influenced by his conversations with his family, Campbell said:

I just – it's the most subject I'm engaged in. I've always – I've worked ever since I've been legally allowed to. I just – I've just been involved in it because my grandpa – I used to spend a lot of time with my grandpa and he always used to take me to work and he was a general manager of a golf course. So I spent a lot of time with him and yeah, and every school holidays I was with him and he was just showing me how he runs things and how he does that and all the operations of everything.

Campbell's experiences seeing the behind-the-scenes operations of the business world have clearly influenced his aspirations. The time spent with his grandfather also appears to have influenced his work ethic and sense of financial responsibility. Describing his plans for the summer, Campbell said, 'I'm going to work as much as possible. I just want to save up as much money as I can. Just save, save, save. Yeah, that's about it.'

Year 2: the post-school year

When I met up with Campbell the following year he had completed one semester at university of basic accounting, claiming: 'It's hard, but it's breezy at the same time, like if you pace yourself, you can do it.' He had performed well on his ATAR, and he enrolled in a university located in Sydney's central business district (CBD). His reasons for attending this institution included that he felt the location of this university would offer more opportunities for internships and the Catholic ethos resonated with him: 'It's more of a small university and it's more of an inclusive community. And it's not like a conventional big university, it's more geared towards helping people who want it and need it.' Though he was also quick to note that they have a '95% employment rate for the business school'.

Campbell described himself as contented: 'I had my first test on Friday, I got 70% in it, so I'm doing really well. I'm happy with it, I'm happy with my courses, happy with the days I'm doing. I'm just really happy right now.' He had made a lot of friends in the business program and already seemed to be distancing himself from his high school friendships; he noted only about 20% of his school friends went to university.

> Yeah, I'd say I am, because like, most of my friends, they just have trade – they're just tradies. So like, they do have their weekends off, they get those two-day breaks. They are working fairly long hours, and it's pretty tough, but at least they have those two days just to chill. While I'm working four days, three days at uni, and then those three days at uni I'm working as well, so like, yeah, I feel that I – yeah, I don't think there's anyone as busy as me in my, like, [in my local area].

We spoke about his time management skills and how he balanced it all-his girlfriend, friends, the same job from high school and his university studies. Because the schedule of university life is more protracted and more online, the previous tension Campbell experienced around financial and academic capital appeared less salient and he tended to prioritise taking time for himself: 'To be honest, my mentality has changed a lot since Year 12. I'd be like, oh, yeah, I'll take a shift any day, I'll do anything for shifts ... but now I value my time more [if] I never get time to myself.' While he had made friends and appeared to settle in well to university life and the sub-stantial commute, he was keeping his eye on other opportunities, thinking about how he could commit more to his job and shift his university studies online.

Lehmann (2009) argues decision-making for working-class students is 'often pragmatic, rather than rational' and tied closely to social context and connections within such a context where new experiences and information can 'gradually or radically transform habitus, which in turn creates the possi-bility for the formation of new and different dispositions' (p. 139). When I met up with Campbell again at the end of his first year, his life had changed significantly and he was excited to tell me about the progress he was making:

> Yeah, like I said, my plan completely changed. So, I thought to myself that in order to get, like a decent, like, job in the future, you only, you

don't only need a degree but you need experience as well. So, it's a funny story. One day on my way to work, I just applied for this job, and then on my way back, I got a call, asking to come in for an interview. So, on Tuesday, I went for the interview, and then ...

The job that caught Campbell's interest was a full-time position in superannuation, working as a call centre operator. When we met he was still waiting to hear confirmation that he had secured the position but it looked very likely he would get the job as they were 'checking my references':

Yeah, so that means – and I also picked up, I picked up another part-time job over the uni break, so I have to drop those two, and then I plan on transferring, if I get into the role, if all goes well. I want to transfer the credits I did this term, because I did pretty well last semester. I want to transfer credits from what I did to an online uni, so, either Macquarie or the University of South Australia ... And study online while working full-time.

Campbell's words here suggest a strategic calculation; he was in a process of working through the pragmatics to ensure the risk was not too severe. And even while he was strategising, Campbell bristled against the confines of his stringent time management:

because like, all I'm doing is I'm locked into a set roster where I'm just working or you're studying, but like, I'm not living. So, like, that's definitely something I want to do by the end of the year, just like, enjoy life.

Here we see Campbell's disposition to explore himself and the world around him in tension with what could potentially increase his social mobility.

Campbell went on to explain that his impulse to apply for the job in superannuation was directly linked to his experiences at university:

Well, we were doing this new topic called financial accounting, and in the introductory lecture, he was telling us about job prospects and how important experience is, and when you're going for experience after the – so, when I finish my degree, I'll be twenty-one. I'll need to have, like, at least a good three, five years' experience to get, like a job that would pay six figures. Well, I thought of it as, hypothetically, if I do the trimester at South Australia Uni, two years, while doing that online and while working full-time, by the time I'm twenty-one, I can already earn that kind of money, instead of waiting that extra three-year, five-year period.

He spoke about taking the necessary time to assure his parents and grandparents he would gain a university qualification and that education would not be sacrificed for career advancement:

Yeah, it's switching from, like this to online and my grandparents weren't too happy about that. But I had to explain to them, like this is going to happen, like yeah. They were just like, oh, no, don't drop out of uni – like, I'm just switching.

Interestingly, amongst this strategising, Campbell insisted he felt a strong sense of belonging to university: 'Oh, a hundred percent, yeah, a hundred percent, yeah.' Campbell drew some important distinctions between his past and current perceptions of university life:

I saw uni as, like, something that opens doors, and it definitely does, and something that was really strict and you had to follow this. But now I realise that it's just, it's on you, and like, you can do what you want, so yeah, that's definitely a big change. Yeah, yeah, yeah, it's definitely just, this is on you, like this is your time that you're using on this, so don't waste it.

As the interview concluded, I asked Campbell about his experiences with pressures around masculinity. For Campbell, the pressure to be a certain type of guy 'depends who you hang out with, and it depends how like, easily influenced you are, because I've just seen so many people crumble and just be who they're not, because of the people they hang out with.' Drawing attention to his friends who do trade work – and have prolonged exposure to working-class masculinities – Campbell explained:

Like, I've had friends that just don't, I don't really talk to anymore, because they're like, hanging with the wrong crowd, and they're doing stuff that I wouldn't do, and I just don't agree with it. And I told them straight to their face, like stop. Like, those people fit in with their schedule, so they see them more often.

Campbell's words highlight the relational aspects of a socially mobile masculinity. Mac an Ghaill's (1994) 'Academic Achievers' and 'New Entrepreneurs' both frequently define their aspirations as different from their working-class male peer group. Furthermore, here we see how the pathways the boys are on significantly influence their exposure to certain gender performances. Campbell telling his friends 'straight to their face' is linked to Campbell's sense of faith and also his understanding of respectable behaviour and the 'bad stigma around [masculinity]'. During this time the #MeToo campaign was prominent in the news cycle and I asked him directly about his interaction with women, given he had attended an all-boys school:

Funny you ask that. I went out for some drinks with [a] girl that's a friend, and – on Tuesday night – and she, we both just got smashed, and I made sure she went home and walked safe and everything. And the first thing she mentioned to me in the morning was, thank you for not taking advantage of me. Not like – not thanks for making sure I was safe, she was, thanks for not taking advantage of me. And that just made me stop and think – like, hell, is society really that bad that it's gotten to the point where girls have to thank you for not taking advantage of them? That's just – oh, that messed me up, it really annoyed me.

As the interview concluded Campbell reflected back on the possibility of a full-time job working in a call centre. He felt like he was on a precipice. At this particular stage in Campbell's life it appeared he could enter the labour market full-time, which called into question his careful consideration of what a university degree actually means. It has been documented that many working-class young people tend to be more risk averse and transactional in their perspective of education (Thomsen et al., 2011) and many see university as a route to a job.

Year 3: new beginnings

When I reached out to Campbell mid-way through his second year of university I was unsure of what he would be doing or where he could be. At age 19, Campbell had been successful in gaining the job in the superannuation call centre and as a result had ended up deferring his university degree for six months in order to take on the role full-time. Furthermore, by his account, he had 'excelled' in the call centre position where out of

> the CSOs [Customer Service Operators] they've trained recently, I've shown the best stats, I've shown the most growth and every[one], all my managers and stuff, they're just praising me for that, so I am feeling proud of myself for doing that.

Working-class students often rely on networks and role models outside of their family (Thomsen et al., 2011) and, by Campbell's account, he had met some inspiring people working in superannuation and he had inspired others. After all, previous to the call centre experience Campbell's aspirations were influenced by family, friends, a university open day and a 20-minute careers advising appointment at his secondary school.

In fact, Campbell had performed so well that his employers had offered him a part-time position so he could return to university full time in his third year. Campbell saw this as an opportunity to blend both worlds and to reap the benefits. Returning to the tension between academic capital and financial capital, Campbell was still adept at balancing his time and ensuring he was getting the most out of everything ('Big juggling act'). He described how he navigated this difficult balancing act:

> Yes. I'm still here at university. Last semester I did four subjects and I got my results, got distinctions all of them. And for this semester, I've dropped down to three subjects because four was just a bit intense and I've taken a lot more responsibility at work, so.

Recognising the risk he had taken and the meticulous strategising, Campbell expressed multiple times throughout our conversation that 'it's worked out really well'. In fact the experience in superannuation inspired him to change his degree from accountancy to a Bachelor of Commerce majoring in management. This highlights an important part of Campbell's journey where his experience on the job influenced his aspirations. When we took a moment to reflect back on how much he had changed since we first met, Campbell was clear that he would have told his Year 12 self to: 'Welcome opportunity, welcome change. Things aren't going to be what you think right now. It's going to go in a whole different direction, and just welcome that change … Don't try to resist the change, welcome it.'

While Campbell struggled through Year 12, partially due to taking on far too much and letting his employment infringe on his studies, he credited the struggle as constructive and essential: 'I definitely think in 2017 I built my work ethic. I really focused on, okay Campbell, this is what needs to get done. This is what you're going to achieve, do it, just do it – no questions asked.' Egeberg Holmgren (2013) writes of the importance of what is said and what is mediated in interaction beyond words. While Campbell was clear that he was a hard worker, and I never doubted that he was, there was also a vibe within the interview of determination and persistence.

The experience of working in the call centre influenced Campbell in a variety of ways and also brought previous dispositions to the fore. Campbell described himself as ambitious – and comfortable in his ambition – 'I'm the type of person who's always hungry. I will never settle for what I'm at right now. So right now I am always looking for the future, I am always looking at what I can do.' Campbell's language felt very different from when we first met. He discussed setting goals: 'I want to say better managing people, better at interacting, better at acknowledging. I'm learning so many emotional intelligence skills, learning so many things that I can apply it and I'm becoming better from it.'

While a call centre is not a place of prestige it could be considered a white-collar workplace with a high degree of professionalism and extensive training. Such an environment has influenced how Campbell performs his professional identity. Giazitzoglu and Muzio (2020, p. 2) address how over time working-class men learn the codes of '"corporate" masculinity associated with middle-class, well-educated men'. In the call centre Campbell was working with people in their 30s so he took care to present an image that would prevent him being judged on his youth: 'I'm the youngest one there and I have an image. I don't know if I do from other people at work, but I definitely in my mind have an image that I have to portray.' Not only did he dress more professionally now, he seemed to have a clearer awareness of what counts in the workplace – and how his skills align with the expectations:

> I actually got the opportunity to speak to one of my, one of the general HR managers within my work, and he was saying that, when back when he was doing interviews and so forth and recruiting, he said that the biggest thing that he looks for is someone's personality and someone's … how someone comes off.

In further dialogues with the HR manager, Campbell noted that there is a view that a degree is not as important as how a person presents themselves:

> Now he said that the degree doesn't really matter. He will hire an employee who has a great work ethic and is someone that will participate and work towards the goal of the whole company over someone with a degree because you can't train work ethic, right? You have to find it, and it comes down to the individual.

As I spoke with Campbell, it was clear he placed great importance on these conversations with managers. He was gaining important insight through this part-time work into how to best position himself in the future, which is learning that cannot be achieved in a classroom. In their research on upwardly mobile men, Giazitzoglu and Muzio (2020, p. 2) highlight that this takes time, but Campbell seemed to acclimatise quickly and this could be due to his familiarity with superannuation, given his parents' work in the profession.

> Okay. I've been speaking to a lot of people in high positions, and people were in places that I would like to be in the future, and they're seeing that in today's day and age, a lot of people have the degree, it's really the experience that separates people. So the reason why I'm still at university is because, yeah, at the end of the day, I just want that piece of paper on my resume. It'll look cool I guess, but it really comes down to the experience in my opinion. That's why it doesn't really bother me, I am going to stay with my degree because that's the decision I've made.

Another important dimension of Campbell's experience was the connections he made between his learning experiences at university and his shifts working in the call centre. This is important because Campbell's words suggest he did not see university as transactional but instead largely as enriching:

> Now I've been learning, I did my management course and I'm taking a course called psychology of work, which delves into the employee psyche and what the, what effective managers do and what, how managers need to adapt in accordance with specific situations. And today for example, I did a lecture on motivation and when it gets work today I'm going to apply that, to apply things that I've learned to my employees and just to really get the fire into them to ensure that we get more productivity and get things done.

Campbell was consistently hardworking and tenacious; furthermore, he was consistently future focused throughout the study. Over time, our conversations became more centred around his area of passion and what resonated with him, specifically, a focus on the white-collar atmosphere where he spoke of networking ('chats with upper management'). As he made the jump from secondary school, to university, to the white-collar corporate world and back to university, Campbell insisted:

my priorities and morals are still there. I still keep in touch with God, I still have – I'm still focused, I'm still driven and I know what I want and I want to get it, sort of thing. So yeah, in terms of my priorities, they're still the same.

Conclusion

Longitudinal research, when well-crafted, allows the researcher 'to understand the negotiations in the young peoples' narratives' where 'choice' is 'an ongoing process that is being shaped, retold, and changed over time' (Holmegaard, 2020, p. 113). With this in mind, Campbell's story centres around pushing himself to work hard in order to get the most out of the opportunities available to him. Campbell could easily have stayed at the service-sector job he had in secondary school but he pushed himself to find a position in the white-collar sector. He was fortunate to be able to access opportunities that will serve him well in the years to come and he understands this; therefore, his sense of agency is focused on capitalising on opportunity. By his own admission his approach to working long hours is unhealthy but, at the same time, he seems to always find something enjoyable about the work he does. And, while he struggles with balance between his social life, his studies and his employment, he clearly feels he belongs in the white-collar world and that he *should* be able to balance all of these different domains. While he certainly is ambitious, able to self-advocate and make the schedule work in his favour, and even though he is on the fringes of the corporate world, it is worth noting that Campbell never presents a subjectivity of corporate masculinity, commonly associated with ruthlessness or aggression (see Gregory, 2016). While his trajectory is commendable – and very different from others in the *First-in-Family Males Project* – from a social mobility perspective, Campbell for the most part is doing a very similar job to his parents. The key difference here is that he secured a job at a much younger age than his parents were able to and, furthermore, he is committed to completing a university degree which he hopes will propel him quickly into positions with increased leadership and management responsibilities.

References

Adams, M., & Coltrane, S. (2005). Boys and men in families: The domestic production of gender, power, and privilege. In M. Kimmel, J. Hearn, & R. W. Connell (Eds.), *Handbook of studies on men and masculinities* (pp. 230–248). Sage.

Egeberg Holmgren, L. (2013). Gendered selves, gendered subjects: Interview performances and situational contexts in critical interview studies of men and masculinities. In B. Pini & B. Pease (Eds.), *Men, masculinities and methodologies* (pp. 90–103). Palgrave.

Giazitzoglu, A., & Muzio, D. (2020). Learning the rules of the game: How is corporate masculinity learned and enacted by male professionals from nonprivileged backgrounds? *Gender, Work and Organization*, advance online publication. doi:10.1111/gwao.12561

Gregory, M. (2016). *The face of the firm: Corporate hegemonic masculinity at work.* Routledge.

Holmegaard, H. T. (2020). Complexity, negotiations, and processes: A longitudinal qualitative, narrative approach to young people's transition to and from university. In N. E. Fenton & W. Ross (Eds.), *Critical reflection on research in teaching and learning* (pp. 107–130). Brill.

Lehmann, W. (2009). University as vocational education: Working-class students' expectations for university. *British Journal of Sociology of Education, 30*(2), 137–149.

Mac an Ghaill, M. (1994). *The making of men: Masculinities, sexualities and schooling.* Open University Press.

Thomsen, J. P., Munk, M. D., Eiberg-Madsen, M., & Hansen, G. I. (2011). The educational strategies of Danish university students from professional and working-class backgrounds. *Comparative Education Review, 57*(3), 457–480.

4 Rashid

Year 1: last year of compulsory schooling

Rashid is a Muslim Australian who attended a private Islamic school in the western suburbs of Sydney serving an Indian, Bangladesh and Pakistani community. The school was located directly next to the mosque which was the heart of the community; the style of schooling was single sex as the genders were separated during the school day. Rashid lives in a very small home that is on the geographical fringe of the Muslim community. His mother works part-time in hospitality and his father works in retail. Rashid is the eldest in his family, which he described as having a cultural pressure attached to it, specifically in regard to being the eldest male. Rashid is very shy and taciturn ('Like I prefer to keep to myself'). He was also one of the only boys in the study to have international travel experience, travelling to Bangladesh to see extended family before the start of university.

Reflecting back on his locale, he described improvements in his local neighbourhood: 'Well when I was younger, it wasn't the best, like lots of things would happen, but they built like residential homes and things like that around our area, so it's not as bad here ...' Here Rashid drew attention to an awareness of his surrounding area and the changes he had witnessed over his lifetime. As we will see in this chapter Rashid's story speaks to the study of 'Islamic diasporic masculinity' as well as 'the cultivation of diasporic Muslim masculinities in specific spatial, temporal, historical and social circumstances' (Fedele, 2014, p. 171). Rashid's transition to university involves navigating the tensions concerning the high cultural expectations relayed through his parents and grandparents and his own anxiety about his academic progress.

When I first met Rashid in his final year of secondary schooling we spoke about the increased pressure with upcoming exams. Rashid described his primary aspiration as 'a fulfilling life', and when probed further what was important to Rashid was being financially comfortable. Rashid was clear about his intended pathway: 'I want to study a Bachelor of Business, and Bachelor of Science and Information Technology, so, a double degree in UTS [University of Technology Sydney].' Furthermore, it was clear he had given this quite a bit of thought with a careful consideration of where this degree could get him: 'I want to work in, like, a technology company, some-thing like Google, or Microsoft, or Intel ... like a company ... like they all have like headquarters in Sydney, so, yeah.'

While university was always Rashid's goal from a young age, his focus on the technology industry was a more recent aspiration. Rashid was even able to make the connection between himself as an 'introvert' and the type of dis-position the IT world may be looking for. Importantly, Rashid also saw close ties between this aspiration and his cultural background. Research by Nathie and Abdalla (2020) demonstrates that students attending Islamic schools often have aspirations in the STEM fields, where mathematics and sciences are typically followed by legal and business studies in terms of course hierar-chy. Rashid perceived that the business part of his studies could potentially lead to him working in the banking sector which would involve charging interest: 'a lot of those jobs lead into the bank and that, religiously we don't deal with interest, so that's some – a sector I want to avoid'. Here Rashid highlighted the Muslim cultural value around *riba*, or exploitative gains. Fedele (2014) describes how 'Diaspora breaks with traditional models of Muslim masculinity through the reformulation of Islam' which can 'involve acts of deculturalisation, deterritorialisation, and de-ethnicisation' (p. 175). Rashid's main social interactions seem to centre around his small Muslim community. Therefore, arguably, foundational aspects of Islam still structure his subjectivity, contributing to how he sees both his present and his future. While Rashid clearly wants to do well, he navigates his desire to strive to suc-ceed and to be the first in his family to attend university around his cultural expectations.

While having high career aspirations, Rashid also described himself as a continual procrastinator, highlighting that his recent underperformance on his mock HSC exams had not fostered a motivation to study: 'I didn't do as well as I wanted to.' Rashid did not have a part-time job and his parents con-sidered his academic progress to be the most important thing at this stage in his life. For the most part, Rashid did not respond well to these academic pressures and could – at times – belittle himself. However, when he consid-ered his overall academic progress during his career as a secondary student, he admitted: 'I guess, like I'm not doing too bad.' As the school year came to a close, echoing the sentiments of most of the boys in the study, Rashid appeared to be chafing against the institutional constraints of his secondary education. He wanted the school year to conclude so he could feel more independent and his perception of a university student centred around hav-ing 'more time and flexibility'. The image of the university student – whether accurate or inaccurate – can be an important source of motivation for young people. As Rashid's secondary school career was about to conclude, he reflected back and wondered about the relevance of what he had learned: 'I'm not really sure how much the education system actually prepares you for anything.' Rashid's words suggest, like many university students regard-less of background, that he never fully connected with his learning. In our interviews, he struggled to describe a teacher he had a close connection with, though he did recount an anecdote where a substitute maths teacher attempted to re-direct a struggling class in Year 11.

When I sought to address how Rashid conceived of his future, we spoke of different pathways young men from the western suburbs of Sydney usually embark upon. In New South Wales he could have left school in Year 10 if he was able to show evidence of an apprenticeship. However, Rashid was quick to mention that leaving school early was never a possibility, 'my parents would never allow that'. Despite Rashid's own struggles with his learning, how higher education is constructed within his Muslim-Australian community is clear. Education is lauded and it carries a certain symbolic currency. However, not all forms of education carry the same weight and as our interview proceeded Rashid described TAFE as an unacceptable pathway. Research from Nathie and Abdalla (2020) highlights that vocational education and training courses are not a prominent feature of Islamic school curriculums in Australia. In reflecting on the value his parents put on education, Rashid asserted: 'Yeah, it's a cultural thing, as well, a lot of it, yeah. They want me to be successful, like they push me, but it's like they do it, so, because they want to see me succeed.' Extending this point further, he noted that his education, and the education of his siblings, was part of the reason for his parents moving to Australia: 'I think too, like, maximise my opportunities of getting like a good education, that's why, one of the reasons why my family moved over to Australia, so … the environment, definitely is quite different.' How education is framed and discussed within the community is important. Furthermore, Rashid's parents do not believe that all universities provide a quality education, as he noted:

> Like obviously, that perception has been made, like the … and … will be like the top of the food chain, and then like maybe, like UTS [University of Technology Sydney] or then Macquarie, and then Western Sydney [University], like obviously, that perception has been built up by like, yeah, so, and that reflects on them as well, like you know, you have to get into this particular uni.

This knowledge base – which stems primarily from family and community connections as well as internet searching – contributed directly to Rashid's aspirations. Rashid expressed some frustration about not having a career advisor at the school, even though the Islamic college that Rashid attended had a much higher rate of university attendance than any of the other schools in the study. This is important because it suggests that, through his school networks and wider community, Rashid had access to important information which supported his aspirations (Patfield et al., 2020; Reay et al., 2005).

> Honestly, like a lot of self-research, and we don't really have a careers advisor here, so, I mean, like you can go to different teachers and things, and well, yeah, I've done a lot of like self-research on the internet and things like that, like you're only using that … guide to look at courses.

Rashid also mentioned he has a distant uncle who works for Western Sydney University and that his grandfather had taken an active interest in his pathway, sitting down with him and going through his university admissions centre guidebook. Adams and Coltrane (2005) note: 'The family typically is considered the main institution for both production and reproduction of polarized gender values' (p. 233) and the role of Rashid's grandfather appears important. Rashid's grandfather stepping in to help Rashid secure a place at university sent certain messages about gender, leadership and being proactive within the family and, perhaps, the community as a whole. While Rashid appreciated his grandfather's investment, he highlighted that it came with a certain pressure. Rashid confessed he was actually quite nervous about getting into university and – if admitted – what the experience would be like without the peer support he had come to rely on in secondary school. Furthermore, Rashid expressed a reluctance to meet new people:

> Like getting in for sure, like getting into my desired course, like especially because I'm not sure if any of my friends will be there, so, like that, like meeting new people and trying to establish, like yeah, that's a bit scary as well.

Aside from uncertainty about what was to come, my conversations with Rashid centred around tepidly setting goals for the following year. Discussing an interest in gaining more independence, he strongly desired to secure part-time employment but only if it did not infringe on his Friday prayer commitments. Friday prayers seemed to be an important opportunity for Rashid to spend time with both his father and grandfather. Also, Rashid expressed interest in experimenting with learning computer code and building an app as well as exploring recent developments in cryptocurrency.

Year 2: the post-school year

When I first met up with Rashid in his first year out of secondary school he had gained acceptance to UTS in the degree of his choice, a dual degree in IT and business. His ATAR was lower than he had predicted but he was able to gain admittance 'because we're in a disadvantaged area so you get bonus points for going to that school'. Describing his exams, which Rashid had been nervous about, he asserted:

> I failed advanced English Paper One and I think I failed Paper Two as well, I got 60% for … general maths, I got high 60s or low 70s for IPT [Information Processing Technology], I didn't get an … and I got I think mid 70s in Business Studies, so yeah, my marks were all over the place.

When I asked him what his family thought of his success in securing a place at a prestigious university, he said:

> My dad was happy, my mum was just like, yeah, you should have studied harder, you would have got 90 easy. She's like, I saw how much you studied and you didn't put in enough effort and you managed to get 85. Imagine if you'd studied properly and consistently.

Rashid had spent the summer in Bangladesh, where he struggled a bit, saying, 'It was alright.' He noted he did not do much 'because my mum was very protective and she wouldn't let me go out a lot so that was a bit – but when I was with my father's side, we went out to eat, went to the movies'. Over the summer he also grew a full beard which made Rashid look significantly older than the rest of the boys in the study.

Universities in Australia have experienced a rise in marketisation, often going to great lengths to compete for students. Zajda (2020) calls our attention to the 'commodification of higher education, with its focus on value-added education and labour market prospects for highly skilled and competent graduates' (p. 55). When we spoke about his first few weeks of university, Rashid noted the carnivalesque atmosphere of O-Week:

> Yeah, … so I think a lot of people were going to all the sessions to try and get a chance because my first session, the business session, she was like – the presenter asked one of the people to come up and nobody put their hand up, like three people, and so one guy went up and then she just handed him an iPad … Because he took the initiative and came up and answered the question, he gets an iPad.

Episodes like this convey many things. Primarily, they indicate the rewards in place for the ideal university student who is proactive and willing to put themselves out there. Furthermore, giving away iPads furthers the perception that the university is a place of high symbolic capital and extensive resources.

Rashid's anxiety about making new friends as he acclimatised to university life was unwarranted as generally his friends from high school ended up at UTS and some of them in his same degree program ('Yeah, there's like five of us, I think, five, six. But they're probably all studying slightly different things'). Part of Rashid's acclimatisation concerned how the university environment recognises a diversity of cultures: 'I'll definitely make use of the prayer room – that's really helpful that that's there.' Coming from a strict Islamic school which separated the genders, Rashid was used to a single-sex learning environment. Furthermore, while Rashid's friendship group was overwhelmingly male, the university environment presented different gender logics and different gender performances. When I asked him if it this entailed an adjustment, he noted that his business courses were quite mixed in terms of gender but that his IT courses were male heavy.

Similar to his original intent, Rashid's plans still focused on a career in IT. Drawing on conversations with his family and his own internet research, Rashid presented a certain strategy in choosing his dual degree, balancing what interested him and what would make him more attractive to employers:

I want to sort of go into a coding background and then also have business to fall back on or to stand out rather than just – and with IT a lot of – it's like business orientated rather than the technical side which is more like computer science and software engineering. I sort of want to … for some type of more technical background in IT.

Where Rashid once desired freedom and independence, he now expressed a bit of anxiety around balancing the workload demands of university life and how to best structure his time. We spoke a bit about the changes he would like to see in himself as a learner as he still appeared to be continually frustrated by what he perceived as his laziness. He consistently drew attention to his struggles with procrastination. Laziness, as a performed identity, is discussed in other studies on working-class masculinities in education (Burke, 2009). Furthermore, not only did Rashid want to become more proactive in his learning environment, he was also keen to capitalise on the wider opportunities available to him despite his introverted nature:

I'm hoping to make a change. I want to try and participate in volunteer stuff and go to the tutor sessions and things like that. It's not really my – something – not the tutoring but the volunteering stuff is like not – something I'm a bit apprehensive about.

In the second half of the year Rashid and I met up again and he seemed satisfied with his progress. He had packed all his classes into three days, which were quite intensive, and he had the rest of the week for himself. This was an important strategic move as his commute to university was just over an hour on mass transport. By cramming it into three days, he also saved a significant amount of the expense of transport. However, it was unclear whether minimising his time on campus would influence his social integration into university life, which is often considered critical for first-in-family students (Rubin et al., 2019). Rubin and Wright (2015) found that working-class students had less desire and concern about making new friends than middle-class students and they may largely see their education in transactional terms (Thomsen et al., 2011). While Rashid is satisfied with the progress he had made in the first semester, he reflected on feeling largely unprepared for the university environment:

Yeah, I'd say I'm less anxious but there's a lot of work in university so … it's quite different to high school [which] doesn't prep you that well for what's to come. So yeah, the workload is very different, it's harder to manage. Yeah, it's clear what you have to do but it's not like high school, so if you miss a lecture or miss a tute, it's not like they're going to spoon-feed you the information or anything like that, it's your own – you have to do that on your own.

Many other students in the *First-in-Family Males Project* also mentioned spoon-feeding. Many noted their teachers worked very hard on their behalf to ensure they attained the best grades possible and, in contrast, university was always depicted as a place where there was little support in place ('because with high school it was easier to cram and whatnot, whereas with university you have to do more prep for the work because of the workload'). Having to work on academic study more independently was an adjustment but it was one that Rashid expected and, in fact, appreciated: 'Yeah, I think it's a good thing. Long term it's a good thing because I assume when you get into the workforce and things like that, you're not going to be spoon-fed information.' This is consistent with the fact that Rashid has always seen university as a step towards employment.

Reflecting on his experiences coping with stress during this first year, Rashid asserted:

> I think I can deal with the stress better, I guess, but even though, despite the workload, the stress and pressure isn't as high as it was during the HSC although the workload might be larger, just because of the implications that were surrounding the HSC and it was built up as such a big thing.

This highlights two dimensions of Rashid's journey. He knows he can work under stress and his words suggest he can separate the temporal rhetoric (e.g. 'built up as such a big thing') from the reality.

While he was clearly developing as a learner, the ideal university student remained an awkward fit. According to his own words, Rashid remained very much the same: 'I'm still pretty bad at time management, especially because I've got so much freedom right now so it's definitely something I still have to work on …'. The struggle with time management was mentioned quite often throughout the study, where the boys often discussed that they could not organise their time or enact the necessary self-discipline around the management of time. Reflecting on this vice, Rashid said: 'Yeah, I think time management is the trigger of the other thing, bad study habits as a result of that, giving adequate time to my subjects, distractions, procrastination, etc., things like that branch off from that.'

The first year of university, when school friends are dispersed onto different pathways, also becomes a time for comparisons. Rashid was clear when he evaluated his progress against those of his peers as they find their way in employment, training or education:

> I have two friends that didn't go to university … So one of my friends does – I'm not sure, I think he's still been working but I'm not too sure what he's doing right now. I think he was looking for work. The other one does sort of like a government childcare job thing, so he's given children to look after. Oh, yeah, and I have one more that was trying to get into medicine but didn't make it the first time so he's doing chemistry this year and he's teaching at that [the Islamic school], because he got a 99.85 ATAR or something.

Rashid seemed comforted to know that in comparison to his peers his transition had been relatively seamless. And, as expected, in securing a place at a prestigious university he fulfilled the expectations of his family, thus important aspects of his identity were reaffirmed (e.g. eldest son, familial pride). Also, it is worth noting here that Rashid, unlike many of the other boys in the study, was not actively pursuing part-time employment. His financial support was a small student bursary and his family's money: 'I want to work part time but I haven't really – I've applied to a few places but I haven't really gone on a proper job hunt or anything like that.'

Rashid described the pressures he felt in terms of his masculinity:

> I guess, I haven't really been exposed to any pressure myself but there's sort of the pressure of showing weakness, guys crying and things like that are sort of looked down upon, I guess. It's sort of associated with guys, they have to be tough and whatnot, so that's something I've sort of noticed.

The all-male social group of his secondary school days was particularly important for Rashid as it influenced his gender expression:

> Yeah, maybe obviously in high school, we'd muck around quite a bit so maybe at times I was quite an introverted person but when I'm around my friends I can come out of my shell a little bit so maybe more like [being] daring maybe for the masculine part …

At university Rashid was exposed to different forms of masculinity that contrasted with those of his cloistered Muslim community; such exposure could contribute to a reformulation of 'traditional models of Muslim masculinity' (Fedele, 2014), though Rashid seemed for the most part to stick to his secondary school peers so his exposure seemed quite limited. So, while Rashid seemed to balance his university life in the CBD with his life in his Islamic community of the western suburbs, the labour involved in such a balance remains a bit unclear. Fedele (2014, p. 178) notes that '[r]ituals are very important in defining new models of Muslim masculinity' and Rashid did regularly attend Friday prayer at his mosque with his father and grandfather.

Year 3: new beginnings

Supported by both family and friends, Rashid had a successful first year at university. He felt he could have performed better academically but he did not fail any subjects and, for the most part, seemed contented. Rashid's summer between his first and second year of university was generally spent lounging around. He did submit some applications for casual work but, according to him, he did not actively chase these opportunities, despite having friends working in warehouses, which was the most lucrative form of manual labour in the western suburbs of Sydney. Nixon (2009) notes that warehousing is part of a 'relatively narrow range of sex-typed "masculine" service niches' (p. 308). Rashid explained:

but I wasn't that proactive [in looking for work] because, I don't know, because I probably could have done warehousing but I don't know if I want to do warehousing, and each time I find a job – but I think I'm a bit too picky because I don't want to do fast food either and one of my friends did fast food and he found out some horrible things about fast food …

Further in our conversation Rashid expressed that his parents were over-protective and that they expressed concerns that warehouses were a place where Rashid would feel uncomfortable. So, while other boys in the study discussed the pressure they put on themselves to find a job or the pressure their parents put on them to earn money, Rashid did not feel these pressures:

maybe do retail or something – it's more difficult than I thought. I guess I have to be more proactive about it, but it's like not so important that really I really have to go and find a job, and that's probably what's hold-ing me back from being more proactive about it. It's not that important for me. So it would be nice, some additional income. Yes more addi-tional income to spend on stuff I buy. It's not that important just right now, but it's something I definitely do want to do, at least casual work. Casual work is probably like the best for me.

As aspirations are socially embedded, and formed relationally through inter-actions with others, Rashid's failure to participate in service sector work meant he was not exposed to a variety of things. Specifically, he did not extend his knowledge around time management through seeing how many university students in Sydney balance their time between university study and part-time labour. Also, he remained largely unexposed to a certain type of working-class masculine culture that can be apparent in factory and ware-house work (see Nixon, 2009).

Not working gave Rashid time to spend with his friends, though, reaf-firming his awkward relationship with time management, he mentioned that they struggled to organise meet-ups. I have written about the importance of unstructured time before and the important role it plays for upwardly mobile working-class men during the transition beyond high school (see Stahl, 2020; Stahl, McDonald, & Young, 2021). While many work aggres-sively, picking up shifts wherever they can and often at the expense of their study, time for reflection cannot be discounted as it often leads to important realisations about what in their aspirations resonates with them. This time of liminality was also when Rashid began to renegotiate his relationship with his family, particularly in reference to attaining his driver's licence:

Get my Ps [permits] I guess was the main thing. My dad was, like hurry up – you need to be a bit more proactive – tell me to go out and drive with you. That's about it. They didn't really have too many – because my brother and sister are such a handful right now they can't be focusing on all three of us. It's all a bit too much for them especially because they are both working. So my brother and sister, especially my brother, take up most of their attention.

Now that Rashid was secure in his status as a second-year student we discussed how he felt connected to the university community. We discussed the importance of belonging to the institution in a social sense and what this may mean for Rashid's long-term trajectory. Rashid was aware that he had benefited from support from his close-knit peer group: 'whereas if I went to uni where I didn't have a lot of friends probably would have played a bigger factor and, you know, probably would have taken a bit of time to adapt and whatnot'. His shyness and the convenience of his friendship group resulted in Rashid only forming transitory friendship groups, usually through required academic work, and according to him these friendships do not take hold 'because the communication is so infrequent. It might just be like a wave or a hi, hello and it's not really how it is with my closer friends.' Furthermore, a lot of Rashid's tutorials were scheduled in the evening, which meant he was often in classes with people older than him. Therefore, Rashid's connection to UTS, at the very best, was fragmented.

While his peer support was integral to his academic success, Rashid affirmed that his learner identity was still very private. He spoke often throughout the interviews of relying on the internet to figure things out for himself:

> Yes I guess, not necessarily social media, but … I Google it or mainly Google it. I am not too proactive about like seeking out tutors and whatnot. I think I should be a bit more … but I usually look up online and see what resources I already have, go over those, see what material the uni has given me, what additional material they have given me and sometimes friends as well.

How Rashid sought help is an important part of his story. While his words suggest he is academically able, Rashid's struggles were around ways to motivate himself. Originally he wanted to do a major in coding but, according to Rashid, 'it's really boring – more boring that I thought it would be. It's a bit difficult to grasp.' As a result, he confessed that he barely passed this class, securing only a 51% which – while anxiety inducing – was an experience that Rashid described as positively contributing to his maturity. He spoke of it not in terms of personal failure but, interestingly, in terms of how much money he would have potentially wasted in terms of HECS debt if he had failed: 'I am going to study harder. Thankfully with our system, you know, I don't have to pay it off immediately or anything like that. I passed – it's like, phew.'

Despite Rashid meandering through his first year at university, he provided examples when he tried to change, to be more proactive and explore the opportunities available to him. After all, given his class background, he did not actually know anyone who worked in IT or business, which limited him. While he had clearly researched these careers online, an over-reliance on this information meant his knowledge remained fragmented. Drawing a connection to stereotypes, Rashid joked: 'I guess people stereotype a lot of people from my cultural background probably work in IT and similar like places, but I don't really know anyone.' Furthermore, confining his social interactions to his small peer group from secondary school could contribute to him not making the necessary connections and gaining needed expertise. Yet, while Rashid was aware of this, he did not seem to perceive it as a problem. This is seen in how he discussed the support he received from the university. Whereas his high school provided limited opportunities to seek career advice, the support at UTS is very different:

> I can go to a careers advisers – they do have career advisors. I went one time. I don't think it was that helpful though, from what I recall, but I guess I am in a better position to state out my options right now … but I don't remember it being too useful. But I want to do finance because I am interested in stocks, but yeah even that – that's a whole lot of reading to do and it's not as easy as it seems.

Rashid has a lot of interests – coding, finance, business, etc. – but he appears unsure how to fashion these interests into being competitive in the labour market. We did not discuss him looking for internships, through most courses do require some on-the-job experience at some stage. Furthermore, as Rashid continued to bring up finance as a career choice, it was also unclear how his aspirations may be constrained by his religious upbringing given the Muslim cultural value around *riba*, or exploitative gains. Arguably, this cultural value serves in contrast to the classed and gendered expectations around the role of the breadwinner and, in Rashid's case, the pressures his parents and grandfather placed upon him.

As Rashid grew older he was exposed to differing pressures and expectations; furthermore, his responses to such things changed. Describing how he positions himself as a student, Rashid now spoke about the importance of dressing the right way and how this is not straightforward. This differed substantially from the first year when Rashid largely seemed to not consider these things, highlighting that he was now thinking more critically about how he wanted to conduct himself and be perceived by others:

> like I don't want to try to look formal but I don't try to look like I am at home sometimes I guess. Like even if I go outside I do the same – maybe for uni a bit – a little bit higher extent than just going out to the shops but that's more – another thing like etiquette again I guess. Because you wouldn't dress, like, the way you do at home, like, you would dress at home to like a business interview. And uni isn't necessarily a business interview but, you know, you've got to sort of dress appropriately.

Striking a comparison to the area where he grew up, Rashid noted: 'So I have seen people come to uni in like suits or a business shirt.' This was clearly a memory that was striking for him. Whereas in Year 12, Rashid associated schooling with procrastination, he now was beginning to see it more as a training ground for white-collar work. Linking back to his exposure to differing pressures and expectations, when we discussed Rashid's masculinity and self-development, he shared that he now attended the gym and had become more aware of what he ate: 'I have been a bit more health conscious, like, I am trying to eat healthier food and trying to put on weight. So that's about it … just get fit to be honest – reach a good weight – put on some muscle.'

Conclusion

Rashid's story centres around living a largely sheltered life. This was not simply because he resided primarily in a Muslim community centred around a faith-based school which shared a site with the local mosque, but because he was shielded from a lot of the real world by both the guidance of his parents and his introverted nature. Throughout the interviews, he reported muddling along as a student and spoke of his uneasiness with his academics and family and cultural pressures. When he successfully gained entry to a prestigious university located in Sydney's CBD, he relied heavily on his networks in order to be successful. Belonging to these networks therefore prevented him experiencing any real sense of struggle. While clearly the lived experience of being a Muslim Australian informs his daily life, Rashid's aspirations and how he negotiates the public and private sphere suggests that he is negotiating tensions around what Fedele (2014) calls 'deculturalisation, deterritorialisation, and de-ethnicisation' (p. 171). Intertwined with his high aspirations, he feels a cultural pressure to do well – to perform well – in Australian society. While it is difficult to discern how Rashid's identity as a Muslim Australian may have shifted over the course of three years, the data suggests that certain elements have been reaffirmed or validated through his upwardly mobile trajectory.

Taking a narrative approach to longitudinal research, Holmegaard (2020) writes that future selves play a role where 'past, present, and future are continuously interwoven and interacting' (p. 117). Both researcher and participant are constantly shifting and this can influence how they interact when they meet sporadically. While interviews can be challenging and unpredictable, in the case of the *First-in-Family Males Project*, the repetition of the interview format opened up important spaces to experiment. I felt that, even though Rashid was often taciturn and generally a private person, the repeated interaction allowed a rapport to be built. Furthermore, the strategies I invested in with Rashid (e.g. humour, digressions) fostered a comfortable atmosphere where his anxieties could be allayed (Stahl, 2016).

References

Adams, M., & Coltrane, S. (2005). Boys and men in families: The domestic production of gender, power, and privilege. In M. Kimmel, J. Hearn, & R. W. Connell (Eds.), *Handbook of studies on men and masculinities* (pp. 230–248). Sage.

Burke, P. J. (2009). Men accessing higher education: Theorizing continuity and change in relation to masculine subjectivities. *Higher Education Policy, 22,* 81–100.

Fedele, V. (2014). Emerging models of Islamic masculinity in the European Maghreb diaspora: Theoretical challenges and possible perspectives. In F. G. Karioris & C. Loeser (Eds.), *Reimagining masculinities: Beyond masculinist epistemology* (pp. 165–193). Inter-Disciplinary Press.

Holmegaard, H. T. (2020). Complexity, negotiations, and processes: A longitudinal qualitative, narrative approach to young people's transition to and from university. In N. E. Fenton & W. Ross (Eds.), *Critical reflection on research in teaching and learning* (pp. 107–130). Brill.

Nathie, M., & Abdalla, M. (2020). Courses preferences and occupational aspirations of students in Australian Islamic schools. *Religions, 11*(12), 663.

Nixon, D. (2009). 'I can't put a smiley face on: Working-class masculinity, emotional labour and service work in the 'New Economy. *Gender, Work & Organization, 16*(3), 300–322.

Patfield, S., Gore, J., & Fray, L. (2020). Degrees of 'being first': Toward a nuanced understanding of first-generation entrants to higher education. *Educational Review*, advance online publication. doi:10.1080/00131911.2020.1740172

Reay, D., David, M. E., & Ball, S. (2005). *Degrees of choice: Social class, race and gender in higher education.* Institute of Education.

Rubin, M., Evans, O., & McGuffog, R. (2019). Social class differences in social integration at university: Implications for academic outcomes and mental health. In J. Jetten & K. Peters (Eds.), *The social psychology of inequality* (pp. 87–102). Springer.

Rubin, M., & Wright, C. L. (2015). Age differences explain social class differences in students' friendship at university: Implications for transition and retention. *Higher Education, 70,* 427–439.

Stahl, G. (2016). Relationship-building in research: Gendered identity construction in researcher–participant interaction. In M. R. M. Ward (Ed.), *Gendered identity construction in researcher–participant interaction* (pp. 145–164). Emerald.

Stahl, G. (2020). 'My little beautiful mess': A longitudinal study of working-class masculinity in transition. *NORMA: International Journal for Masculinity Studies, 15*(2), 145–161.

Stahl, G., McDonald, S., & Young, J. (2021). Possible selves in a transforming economy: Upwardly mobile working- class masculinities, service work and negotiated aspirations in Australia. *Work, Employment and Society, 35*(1), 97–115.

Thomsen, J. P., Munk, M. D., Eiberg-Madsen, M., & Hansen, G. I. (2011). The educational strategies of Danish university students from professional and working-class backgrounds. *Comparative Education Review, 57*(3), 457–480.

Zajda, J. (2020). Globalisation and neo-liberalism in higher education: Australia. In J. Zajda (Ed.), *Globalisation, ideology and neo-liberal higher education reforms* (pp. 47–57). Springer.

5 Manny

Year 1: last year of compulsory schooling

Manny is of Pacific Islander heritage, specifically Samoan, and he attended an ethnically diverse state school in the northern suburbs of Adelaide. He had some familiarity with the university context as he was involved in a specialist maths program in Year 12 which required him to go to the university one afternoon a week. He is the eldest in his family and a consistent theme in the data was he was very family focused. Manny openly framed his aspirational trajectory in terms of his pride in his heritage, though he also expressed some frustration at the rigid practices and expectations: 'Samoan culture is very strict– when you're the oldest one you have to deal with everything.' Manny described one of the best parts of his week as 'Go to church and just chill with the fam' which occurs on a Saturday 'from 9:00 until 2:00 usually'. His extended family is transnational, with some of them still residing in Samoa, some in Australia and New Zealand, and an aunt who lives in the United States. Manny also moved around quite a bit in his childhood, mainly in Sydney and Mildura. He described his local neighbourhood as 'ghetto-y' and 'sketchy', where he feels he needs to be on guard. Manny's transition to university involved a fragmented trajectory as he struggled to find himself and spaces where he could feel valued. This struggle was hampered by the effects of poverty.

Scholars have argued that 'talking' can be viewed as an act associated with the feminine and that young men may feel anxious about engaging in discussion concerning themselves and their experiences (Francis, 2000; Robb, 2007). McDowell (2000, p. 209) contends that many working-class boys in her research 'were not verbally adept, perhaps unused to exploring their views and feelings with a stranger', whilst many 'tended to have restricted social lives, further limiting the conversation'. Manny was slow to engage with the interview method and could often become terse and monosyllabic, though over time he became more open. When I first met Manny in his final year of secondary schooling we spoke about the stress involved with various assignments and upcoming exams. While Manny admitted the experience had been stressful, he seemed committed to performing an 'easy-going' subjectivity: 'Well it's been kind of hard with all the different subjects but it's been fun going through your subject but keeping chill, it's pretty cool because I'm a chilled person.' The notion of easy-going-ness or 'chillness' was mentioned several times throughout the interview and it seemed Manny valued being seen 'as a chilled dude that just goes through life pretty chilled and doesn't get down and stressed'. Butler (1990) writes that masculinities are performed through repetitive acts and deeply tied to social context. The performance of 'easy-going' carried a certain currency within Manny's disadvantaged school context where the critical mass of students would not pursue university. Furthermore, this performativity about the 'relaxed guy' also seemed tied to his own sense of well-being where he describes himself as 'Just being happy with everything.'

During the data collection, I was consciously aware I served as an audience to the participants. Clearly, the interview in itself can work as an important setting for *doing gender* (Egeberg Holmgren, 2013) where consciously or unconsciously certain identities are performed. However, while Manny drew heavily on the 'easy-going-ness' in the subjectivity he presented, it was fragile. He asserted that, depending on the circumstance,

> I get frustrated a lot but I don't really show it because I'm a chilled person. I don't let people annoy me a lot, but just when people are really loud and I'm trying to do work in the senior school.

Nichols and Stahl (2017) highlight that the 'easy-going' Australian male is someone who 'was able to let go of negative emotions associated with conflict arising from competition' (p. 175) and that presenting an 'easy-going' social identity mitigated the risks associated with high achievement. Some of Manny's words highlight both the necessity of performing a relaxed identity and how such a performance can become an issue when those surrounding him perform a similar relaxed identity: 'Yeah kind of a lazy student but I do end up doing my work after a bit. I can be annoying in class because I tend to talk a lot.'

Manny described himself as a learner as easily distracted and slow to take initiative. Laziness, as a performed identity, is discussed in other studies on working-class masculinities in education where it can – in a contradictory sense – exist alongside performances that suggest a natural intelligence and entitlement to a good education (Burke, 2009, p. 96). Manny spoke of procrastination and how his good relationship with teachers often leads to them giving him extensions on assignments. A main currency structuring the relationships he had with teachers was his humble and polite demeanour as well as his humour, which allowed him to lighten the mood when difficult situations arose. When I asked him how his teachers would describe him, Manny said: 'Yeah, they would say I was – I don't want to sound snobby but a smartish kid. But I could do better if I put my head on most of the time.'

Given that Year 12 final exams were weeks away, I spoke with Manny regarding his plan of action to ensure his success. Rather than calling attention to the risks of underperforming on exams, Manny instead highlighted that 'It's stressful but it's still fun' and that he and his peers had a sense of comradery: 'we all get together if we need help and ask questions with each other'. Studying together with his school friends created some tension as it pulled him away from his wider friendship group. Unlike other boys in the study, Manny had a wide and diverse group of friends and there was some cross-pollination between his school friends, his neighbourhood friends and his church friends. Not too concerned about his exams or ATAR, Manny seemed more focused on the search for a part-time job and his endeavour had been largely unsuccessful thus far. His family shared a car and, while Manny did have access, it carried with it a responsibility of picking up his younger siblings during the week.

As previously mentioned, family was very important to Manny and he described having a family of his own as one of his main aspirations. When asked whom he admired he spoke of his parents' immigration from Samoa and how hard they worked to provide for the family. These experiences around 'hard work for a hard day's pay' were formative for Manny and he wanted to enter employment as soon as possible. His father was employed in a local factory and his mother worked as a receptionist:

> coming straight from Samoa and it's pretty hard because they had to work their way into New Zealand and then to Australia, and my mum worked two jobs when I was little and my dad wasn't the best when I was little. But he's been working hard ever since. So I just look up to them because they work *so* hard.

This motivation of making one's parents proud echoes other research on first-in-family students (Capannola & Johnson, 2020; Wong, 2018). As he rounded off the last few weeks of schooling, Manny discussed his positive feelings regarding the progress he had made compared to others who left school early[1]: 'Yeah most people don't expect half our grade to make it through this year.' Though he accepted that his attendance had been fairly poor, he still felt a sense of accomplishment in finishing Year 12. He spoke of his passion for maths and physics and how his current Year 12 class only had five students, although it began the year with significantly more. However, echoing other studies on working-class experience in higher education, Manny's views of university were hazy, confirming Thomsen et al.'s (2011) finding that 'working-class students' expectations of university studies are diffuse, vague, and often implicit' (p. 474). What is clear is that success at university is characterised as a successful return on investment where the aim for Manny is to secure a good salary, as noted in other research (see Lehmann, 2009). Another factor that placed Manny at a disadvantage was he did not have access to the internet at home, which probably would have substantially assisted him in Year 12. As his time at secondary school came to a close, Manny spoke of his aspirations and plans for the future. He planned to study engineering and, when asked about his rationale, Manny voiced: 'I just kind of thought I was really good at maths and stuff and I enjoy it and

I like physics.' He is leaning towards 'probably civil engineering or mechanical. I'm still in between those two.'

Year 2: the post-school year

In his first year of post-compulsory schooling, Manny attended University of South Australia, located close to where he lived. He was enrolled to study mechanical and mechatronic engineering, a competitive program. Manny's ATAR was lower than expected but it was bolstered by his socioeconomic and ethnic status as well as doing specialist maths in Year 12. He was credited with 14 bonus points, which secured his entry into the university program of his choice. We spoke during the first few weeks of university and, according to him, he was finding the course quite enjoyable though he cited a high level of revision of what he covered in Year 12 and an overemphasis on civil engineering: 'And that's basically civil engineering, because in the first year of engineering you're basically doing all the basics of engineering, doing different parts of each type of engineering. So, the sustainable bit is for the civil engineering part.'

While being admitted to the Mechanical and Mechatronic Engineering program was a source of pride, Manny openly admitted that he was out of his depth in some content areas. This echoes Clark's (1960) definitive work on 'unbounded expectations' which, when combined with the reality of poor academic preparation, can become a source of friction. Higher education, in Clark's words, can 'cool out' the high aspirations many disadvantaged students possess at the end of secondary school. Manny described some of his difficulties:

> And then we've just got the super annoying class. I have to learn about materials and the structures and how much – and failures and stress, and different stuff ... It's kind of boring, because it's basically chemistry, which I never did at high school, so I was completely confused for the first couple of weeks ... Because the first lecture confused the heck out of me, because I was like, I don't have a clue what he's saying, but I'm just going to nod my head and say yes.

Embedded in this story is both the situation and Manny's response. While the 'easy-going' and 'relaxed' learner identity was an integral aspect of Manny's high school learner identity, it did not appear to carry the same currency at university. Regardless, Manny was quick to assert that it was only in the one class that he felt out of his depth and he found the other subjects to be 'alright'.

University does not offer a pre-constituted friendship group and the boys in the *First-in-Family Males Project* often had to orient socially to new people. Such a process called on them to, depending on circumstance, perform an 'easy-going' subjectivity (Nichols & Stahl, 2017). Manny perceived his fellow university students as similar to him (e.g. 'easy-going') and drew on his friendliness, politeness and sense of humour – which worked well with his secondary school teachers – to extend his social networks:

> Oh, I've talked to so many different people, like I don't even know them. Because I always find something to talk about, so I was like, hey, because like, in tutorials we sit wherever, so I just sit wherever there's a seat, so I'm just like, hey, I'm Manny, and then meet new people, and they're like, where did you go? And they went to this school – I know a person from that school.

One friendship that proved particularly beneficial for Manny was with a student who had previously failed the course and was re-taking it. This friendship provided some valuable insights for Manny not just in terms of academic learning but also navigating the online learning system and getting access to the information that was often unavailable through the institution itself. It is Manny who raised the issue with me that the introductory engineering course was quite male dominated ('it's just a dude fest'), which seemed to surprise him.

Gaining employment was important to Manny and over the summer he was able to secure part-time work at a local fast-food chain. He now worked eighteen hours per week, typically Sundays, Mondays and Tuesdays. Rubin et al. (2019) and others call attention to how working-class students are more likely to work to support themselves through university, which can have consequences for their social integration, as otherwise they have 'less money to purchase items associated with social experiences (e.g., tickets, entrance fees, food, and drinks)' (p. 91). Taking on this work required Manny to be adept at balancing his time between academic work, familial responsibilities and church commitments. However, he did not seem to struggle and he asserted that he had put effort into restraining himself from the temptation to binge watch entire seasons of television shows.

> Yep, I've got a draft due on – oh, it's tomorrow, yeah, I have a draft due tomorrow. I've already finished the cultural forum. I got an assignment for computing techniques due next week. Yeah, and another computer techniques thing, and a practical due two weeks from now.

A continual source of pride for Manny is his identification with Samoan culture and he is heavily invested in 'being the first person in my community to go to uni'. He reiterated this as sort of a mantra: 'Yeah, I'm just like, yeah, I'm going to uni', almost singing it out in the interview. Focusing on masculinities undergoing social change, Mac an Ghaill (1994) writes of the interplay of 'family/kinship relationships, peer networks, media representation, and school and workplace experience – that provides a filter through which masculinities are culturally produced and reproduced' (p. 75). Manny spoke about his parents feeling proud of him, and when I ask him to explain a bit further he said:

this is sort of cool, because everyone recognises me in my Samoan community, and it's like that you're just going to uni, because not many people of my culture go to uni … not many people in my family go to uni.

This celebration of Manny's achievement came with a certain pressure to do well. When I ask him specifically about this Manny did not seem to be affected by the expectation, instead reaffirming his relaxed and 'easy-going' attitude. However, his words suggested that this disposition seemed to be receding, as Manny spoke openly about the high standards he set for himself:

I want to keep my grades, at least distinctions, because that's what my teacher told me to … but I'm just trying to keep it at a distinction level. I wouldn't mind a credit, but if it gets down to the P's and stuff, I'm just going to be like, what is wrong with me?

Family is a significant part of Manny's lifeworld and, as to be expected, it informed his transition to university life. When I asked him if his relationship with his parents changed with his newly acquired freedom away from the confines of schooling, he said it had not:

A: No, I'm just super close to my parents, especially my mum, and my … yeah, I'm really close to them.
Q: Okay. And I mean, do they ask you lots of questions about university?
A: Not really, because they always – they treat me like I'm a full-time worker right now, because they're like, oh, you must be tired, you have some food. And I'm like, thanks, mum.
Q: Do you feel like a full-time worker?
A: Oh, no, because I do part-time work too, and I'm always, like in my spare time after uni, I'm always working, and my friends are like, ah, you must be so tired. And I'm like, yes, I'm very tired.

Manny's schedule was exhausting and we spoke about him being stretched too thin. However, according to Manny, there was nothing that could be cut back. He needed to work to pay money to his parents for food and rent. His academic labour was demanding and his chosen course was very competitive. Also, his participation in church activities was an important part of his identity and something he looked forward to. What seemed to fall by the wayside a bit were his friendships from secondary school which, by his own admission, he did not have time to maintain. However, Manny remained positive. As we concluded our first interview of his first year, Manny stated: 'I find uni cool, because it's just like free, and you can do anything. Like you have the options to do anything.'

When I met up with Manny towards the end of the first year he seemed to be muddling through. The competitive and demanding nature of studying engineering without the proper subject foundation in place at the secondary level had contributed negatively to his development. When I ask him how it went academically he said: 'I should have done better really … I should have really handed up the stuff that I didn't hand up', signalling that he had suffered in the areas of time management and motivation. Whereas in the previous interview he was more forthcoming and open, there was now a shame present that made Manny more taciturn, especially when discussing his lack of motivation or his practices of procrastination. I noted his reluctance to explain that he had to take a supplementary exam because he failed one of his assessments. According to Manny, this is an opportunity that comes to the fore when 'the lecturer feels that you deserve to pass it, you can try that exam all over again'. Despite the pain around managing the academic demands, he still continued his part-time work at eighteen hours per week.

As Manny constructed his subjectivity we can identify a struggle over 'the production of the subject position "university student"' (Burke, 2009, pp. 83–84), a process of meaning making aligned with the social order of things. Whereas earlier in the year his easy-going disposition seemed to be fading as Manny became more captivated by the ideal university students (e.g. studious, outgoing, positive about academic work), now when we spoke Manny presented a similar subjectivity to that in high school:

> Still pretty chill. I'm not too stressing even though I didn't do as well as I probably could have, I just move on and try and improve for this semester.
>
> Yeah, I don't really feel pain from university because I have been – I haven't been that annoyed at stuff or, yeah. I invest my energy in stuff but I usually, if I under-perform from what my actual expectations are, I do usually just shrug it off. That's just me, I don't really dwell on pain or shame if I ever feel it … Yeah. I was kind of ashamed when I failed – I got an F1 in … exam but I was like, oh, well, hopefully I do well in the sup exam. If not, try again next semester.

When we spoke about what he took pride in as he completed his first year of university, Manny asserted:

> It feels pretty good, but then also I feel like I've fulfilled my parent's aim because they aimed for their kids to go to uni when they migrated here to Australia, so I feel kind of proud for fulfilling that.

The close relationship with his parents is a powerful part of how Manny constructs his identity and navigates the everyday. On the other hand, he noted that, while this has always been their aim and he has continually worked towards it, many of his extended family do not quite understand what university life entails, a common theme in the literature on first-in-family students (Spiegler & Bednarek, 2013).

> I rocked up to a family function on the – during the holidays and they all acted all surprised when they heard I was at uni because half my family don't really go to uni, they usually drop out of high school and go straight into the workforce.

While the first year has presented various challenges, overall Manny seemed well positioned to continue his studies. He had a friendship group in his course whom he found supportive. Furthermore, he saw university as an affective and relational place and not just a space for the accrual of qualifications: 'Yeah, it's about connecting with people, creating relationships with people that you can work with in the future.' He commented further: 'also getting ready for the real world, it's like a bridging bridge between high school and real working'. Furthermore, the experience of university compelled Manny to reflect on his aspirations going forth:

> Because there is stuff that you want but I don't know if I really, really want them. Because usually if you really want something and then you get it, then you feel like, oh, it's not as good as I thought it would be. Like getting a new phone or something, oh, this phone's so cool, but then you get it and then you're just like, oh, it's just a phone, don't feel satisfied with you trying ... something, but probably, I don't know, I was going to say job but then job's just like, you get the job and then you're just like, it's just a job. I don't know, probably a family. Yeah, probably a family because I don't want to be alone.

Where other participants spoke about the importance of a career and saw university as a means to an end, Manny saw paid employment as just a job. This is not to say he did not desire a career, but it is interesting that he did not position it in those terms. In discussing his aspirations, it is relevant that family continued to play a significant role. We spoke about his recent eighteenth birthday and the responsibilities of adulthood, for example when he had to assume a different role in the household when his mother travelled out of state for a family funeral: 'I've become ... responsible now because I'm an adult now and my mum – my own family has been going through stuff ...' and 'So, I have been carrying the mum role in my family because my dad's here so I have to carry the mum'. He was describing when he had to cook and take his younger siblings to school, although he explained that it is quite common in Samoan families for the eldest child to look after the younger ones. Adams and Coltrane (2005) note: 'Men are resisting, but some are learning how to share in the everyday tasks of cooking and cleaning, and many are developing the emotional capacities and understandings that enable them to share in the upbringing of the next generation' (p. 243). Describing how he sees masculinity and expectations associated with masculinity, Manny said: 'Just not being a bad example to younger males and trying to – and not being discriminative to females and other males.' When I asked him his perspective on Samoan masculinity, he said:

A: Samoans are different.
Q: How so?
A: Well, males have to be able to know when to do stuff, do things when people come over, we have to know our role in different situations.

Q: Okay, ... an example?

A: So, in Samoan culture, usually the oldest male or female, doesn't matter really, they have to get coffee or tea and stuff or refreshments for people who come over.

Q: Got you, okay, to make people feel – be hospitable.

A: Yeah, it's just a ... thing, you have to do it, unless you're going to get a – you're probably going to get a look from your parents ... do it.

Q: Got you, okay. So that's interesting. I mean, do you, in society or even in high school, whatever, do you feel there is a certain pressure to be a certain type of guy?

A: Kind of. High schools nowadays, you're going to have those dudes that always tell you ... you have to be with some chick or you have to act gangster or hip. I sound old saying hip. Yeah, you have to be strong and not be in terms, whipped by your girlfriend ... have a girlfriend, you have to be the strong one in your relationships, from what I've been told.

Manny's words powerfully delineated a certain set of cultural expectations embedded in family life. While these are continual, we see how he framed the pressures to a embody a certain type of masculinity (e.g. strong, dominant, cool) as something adolescent and tied to secondary schooling as opposed to university. Regardless, if these pressures are 'temporal' and 'spatial' – integral in this case to schooling – for many boys they are the product of sustained involvement with such gender logics. Clearly the male-dominated engineering course Manny attended ('it's just a dude fest') has its own logic but Manny remained less forthcoming about it, perhaps being too close to it.

Year 3: new beginnings

The next time I met up with Manny was a year later when he was in his second year at university and exams were coming up. We spoke about his experiences in his second year and what was motivating him currently. He expressed some frustrations but also resilience. From a psychosocial perspective (Reay, 2005), this all suggests Manny was immersed in the emotional dynamics of university participation and that, through this affective process, he was trying to make the experience work for him. However, he was concerned that he had not chosen the right courses and could feel himself becoming disengaged from them:

> Some of them, some of them not really. I am in between wanting to change and not wanting to change courses because I'm not really like some of the stuff that we're actually doing and I'm not really enjoying it. I mean, you don't really want to do something you don't enjoy.

It was not always clear from the interviews what Manny had failed and resubmitted but it appeared that he was redoing parts of his first year over again ('... well this semester's been kind of a risk in a way because I'm redoing classes with people I don't even know'). What was clear is that one course had gone poorly for him and it had influenced his perception of himself and his capabilities as a university student. While in the previous interview Manny was reluctant to speak about his failure, now that a whole year had passed he was a bit more forthcoming:

A: No. I'm not like super smart. I believe in God and everything and he helps me. I've also got other people helping me along like friends and other influences in my life.

Q: So you have a support structure. So when the going got rough before, last year, whatever, last time we spoke, how did you use your support structures to your advantage?

A: My parents, kind of talked to other people I look up to, can't think of them right now. I just talked to some people about what I'm doing and they were like, oh, everyone, pretty much know that everyone fails every so often. You just got to get back up and go again.

Q: Well it's probably pretty good advice.

A: Yeah. I'm just like, okay, because I have a massive fear of failing because my friends since I was a kid they've held me up to a standard where if I fail they're like ah, you should be doing better and I'm like, 'Okay …'.

We are reminded here that Manny originally felt quite out of his depth because of the jump in content knowledge and this seemed to have caught up with him. While he saw himself as a capable but relaxed learner, he now called attention to the fact that he is 'not like super smart', highlighting that, within the space of the university, he had encountered people whom he perceived as smarter than himself. This was isolating. Manny attended a school where a very small percentage of students, particularly males, attend university; therefore his experiences as a high school student probably centred around, in terms of academics, being a big fish in a small pond. However, Manny's story is more a story of resilience than defeat and he openly discussed the changes he had made to ensure his success:

> In a way, I lessened the amount of stuff I tend to watch and then I just been trying to smash out all the assignments I can, try and change what I did because last year my main reason for failing was not handing [assignments] up. I would finish them but then I wouldn't hand them [in].

Doing the work but feeling reluctant to actually submit the assignments online created a perplexing situation for him where he did not fully understand his actions. Manny was unable for the most part to explain the reason for his inaction and when we discussed it he said:

A: I don't know, it's a walk and then I'm just like too lazy, I'll do it tomorrow. That's only 10%, it's fine. And then the day after I have something on and then it's 20%. Once it gets to 40% then I'm like no, I'm just not going to hand it in.

Q: Okay, but you did the work.

A: Yeah, I did the work and I assumed it was right, I didn't check.

There are echoes here of Manny's 'easy-going' learner identity. Here the relaxed attitude dipped into carelessness and the nature of high-stakes assessment became a source of frustration. When we discussed strategies Manny said he relied heavily on the textbook to understand the chemistry content and did not look to YouTube or Wikipedia. Manny did not reach out for the support services which were in place. Instead, from his account, it seemed like he watched the educational system at work, feeling almost helpless to take it on.

When we spoke further about how he was engaging in higher education Manny cited two key barriers that had influenced his progress. First, although he excelled at maths and was in an advanced program at secondary school, the quality of his written communication has always been a weak point: 'Probably the writing aspect and stuff. I did ESL, my school put me in that so I didn't really get the whole writing concept with the fancy referencing and stuff.' Although he acknowledged that in engineering the writing counts for very little, 'it's all about your numbers and graphs and stuff and then little words, using the right terminology, and they're all good,' it continues to plague his self-confidence. Secondly, he lacked the basic chemistry skills typically acquired at the secondary level and this limited how he accessed the course content in the engineering degree: 'Yeah and a little bit on the chemistry kind of thing because I didn't do chemistry at all [at secondary school].'

Socially, at university, Manny also seemed to have changed his approach. Given that he had to retake a significant portion of his first year classes, he no longer described himself as vivacious and content to speak with any student who sat beside him. Now he stuck very closely with a fellow student who was also a church friend and perceived the other young men in his course as either conceited or clique-y.

> It depends on the dude, there are some dudes [in engineering] that are pretty high on snob meter and then you get the just before the snob meter and then you've got some of the normal people but they're kind of rare because some of the uni boys they're like if you're not getting HDs you're below them.

The masculinities Manny was exposed to at university contrasted significantly with those he interacted with at secondary school, which was an environment where Manny was well-liked by both students and staff:

> Well the dudes at my high school, only some of them were snobby, we had like one dude who was snobby because he was super smart but then the rest are down-to-earth dudes who aren't as smart. I like the down-to-earth people, I don't like the snobby people that are up themselves.

Here Manny equated being 'super smart' with 'snobby', outlining his perception of a certain type of university student. Furthermore, he constructed himself in relation to such a perception where he saw himself as less academically able and more grounded. In his account overall, Manny seemed to be accepted by his classmates even though he did not go out of the way to speak with them. He also made it clear he did not have the money nor the time nor the interest to reify these friendships outside the classroom at the local pub; this constraint appeared to frame him as an outsider: 'Yeah, I guess … and also I don't really drink as much as most uni students, I don't actually drink at all so half the dudes are always talking about how they went to town and how they drank this.'

Manny was still doing part-time work at the fast food place with a minimum of two shifts per week. He expressed some frustration about this: 'They've recently upped my hours and I'm like, "Why?" It's exam time, it's exam time.' Furthermore, while he did not have abundant spare time, Manny also spent his weekends at a 'mini scouts thing, mentoring little kids and stuff', citing 'I like chilling with kids … because I'm pretty much a big kid in an old body.' While he was passionate about this volunteer work which he found rewarding, it required time which essentially he did not have:

> Oh yeah, I'm actually going on a camp this weekend for my church. It's supposed to be the whole weekend but I had to cut it short on Saturday because I have to go to a Safe Place Training[2] for the kids and stuff and then I've got work on Sunday so I go to half my camp because of my other two things … And then after work I have to study for my exam which is on Monday.

This engagement in volunteer work offered a space where Manny could feel valuable (Stahl, 2015), something his words suggest he was not getting at university. While Manny was clearly passionate about working with young people, one cannot wonder if he was hiding in these enjoyable and largely positive activities when he should have been figuring out how to navigate his academic work. It is clear he felt a sense of shame at his underperformance which resulted in him feeling like an imposter, not willing to expand his social circle any further than he had to. University life, which used to be filled with opportunities, now seemed compartmentalised. Despite the hours he put in at work, when we talked about money, Manny acknowledged this year was harder than the last:

> A little bit because I've got a family of six plus my uncle that came from New Zealand so there's a whole bunch of us and then I have to work and then I get Centrelink and then I have to share the bills and everything with my dad who only works … because my mom doesn't work.
> Yeah, these last three weeks has been draining. I had work yesterday when I wanted to study for my maths exam, it was three to ten, I got home and I was like, whoa, and also my parents were moving houses at

the same time so I had to fill out forms for my mom because my dad doesn't know how to fill out forms, so I've been filling out house paperwork for the last three weeks too, so I'm like why? Can someone else know how to fill out forms please?

Not dissimilar from other second-generation immigrants, Manny here called attention to his expanded role in the family and how he served as an important resource and his skills ensured their security. Since we last spoke Manny's family had undergone some significant changes. His mother was laid off from her job as a receptionist, did some home childcare to help supplement the income, but then was diagnosed with cancer which she was slowly recovering from: 'Her health's better now, she just can't really find work mostly because she's old now because once you get past 40 no-one wants to hire you.' Manny's family still shared the family car and this structured the family dynamic and contributed significantly to his time pressures and his responsibilities: 'I pretty much use the car so at uni I have to drive here, do work, 15:00 pick up my siblings, drop them home, sometimes I come back.' As Manny reflected back he considered other avenues he could have taken and what led him to where he currently was. Whereas just a year ago Manny took pride in being one of the first in his family and community to attend university, he now seemed disillusioned with life at university and the doors a university degree could open for him:

A: You don't really need a degree to get money. There's plenty of jobs out there that pays still around a high amount to live off.
Q: Yeah, like construction work – they get paid well.
A: They get paid pretty well without a degree.
Q: Yeah, but you could have gone into that but you chose to go into university.
A: Yeah, because I am absolutely useless with tools.
Q: Okay, so you want to use your brain.
A: Yeah, most likely, yeah. Mostly because my parents, my parents came from another country and they want a better future and since most of my culture don't really go to uni so I'm like, yeah … Yeah, everyone in my community is like, 'Oh, you're the dude that goes to uni.' I'm like yeah, I'm not failing at all.

Manny highlighted a community pressure here as he was 'paving the way' and 'inspiring others', which Capannola and Johnson (2020) note is an important part of the identity work of being first-in-family. Manny's words here highlight a private burden he faced where he felt that he had to keep his struggles at university largely to himself, which must have been an isolating experience. The image of the university student in his community is one of success, ease and the pursuit of upward mobility. It is not an image of scraping by. This last comment stuck with me and it alludes to the effort Manny was putting in to hold up a successful learner identity when his true learner identity was much more fragile and his work at university was precarious.

I've set myself to a high-ish standard and if I don't reach it I'm like, 'I'm all right.' I'm not one of those guys that 'I'm the best, I got a HD.' Even if I get a HD I'm like, 'Oh, I'm still all good.'

This suggests a conflict between having high standards – thus suggesting an investment – and remaining neutral whatever grade is attained. The carefree Manny from the previous year who described uni as 'fun' and filled with 'freedom' was no longer present. Steadily, over time, the university experience seemed to have become not only more associated with work but something to be endured. Reay (2001) notes that for working-class people education is something to be 'got through rather than go into' (p. 335). To change the tone of the conversation, I asked Manny where he was happiest:

A: With people generally, more kids … because kids are cool.
Q: Yeah, relaxing, less stressful than memorising chemistry.
A: They can be stressful, not as stressful as trying to memorise a whole textbook for an exam next week which I have not really studied for.

Manny's sense of personal authenticity appeared changed since the first year at university. He now voiced that he is suspicious of people who feel a need to validate themselves through having too many friends. As he became increasingly involved in volunteer work, Manny contrasted his experiences working with young people with the 'snobby' university space. Negotiating this tension contributed to his identity formation:

I don't know … through volunteering I feel more comfortable, at work I feel comfortable. I generally try and be comfortable but then there's certain spots where there's people that are kind of snobby and I'm like, [inaudible] shell a bit by myself.

What is clear is that Manny, like many working-class students, no longer felt he 'fit in' with the university space and he thus felt uncomfortable. These feelings contributed to what Reay (2001) calls the 'difficult uncomfortable configuration of working classness with academic success' (p. 339); furthermore, Manny's words suggest these feelings worked to undermine his pride around being first-in-family. When I queried what attracted him to engineering, I learned that Manny was actually considering a change of degree course entirely:

I was actually looking into teaching but I don't know. I'm a good people person, I'm pretty good with kids. I volunteer a lot with all these kid programs and stuff … Yeah, it's always there for me to go into but my parents just told me continue with this course until there's a certain point where you're like no.
Yeah, I've always had the thought in the back of my head where I'm like maths teacher, pretty chill you know, work with people and doing maths … because maths is fun. I like maths, physics not so much, I like physics

but not as much as maths and then chemistry I hate so much because I have no clue about it.

As Manny vacillated in his aspirations between engineering and teaching, he picked up extra shifts where possible to avoid what he saw as the drudgery of academic work. This also possibly prolonged his exposure to working-class masculinities (Nixon, 2009). Our interview ended on an upbeat note because his volunteer work had secured him a free trip to the Gold Coast to work with a youth volleyball tournament. I asked Manny what was next for him:

> I want to figure out what I want to do and stick with it. I can't just keep going through life not really knowing what I want to do because to a certain point I'm just going to be like I still don't know what I want to do.

Conclusion

Manny's story is complicated and it centres around balancing responsibilities while struggling to find both validation and fulfillment through his education. His story is infused with experiences with family unemployment and poverty and Manny's words remind us that the transition to university for many students is longer than just the first semester or, in fact, the first year. Furthermore, his experiences highlight that equity programs are important but should be more personalised and sensitive to how the needs of students change over time. Manny's struggles with masculine subjectivities remind us of Burke's (2006) argument that 'aspirations are discursively fashioned through gendered power relations and identifications [and that] regulatory and competing discourses make available a range of masculine identifications' (p. 720). How Manny positioned himself in relation to the masculinities he encountered changed significantly from the first year to the second year. The original friendly Manny who enjoyed meeting new people became more reserved with the realisation he had very little in common with students in his course in terms of lifestyle. In terms of masculinities, as the eldest male in his family Manny felt a certain responsibility and sense of pride in attending university, but he seemed to find the overly masculine nature of engineering off-putting. Therefore, while he may have felt an early sense of belonging, this seemed to dissipate over his two years at university. Holmegaard (2020) writes that interviewing young people repeatedly about their choices and transitions can open up a 'space for reflection created in the interview [which] can support reflections that the young person would not otherwise have made, and this is reinforced in a longitudinal study' (p. 125). With Manny, I often felt our dialogues did foster this reflection. He seemed to realise university was a good place for him but the subject area of engineering actually held little interest. This created a tension where I had to hold back from assuming the role of counsellor, given my familiarity with his particular institutional context.

Notes

1 In most states in Australia students can leave school early if they secure an apprenticeship or some other form of training.
2 Manny was referring to a training centre that provides training and certifications for those working with young people.

References

Adams, M., & Coltrane, S. (2005). Boys and men in families: The domestic production of gender, power, and privilege. In M. Kimmel, J. Hearn, & R. W. Connell (Eds.), *Handbook of studies on men and masculinities* (pp. 230–248). Sage.

Burke, P. (2006). Men accessing education: Gendered aspirations. *British Educational Research Journal, 32*(5), 719–733.

Burke, P. J. (2009). Men accessing higher education: Theorizing continuity and change in relation to masculine subjectivities. *Higher Education Policy, 22*, 81–100.

Butler, J. (1990). *Gender trouble: Feminism and the subversion of identity.* Routledge.

Capannola, A. L., & Johnson, E. I. (2020). On being the first: The role of family in the experiences of first-generation college students. *Journal of Adolescent Research*, advance online publication. doi:10.1177/0743558420979144

Clark, B. R. (1960). The 'cooling out' function in higher education. *American Journal of Sociology, 65*, 569–576.

Egeberg Holmgren, L. (2013). Gendered selves, gendered subjects: Interview performances and situational contexts in critical interview studies of men and masculinities. In B. Pini & B. Pease (Eds.), *Men, masculinities and methodologies* (pp. 90–103). Palgrave Macmillan.

Francis, B. (2000). *Boys, girls and achievement: Addressing the classroom issues.* Routledge Falmer.

Holmegaard, H. T. (2020). Complexity, negotiations, and processes: A longitudinal qualitative, narrative approach to young people's transition to and from university. In N. E. Fenton & W. Ross (Eds.), *Critical reflection on research in teaching and learning* (pp. 107–130). Brill.

Lehmann, W. (2009). University as vocational education: Working-class students' expectations for university. *British Journal of Sociology of Education, 30*(2), 137–149.

Mac an Ghaill, M. (1994). *The making of men: Masculinities, sexualities and schooling.* Open University Press.

McDowell, L. (2000). The trouble with men? Young people, gender transformations and the crisis of masculinity. *International Journal of Urban and Regional Research, 24*(1), 201–209.

Nichols, S., & Stahl, G. (2017). 'Gotta get that laziness out of me': Negotiating masculine aspirational subjectivities in the transition from school to university in Australia. In G. Stahl, J. Nelson, & D. O. Wallace (Eds.), *Masculinity and aspiration in the era of neoliberal education: International perspectives* (pp. 166–184). Routledge.

Nixon, D. (2009). 'I can't put a smiley face on': Working-class masculinity, emotional labour and service work in the 'New Economy'. *Gender, Work & Organization, 16*(3), 300–322.

Reay, D. (2001). Finding or losing yourself? Working-class relationships to education. *Journal of Education Policy, 16*(4), 333–346.

Reay, D. (2005). Beyond consciousness? The psychic landscape of social class. *Sociology*, *39*(5), 911–928.

Robb, M. (2007) Gender. In M. J. Kehily (Ed.), *Understanding youth: Perspectives, identities and practices* (pp. 109–145). Sage.

Rubin, M., Evans, O., & McGuffog, R. (2019). Social class differences in social integration at university: Implications for academic outcomes and mental health. In J. Jetten & K. Peters (Eds.), *The social psychology of inequality* (pp. 87–102). Springer.

Spiegler, T., & Bednarek, A. (2013). First-generation students: What we ask, what we know and what it means: An international review of the state of research. *International Studies in Sociology of Education*, *23*(4), 318–337.

Stahl, G. (2015). *Aspiration, identity and neoliberalism: Educating white working-class boys*. Routledge.

Thomsen, J. P., Munk, M. D., Eiberg-Madsen, M., & Hansen, G. I. (2011). The educational strategies of Danish university students from professional and working-class backgrounds. *Comparative Education Review*, *57*(3), 457–480.

Wong, B. (2018). By chance or by plan? The academic success of nontraditional students in higher education. *AERA Open*, *4*(2), 1–14.

6   Dominic

Year 1: last year of compulsory schooling

Dominic is of Indigenous heritage and he attended a state school in the northern suburbs of Adelaide. The eldest in his family, he is what would be described as a high achiever. While many boys in the study suffered through maths, Dominic asserted: 'Oh I've always been good at maths'. This affirmed his commitment to study civil engineering at university, which he had heard has good job prospects: 'I don't want to sound cocky or anything, I am one of the top students in this school for my year level anyway.' As he concluded his last year of compulsory schooling, Dominic was working casually as a pizza delivery driver, a job that brought him very little satisfaction but he considered essential to set him up financially for university the following year. Dominic's masculine subjectivity embodies many facets of Mac an Ghaill's 'Academic Achiever', seeing education as part of the ladder to social mobility. He was not 'unambiguously pro-school' but rather complied as he saw it as a means to an end (Mac an Ghaill, 1994, p. 59). Dominic's transition to university involved a commitment to hard work and diligent study. He valued the importance of getting ahead through his education and saw university in largely transactional terms, believing that the experience would give him access to the career of his choice.

   Dominic's heavy involvement in mathematics at secondary school was important for a variety of reasons. First, maths served as an entry point into understanding where he could excel:

> when I first started to love maths was in primary school, second year I'm pretty sure. I was the best in class so that kind of inspired me to do – keep going better, see how far I could go but besides that not really anyone else.

At the secondary level, his advanced maths skills provided him with the opportunity to be on a university campus through a specialist program. It also made him a more independent learner as the maths he was studying was, according to him, beyond the capabilities of the teachers at his secondary school. The further Dominic became involved in maths, it appeared that he was able to construct himself in ways that reaffirmed the strengths in his learner identity. Maths also served a primary social function with a close-knit group of peers all focused on capitalising on their maths skills as they progressed into higher education: 'We're supposed to be able to help each other, so we do gain that kind of bond to trust and be a group, so yeah you could say that'. Despite having this experience at university, Dominic expressed some hesitancy. When I ask him specifically about his feelings regarding the following year, he stated: 'Yeah, see how it goes, that's a bit of a blurred side of it, I don't really know what I'm getting into too much. Like, I'm sure I'll like it anyway.'

Dominic described his immediate locale: 'It's a very nice area, people consider it a bogan area but I don't … that, I would love to live here my whole life but I know that's very unlikely.' Integral to his aspirations was his commitment to studying civil engineering, which would take him beyond the northern suburbs: 'Yes because going into my course, and being civil engineering, probably have to move states and maybe move countries.' Drawing upon what Friese (2001) refers to as the 'ontologies of belonging and identity', research continues to document how working-class young people struggle with both attachment and pathologisations of place (Stahl & Baars, 2016; Stahl & Habib, 2017). As Thrift (1997) states, 'the difference between location and place is that places have meanings for us which cannot be reduced to their location' (p. 160).

Browman et al. (2017) focus on how low socioeconomic status students perceive socioeconomic mobility and how this may influence their academic persistence; they emphasise that students' perception of education can be connected to 'a desirable future, characterized by stable employment and a respectable income' (p. 45). Dominic's father completed Year 12 and went directly into working as a mechanic and, Dominic says, 'so he earns pretty good'. Furthermore, his family had some recent experience with post-compulsory study: during Dominic's final years of compulsory schooling his mother – who dropped out of school in Year 10 – was enrolled in an accountancy course at TAFE and she earned a qualification. As a result, Dominic entertained the idea of being an accountant but eventually dismissed the idea when he 'did a course on business thinking and I was just sitting behind a computer all day and that's not my thing. I couldn't sit there all day.' Prior to Dominic's mother beginning her course, the family had suffered financial hardship but since gaining her qualification and subsequent employment, the financial situation of the family had improved. Having a father as a mechanic assisted Dominic to get a car when he got his licence. Such a purchase allowed him to transverse his immediate locale and see a lot more. It also positioned him advantageously to work as a pizza delivery driver, which was a form of employment which required a car.

When asked about what he wanted at this stage in his life, Dominic was quick to respond with 'I don't want to be, like, rich' then elaborated:

Yep, well obviously getting a job, a good strong healthy job would be one of my first priorities. Then moving out, getting my own house, starting a family if possible. Yeah, I don't want to live a wealthy like … job life, just want a standard life – enjoy it.

Within this articulation of Dominic's aspiration, we see a distancing from middle-class forms of entitled aspirations and a downplaying of his high aspirations. In scholarly accounts of upwardly mobile working-class masculinities, this modesty Dominic presents is quite common (see Miles et al., 2011; Savage et al., 2001; Stahl, 2015). While Dominic embodies a high achiever learner identity, this appears at times to be an awkward fit at the state school he attends, which has few students who are bound for university.

When asked about his learner identity in the last few weeks of Year 12, Dominic suggested that 'people look at me [as] pretty successful, hard working. I'm very organised in my life, or used to be anyway. This year's got me all binded up, can't really do much else than just study.' Furthermore, upholding this learner identity involved a certain pressure and had implications for the family dynamic. When I spoke with Dominic about being the eldest, he said, 'Oh I set a high standard for everybody, which is hard for my sister because she's not doing too well in school, so she kind of gets the bad end of the family reputation I guess.' Similar to the experiences of other participants in the *First-in-Family Males Project*, Dominic also called attention to the sacrifices he had made in Year 12, specifically around how the demands of study have limited his family time. And, while his time with his family had been significantly reduced, Dominic was quick to assert that he was looking forward to a family holiday after his exams.

Dominic has Indigenous heritage, and is White in appearance. When I asked him about his Indigenous status, he alluded to an identity conflict, saying: 'Yeah just kind of go with the flow, just go with it. But because I'm Aboriginal somewhat people don't see me as that, I don't really see myself … as well.' Perhaps because I am White, I sensed Dominic was reluctant at this stage to speak further on the matter so I did not probe. In regard to the support available at his secondary school, Dominic described a space in the library:

yeah there's an area for all us Aboriginals, we can go in there and study any time we want … I do have [access to] the Aboriginal area, so that side of it that I can go to … but I don't often.

As Year 12 came to a close, Dominic claimed that he was going to work much harder: 'Just probably push myself harder than ever … strong and not give up which I haven't done yet, which I've seen a lot of other people fail'. Aspirations are formed relationally through interactions with others as well as observations. Seeing people give up on their studies during the crunch period of Year 12 contributed to how Dominic produced himself as a student who was upwardly mobile. Numerous times in our interviews Dominic drew attention to other students whom he perceived as underperforming, 'Yeah it's very hard. I still know a lot people in my year level have no idea where they're going next. So I'm glad I know where I'm going.' Being a determined student with high career aspirations in a school where this was uncommon seemed to also carry some responsibility. He described some of his close friends dropping out because 'some just couldn't handle it so they just dropped out, but now I've kind of encouraged them to go back and finish because they need to do something'.

As Year 12 drew to a close and exams were on the horizon, Dominic admitted he was struggling though he was resilient. Employing an automotive metaphor, 'you just got to put your foot down, just got to do it', he noted: 'I'm running off fumes.' When we discussed how Dominic was dealing with this stressful time, he highlighted the tremendous pressure that he puts on himself:

> Because there's always, I know I can try harder and I can do more than I'm doing now. It's just I need to push the limits which is pushing the limits because I push everything, which is going to be hard.

Dominic's story was one of sacrifice and determination. He appeared willing to put everything social and familial off to the side in order to gain the best ATAR possible.

Looking towards university on the horizon, Dominic worked to normalise his aspiration through noting that 'most of my friends are going to university'. These were mainly the boys from his maths enrichment program. Also, his girlfriend of three years planned to attend university to study teaching. At this stage in his academic career, it was important to Dominic to frame higher education as a place of further opportunity where he would be amongst like-minded people and away from 'failures'. Always a high achiever striving for more, Dominic asserted: 'Obviously I want to try and be better than the rest so I can get the better opportunities than most people, so yeah that's what I'm trying to do.' We discussed how Dominic's life will potentially look very different from the life of his parents. Dominic took care with his words here and did not want to judge his parents harshly: 'But I'm the first into university in my family. Hoping it's better than their life … [but] I don't want to say that their life is bad or anything.' In thinking of how hard his parents worked to raise four children while advancing their own careers through education and training, Dominic said: 'Yeah but I hope I get to a bit better, just lead myself onto a better life.' When he discussed various notions of success and failure Dominic called attention to university as a pathway to employment and thus a means to an end. Yet, he seemed aware that a degree does not ensure a job: 'I would see myself as a failure if I left university and I couldn't get into a job straight away. I know sometimes that's pretty hard.'

Year 2: the post-school year

When I met up with Dominic in the first few weeks of his course I found that his ATAR had surpassed his expectations and he was enrolled at the university closest to his home in a course on civil engineering and project management (a four-year degree). This is not the most prestigious university in the state though, by his account, it seemed that Dominic could have gone to that university. Instead, Dominic had selected a university that was familiar to him because one afternoon a week in secondary school he attended a specialist maths course. We spoke about the structure of his course, how everyone was completing the foundation subjects together before they specialised and also about the gender imbalance (he estimated there were 'about 15 girls out of like, the 150 students, I think'). Dominic appeared relaxed ('I found it pretty easy the first couple of weeks') and mentioned he had seen some old friends from high school and made some new friends as well, though very few of his high school friends had actually made the transition to university ('We had 8 friends [in the group] and only 4 went, so 50%').

> I'm in a good place yeah; I've just started to get into the progress of doing lots of study, working around my work and family … but yeah. I'm going there only 4 days a week out of the 5 …, I got Monday off. But I try and stay there from 9 until 5 or something like that, but most of my classes finish at 4 so I just study a bit after, just trying to keep up with it all and try and get ahead.

However, while he described himself as being in a good place, when I asked him what had been rewarding so far, Dominic asserted: 'Rewarding, I don't know. I actually don't know … there's nothing really rewarding about it at the moment', suggesting a certain hollowness in attending university. For Dominic university was largely a means to an end and he approached it with the same efficiency that he did his studies in Year 12: 'Yeah, [it's] just school really, just do my assignments. I'm learning more though, I'm learning more about the specific thing I want to do so that's good. There's nothing really rewarding … it's just work.' Though, within this, Dominic was generally satisfied with the quality of the teaching and felt he had selected the right topic area.

   Similar to how he constructed his learner identity in high school, Dominic appeared to maintain his motivation through comparing himself to other students. As his first few weeks of his course came to a close he was aware of people who were dropping out. According to Dominic:

> Yeah, like you can tell people that are slacking off and not going to do so well compared to those who will. But I'm hoping, I feel like I'm in the middle ground, like sometimes I do [slack off] but I feel like I'm moving to the side a bit more.

This indicated that he was managing to maintain his motivation. Research on the learner identities of working-class boys suggests a desire to be ordinary, as they feel comfortable occupying a middling position, devoid of distinction (Stahl, 2013, 2015). This is in contrast to work on upwardly mobile working-class masculinities, where men have been documented to be boastful, rationalising their socially mobility as the produce of their skill and hard work (c.f. Giazitzoglu, 2014, para 4.9; Mac an Ghaill, 1994). While Dominic did not consistently occupy this position, it is interesting that when he went to university and entered a competitive program he occasionally adopted this subjectivity. In the safe space of the interview Dominic described himself as hard working: 'when I get my head down I get my head down and do work, get it done really well. Like I don't get distracted or anything like that, like I get the work I need done when I can.' When I asked Dominic if he felt like a university student, he was quick to reply that he did but was clear that he had not fully engaged in the university culture:

> Yeah, like when I walk in there I feel like I'm actually a uni student, like the typical, carry bags, all the textbooks and stuff, all around doing hard work, putting your head down. But I haven't done any of the community stuff, like they have events all the time, every week or so often.

Acclimatising to the culture of the university can take time for some students. Furthermore, the first couple of weeks of university study can often involve substantial shifts as students juggle and rejuggle their timetables for lectures and tutorials. Dominic's acclimatisation appeared to occur largely without obstacles:

> Yeah, I'm sort of like getting into it more and more, like feeling more comfortable and where I'm going and who I'm with. Like don't have to be … I feel like it was more of a competition at first, but then now it's just like different.

When asked about Indigenous support programs, he seemed to be not very interested: 'I believe they do [have support services], they probably would but I haven't really looked into it that much, even though I am Indigenous myself.' He called attention to how at school he rarely used the support structures and relied mainly on his friends.

Neither Dominic nor his parents know any people working in the field of civil engineering. Compared to other boys in the study at this stage, Dominic seemed more focused on academic persistence in relation to his own employability. There exists a relationship between low-socioeconomic-status students' perception of socioeconomic mobility and their academic persistence (Browman et al., 2017). Working-class students rely heavily on their investment in their academic progress in order to feel a sense of belonging (Mallman, 2017). Through engaging fully in academic practices as a process of inculcation, working-class students may experience alterations at the level of the habitus (Lee & Kramer, 2013), which may or may not foster a sense of entitlement.

However, interestingly, Dominic does not see joining university clubs and student groups as integral to accruing social capital to bolster his employment prospects. While he was making friends and there seemed to be no apparent barriers to acclimatising socially and academically to university life, Dominic actually held himself at a distance from his classmates: 'So it's like kind of, you think it's going to turn in to a competition later on.' Dominic cited a few examples of the competitive atmosphere in the engineering course where people 'just make themselves look stupid by being so rude and stuff'. Dominic's sense of success or failure which structured his aspirations was aligned with what we discussed when we first met where his anxiety was around getting the degree but not getting the job: 'So I've still got the goal, just maybe third or fourth year I'll get a casual job as an engineer just working ... so I can get into the workforce early before all the others.' Despite being quite new to university study, Dominic spoke about wanting to go to the career expos when they are held and articulated a sophisticated understanding of what he would have to do to become a competitive candidate to an employer:

> you've just got to stand out from the crowd, I say, highlight what you're good at and, I guess ... in the community so that you know that they look out for you. That they will look for you in the future you're going in.

One factor that helped with Dominic's acclimatisation to university was that his independence was a significant part of his learner identity throughout high school. He described how his parents had long since had a hands-off approach to his trajectory:

> Yes, they know I can control my own life ... I don't need them as much anymore, which might help them ... I don't even really rely on my parents too much really ever. Once I got in high school I was basically myself – my own goals.

Now at university, though albeit only in the first few weeks, Dominic said his relationship with his parents had changed:

> With my dad it's gotten better, like it has got a lot better. Like we talk a lot more than we used to, but like it's always been the same. I'm not really a very emotional person when it comes to family and stuff like that.

This reinforces arguments made by Adams and Coltrane (2005) that men and boys often 'maintain ambivalent connections to families which can have implications for their emotional development' (p. 230).

While Dominic presented an identity that involved being unemotional, it was clear that he was. Powell and Takayoshi (2003, pp. 395–396) suggest that all relationships are formed through 'an attentiveness to the personalities, desires, needs and knowledge of the people involved; an attentiveness to the give-and-take of human interaction; an attentiveness to participants as human beings'. In my dialogues with Dominic over the course of the study I did need to be extremely attentive. As a deeply private person who was very invested in his aspirational trajectory, sometimes it was the smallest detail that Dominic uttered that allowed me to build the necessary rapport.

Throughout the *First-in-Family Males Project*, during the process of transition to university many of the participants expressed frustration around 'time management' and 'scheduling'. A balance between the academic demands of university life and part-time service work seemed elusive to some. In his first few months of university study, Dominic went from casual employment as a pizza delivery driver to a more substantial schedule. He admitted that this rigid schedule left very little time for sleep and 'Like I used to like watch TV programs but that's gone out the window.'

When I met up with Dominic towards the end of his first year in university, he described himself as still being in a good place: 'I don't know why [but] I just feel more in control.' He discussed adopting better strategies to navigate university study and the topics covered in the second half of the year seem to resonate more with his passion areas within civil engineering: 'Yeah, now I am feeling, now I know what's coming and I feel confident … and I am excited to see where I am going and I am doing my study as well.' Describing his journey in affective terms, this is in contrast to his more transactional approach I witnessed at the beginning of the year. As his aspirations were slowly being realised, Dominic noted:

> Yeah, I feel pretty confident what I am studying – I am enjoying what I am studying at the moment, so I feel like I am confident that once I leave university that I will still be motivated to do what I want to do. So I feel like the course I've picked is good. In terms of going to university it's a good decision. I have seen some of my old friends who have moved onto full-time jobs and getting a lot of money, but I just think about how much more money I will be earning once I finish my degree.

While Dominic had always constructed his identity in relation to others' successes and failures, here Dominic's words signify a change in disposition from the previous year. Where before he asserted 'I don't want to be like rich', now that he was at university and exposed to a certain level of competition in his course, he considered his present position and his future. He acknowledged that he was motivated by the prospect of earning a good salary.

Furthermore, the stressful moments at university of group assignments and exams also worked to strengthen his small friendship group. Dominic noted:

> if I ever had some trouble just turn to them – same for them turn to me. Just keep each other focused really and just feel more motivated to go because you've got friends that you can actually talk to and fit in.

Dominic made important comparisons here to his friends from high school who, aside from his small group in the maths enrichment program, largely had interests and aspirations more aligned with traditional working-class masculinities. Given Dominic's proactive spirit and desire to position himself advantageously for his future, he expressed concern about the people he knew from his secondary school who were not working: 'Some aren't working at all – don't have plans to do much – I worry for them people.' Drawing on the work of Giazitzoglu (2014), it would appear a significant dimension of upwardly mobile masculinities is the othering of those from similar backgrounds who did not capitalise on the opportunities available to them. An active 'entrepreneur of the self' in constructed here in contrast to notions of stagnation, ignorance or a lack of ambition.

Despite being only eighteen, Dominic towards the end of his first year was also working as a Senior Manager at the pizza shop (approximately 25 hours per week), which allowed him flexibility to determine his schedule, a certain amount of responsibility as well as a higher pay scale. 'So I just do two nights as manager like controlling the whole store by myself – just controlling everybody. It's basically what I was doing before but I am in control – like I am the boss basically.'

On a symbolic level, becoming a Senior Manager meant something for Dominic in terms of the formation of his aspirations and his perception of self. Assuming a senior position reinforced Dominic's belief that hard work pays off, as evidenced by his high ATAR and good performance during the first semester of university. Dominic now seemed more comfortable with acknowledging that he was a motivated and competitive individual. Integral to his disposition to do well, he was open in vocalising: 'I was like, yeah I want to go up – every place I want to go I want to get to the top. I want to be the best.' It has been documented in work on first-in-family students that a 'key driver' is a 'desire to prove to themselves or others their abilities' (Wong, 2018, p. 6). While not discounting the many issues with the construction of some university spaces as prestigious while others are less so, Dominic's desire to 'be the best' is interesting considering that he chose to attend the university closest to his home, rather than a university in the city with higher symbolic capital. It is unclear whether this was Dominic's decision or if his ATAR determined this. When asked how he balanced his work with his study, Dominic emphasised his skills of self-discipline and time management:

> I just manage time you know – like I study when I can so at uni I put my head down, so Monday to Thursday I am here 8 till 4 everyday even when I don't have lessons and then I do all my work and then I work basically 5–11 or 5–1 whatever day it is – because it always changes, then sleep when I can, and then yeah repeat the cycle.

As the year closed Dominic had increased his independence both in university study and in his part-time work. This autonomy was satisfying to him. When we discussed the way his lifestyle had changed since he was in his last year of compulsory schooling, he reported: 'Well my lifestyle hasn't really changed much. I am not living at home now, that's the only really thing. I have moved in with my girlfriend.' Only two participants in the *First-in-Family Males Project* were able to move out of home, with the other participant living on the university campus (cf. Stahl et al., 2020). Dominic disclosed that he and his girlfriend were living together in rented accommodation just a few blocks away from his parents. I commented that this seemed like a significant change, but Dominic was quick to downplay it: 'Not really, before even when I was at home I was kind of supporting myself anyway because they are always working and stuff like that. Not much else has really changed just study … [still] working hard.' Reflecting back on how his life had changed since the beginning of the research, Dominic said:

> I do think about it sometimes. When I was in high school and I looked at university students, thinking they were all high and mighty, but it hasn't changed much really for me. Like I'm just still doing the same thing, studying hard and working hard and doing what I can do to improve. So there is not much to change. It's just more flexibility in what I want to do – enjoying my own life and being an actual adult – not having to rely on parents to pay for things and do anything like that.

Aspirations are largely structured by discourses and experience. Paramount to Dominic's aspiration was a future career. According to him:

> Yeah, I have heard a lot of rumours that once you get a degree it's very hard to get a job. I don't know why, because you don't have the experience compared to if you do an apprenticeship or something like that.

When I asked if it was too early in the game to be so concerned with employment, Dominic disagreed: 'It's never too early, like you can always do better than you are now – always trying to improve. But just take it as a learning experience now and see how I go.' Dominic confessed that he was anxious about the fact that he was not networking enough and this could pose a potential barrier to his success: 'I know, yes, I need to work on my networking skills quite a bit. I haven't really engaged in talking to anyone senior compared to what I should be.' Again, this echoed his previous words concerning the pressure he put upon himself but there was also a fear here of wasting opportunities, or even downward mobility. Despite it being only the end of his first year, Dominic was clear about his ultimate goal: 'just get a full-time job and just start earning some money and living the good life and do what I need to.'

While Dominic was clearly ambitious and competitive, these qualities did not always sit comfortably with him. Arguably, for working-class boys there are many potential barriers to their engagement with education; perhaps the most significant is the duality that burdens working-class boys, the 'habitus divided against itself' (Bourdieu et al., 1993, p. 511), where working-class boys must keep their identities intact while attempting to position them-selves as respectable in relation to the field. When I asked Dominic if he ever felt at a disadvantage at university, he said he did not, asserting:

> No, never feel a disadvantage – I don't have anything wrong with me or anything like that. So I always feel like I'm equal to everybody else. Like I am not advanced to anybody else or anything else. I am just equal, trying to do the best I can really.

In response to this I alluded that he seemed to have a very high work ethic and the ability to balance many things at once. When this came up in the interview, Dominic was quick to project an identity of being ordinary; he must have found comfort in occupying a middling position (Stahl, 2013). He asserted: 'I don't feel that way, I feel like I am just doing what I can get past, to get through – I have my standards.'

The notion of standards led us to speak about masculinity, which was being discussed very robustly in the media, particularly #MeToo and toxic masculinity. When Dominic described a good man he emphasised the impor-tance of family responsibility and how mutual support worked in his own relationship: 'there for them and support them just as they can support you too'. He acknowledged:

> yeah, I don't know why there is so much talk in the media about men's masculinity these days. Like it shouldn't be a thing. We are not going back to the 80s where women had no rights or anything like that.

However, while voicing this viewpoint, Dominic also drew attention to the pressures around masculinity that may be particularly pertinent in the transi-tion from boyhood to manhood. He was aware of common and problematic stereotypes of masculinity and how 'most of a time you want a guy that's thin, abs, muscles like that, but you also want him to be smart, tall – be able to support a family – be the superman basically and do everything.' While he did attend the gym regularly and played basketball non-competitively once a week, he noted: 'No, I am not the standard of most guys – like being big and strong and stuff like that.'

Year 3: new beginnings

When I met up with Dominic in his second year of university, we spoke of his sense of resilience and determination to complete his degree no matter what. His mood seemed different – more downtrodden and less excited by what he perceived university could offer him. His life outside of his university studies had also changed. He had broken up with his girlfriend and moved back home and this was clearly a sensitive subject ('Yeah, [the relationship] was not making me focus on uni. I saw that it was a bad thing, I moved on, and that made me focus on uni more. Focus on myself. It's how it was.').

Dominic's rationale was interesting here as he framed the ending of the relationship in terms of a distraction from his aspiration to do well at university. His determined spirit highlights that in the neoliberal 'individualised' model the self is not fixed, but is rather constantly made and remade to secure one's advantage (Beck, 1992).

Ending the relationship and then ending his lease served as important milestones – or critical moments – in the transition to adulthood. According to Dominic, the year was financially challenging mainly due to this break-up: 'It's been tight for me personally, but it's because I'm supporting myself. I don't rely on my parents for anything like that. Obviously, I'm working often.' As being independent was important to him, Dominic was quick to note he budgets so as to not be a burden to his family:

> But I do pay board and stuff like that. It's not like I'm sliding off them. It's been tight, but that's my own budgeting. I let myself down a little bit by budgeting too tightly, and job dropped off a little bit for a little while … I only dropped down to ten hours a week, which is not enough, and what I needed is high [number of hours]. It was tight for a while, but now I'm back up to 20 hours a week. Now I'm doing pretty well.

We spoke about resilience and Dominic noted: 'No, if anything I feel like negative things push me in to do better. I can focus on myself more, and get away from that negative thing.' However, Dominic also noted: 'Definitely feel a lot more stressed at uni than anywhere else', but at this stage, he seemed quite committed to the aspiration he set forth for himself back in secondary school. As he had progressed from boyhood to manhood, Dominic asserted:

> You do sometimes think about, 'Is everything I'm doing worth it in the end?' But it always comes back to yes, of course it's going to be worth it. I'm going to get to the end. I'm going to achieve. I'm going to be what I want to be.

Adding to Dominic's current mood, some of his close friends had dropped university study or had switched to studying a different aspect of engineering. As a result, Dominic was back to making new friends but this also contributed to him doubling down on his strong-willed nature. He was still very anxious about employment, reiterating some of the same concerns of the previous year, though now he said: 'I'm looking on the careers website' and 'Try and be at all my lectures, make sure they know who I am so everything happens.' Such an approach suggests Dominic was aware of the level of competition and as a result he was positioning himself to secure his advantage.

Where previously Dominic spoke about being quite distant from his family, he now saw them as a source of some pressure: 'But it's not like I'm stressing over I have to get this. I've got a bit of expectation by my family towards that, puts a bit of pressure on.' While he was only halfway through his four-year degree in civil engineering, Dominic noted his family had framed him as potentially having significant earning capacity. Addressing this familial expectation, Dominic noted:

> they have this high expectation of me now that I'm going to be earn-ing this big amount of money after all this stuff. Every time I see them they're like, 'Oh, you're going to be earning so much money when you finish this career.' But there's obviously that fear that I could end up failing in the end. I don't think I will. I hope I don't.

Dominic's family perceived that university opens up opportunities not nec-essarily to do the engineering work Dominic was passionate about but to earn a high salary. Marginson (2016) notes that, while polices are in place to enhance equity in Australia – 'to modify the extent to which these forms of stratification reproduce each other', there is only increased 'potential for upward social mobility' as opposed to social mobility itself (p. 421). While Dominic appeared to be making the right moves to secure an advantage, his employment future, like many undergraduates across Australia, remained hazy. After a short pause, Dominic noted:

> Even if it doesn't work out, I always can go on something else, or I can fall back on something else. I've always got a back-up. I'm not too wor-ried … It's family, even if I do fail they'll come around to that.

Dominic still presented a subjectivity of being resolute in his aspirations, but how this was reaffirmed had changed over time. Whereas in high school we saw him encouraging students who dropped out to go back and finish their compulsory schooling, he now pulled himself away from students who fail and aligned himself with those whom he considered equally tenacious: 'I stay very academic, very driven, all that stuff. I surround myself with those people.' Furthermore, connected closely with his focus on doing well and not making excuses for himself, Dominic went on to assert: 'Anyone can achieve. All people in my high school could have done this, but it's just they didn't choose to.' He explained that he was no longer in contact with his high school friends who were not in the maths enrichment program, having purposely distanced himself from them.

As we concluded the interview, I asked Dominic where he felt he was strug-gling. He had had a confronting year with the breakup of a long-term relation-ship, a reduction in work hours and having to end his lease and move home. Through this hardship what had come to the fore was something that was per-haps always crucial to Dominic, which was ensuring his financial independence:

> Where am I struggling? Probably financially at the moment … but I'll get over it. Achieving, striving. Uni's doing pretty well. I think I'm, obvi-ously like I said, my best semester. I'm striving in that at the moment, but I hope that continues as I can go on …

Dominic is transactional and logical in his approach to higher education and he sees it as a means to an end. When he struggles, he does not draw upon the support services present at the university and there is no evidence in our dialogues of him connecting closely with the support services aimed at Indigenous students. These services are present at the university but, perhaps due to low numbers of Indigenous students or restricted funding, receive less recognition than in other universities in the study which invested more in outreach and personalised support.

Conclusion

Where at first, Dominic's story was one of resilience and self-sacrifice, it also works to illustrate how context and circumstance influence the alignment of aspirations. Not only was Dominic aspirational ('I want to be the best'), he was agentic in strategically realising these aspirations. Comparing Dominic's journey as a learner with scholarship on belonging and widening participation, a key difference for Dominic is he does not actively seek to belong to the university space – instead he is more focused on belonging to the labour market. This informs his view of his education as not necessarily enriching or enjoyable, but instead, adopting a transactional approach, as a means to an end. When Dominic encounters barriers, these experiences seem to reaffirm his aspiration to do well which involves making the necessary sacrifices. His sense of resilience bolsters him through the continued exposure to a competitive subject area.

As DuGay (1996) writes, within a neoliberal governed state, individuals are compelled to become 'entrepreneurs of the self'. Dominic's words, especially during the second year of university, implied that he had doubled down on his aspiration to *be(come)* upwardly mobile through his university studies. The onus for Dominic was always on himself and he rarely contextualised his experience with any reference to family, poverty or Indigenous status. At times, he seemed to be pursuing his aspirations at the expense of his relationships with his peers as well as his well-being. Egeberg Holmgren (2011) writes of 'co-fielding', a concept developed to address methodological challenges derived from the reflexive use of knowledge (in her case in feminist theory) and the overlapping positionings that were made part of interviewees' presentation of self in interaction with the interviewer. I raise this point here because I often felt through the three years that Dominic and I had close and aligned dispositions in multiple areas. Not only did I identify with aspects of his struggle, I had to work actively to not let it be known I championed him, wanting to see him do well and his various sacrifices pay off.

References

Adams, M., & Coltrane, S. (2005). Boys and men in families: The domestic production of gender, power, and privilege. In M. Kimmel, J. Hearn, & R. W. Connell (Eds.), *Handbook of studies on men and masculinities* (pp. 230–248). Sage.

Beck, U. (1992). *The risk society.* Sage.

Bourdieu, P., Accadro, A., Balazs, G., Beaud, S., Bonvin, F., Bourdieu, E., Bourgois, P., Broccolichi, S., Champagne, P., Christin, R., Faguer, J.-P., Garcia, S., Lenior, R., Oeuvrard, F., Pialoux, M., Pinto, L., Podalydes, D., Sayad, A., Soulie, C., & Wacquant, L. J. D. (1993). *The weight of the world: Social suffering in contemporary society.* Stanford University Press.

Browman, A., Destin, M., Carswell, K. L., & Svoboda, R. C. (2017). Perceptions of socioeconomic mobility influence academic persistence among low socioeconomic status students. *Journal of Experimental Social Psychology, 72*, 45–52.

DuGay, P. (1996). *Consumption and identity at work.* Sage.

Egeberg Holmgren, L. (2011). Cofielding in qualitative interviews: Gender, knowledge, and interaction in a study of (pro)feminist men. *Qualitative Inquiry, 17*, 364–378.

Friese, H. (2001). Pre-judice and identity. *Patterns of Prejudice, 35*(2), 63–79.

Giazitzoglu, A. (2014). Qualitative upward mobility, the mass-media and 'posh' masculinity in contemporary north-east Britain: A micro sociological case-study. *Sociological Research Online, 19*(2), 1–11.

Lee, E. M., & Kramer, R. (2013). Out with the old, in with the new? Habitus and social mobility at selective colleges. *Sociology of Education, 86*, 18–35.

Mac an Ghaill, M. (1994). *The making of men: Masculinities, sexualities and schooling.* Open University Press.

Mallman, M. (2017). The perceived inherent vice of working-class university students. *Sociological Review, 65*(2), 235–250.

Marginson, S. (2016). The worldwide trend to high participation higher education: Dynamics of social stratification in inclusive systems. *Higher Education, 72*, 413–434.

Miles, A., Savage, M., & Bühlmann, F. (2011). Telling a modest story: Accounts of men's upward mobility from the National Child Development Study. *British Journal of Sociology, 62*(3), 418–441.

Powell, K. M., & Takayoshi, P. (2003). Accepting roles created for us: The ethics of reciprocity. *College Composition and Communication, 54*(3), 394–422.

Savage, M., Bangall, G., & Longhurst, B. (2001). Ordinary, ambivalent and defensive: Class identities in the northwest of England. *Sociology, 35*(4), 875–895.

Stahl, G. (2013). Habitus disjunctures, reflexivity and white working-class boys' conceptions of status in learner and social identities. *Sociological Research Online, 18*(3), 1–12. http://www.socresonline.org.uk/18/3/2.html

Stahl, G. (2015). *Aspiration, identity and neoliberalism: Educating white working-class boys.* Routledge.

Stahl, G., & Baars, S. (2016). How 'space' and 'place' contribute to occupational aspirations as a value-constituting practice for working-class males. *Education + Training, 58*(3), 313–327.

Stahl, G., & Habib, S. (2017). Moving beyond the confines of the local: Working-class students' conceptualizations of belonging and respectability. *Young, 25*(3), 268–285. doi:10.1177/1103308816669451

Stahl, G., McDonald, S., & Stokes, J. (2020). 'I see myself as undeveloped': Supporting Indigenous first-in-family males in the transition to higher education. *Higher Education Research & Development, 39*(7), 1488–1501.

Thrift, N. (1997). 'Us' and 'them': Re-imagining places, re-imagining identities. In H. Mackay (Ed.), *Consumption and everyday life* (pp. 159–202). Sage.

Wong, B. (2018). By chance or by plan? The academic success of nontraditional students in higher education. *AERA Open, 4*(2), 1–14.

7 Logan

Year 1: last year of compulsory schooling

Logan attended a low-fee independent private school in the northern suburbs of Adelaide. His parents were separated; his mother worked in child
care and his father worked at a local chicken factory. As the eldest in his
family, Logan has one younger brother. When I first met Logan in his final
year of secondary schooling, he was positive about his progress and about his
future. Many of the boys struggled with the demands of Year 12, but Logan
described it in astutely pragmatic terms: 'It's been fun, it's been stressful,
I think it's been what Year 12 is supposed to be. There have been a lot of
highs and a lot of lows, but overall I think it's been a good year.' He was in
a long-term heterosexual relationship, had long hair tied back in a bun, and
was a popular and well-regarded student. Logan's transition to university
was marked by a fragmented search for fulfillment, especially in his second
year. Whereas he excelled and enjoyed secondary school, Logan struggled at
university and his experiences suggested he was isolated.

Academically, Logan would be described as an 'all-rounder'. He performed
well in multiple areas of academia, excelling in the classroom while also playing basketball and participating in the performing arts. Skelton and Francis
(2012) describe the all-rounder – the so-called 'Renaissance child' – as being
skilled not only in academics but also in 'the development of social contacts
and skills, thus contributing to an "all rounder" curriculum vitae that enhances
their prospects in a competitive higher education and labour market' (p. 443).
For young men, being an 'all-rounder' carries a certain currency and can
serve as an important ideal to strive for (Imms, 2007). The all-rounder has
been often reified through institutions as an idealised version of selfhood/
studenthood. Always upbeat and cheery, Logan was committed to studying
biological science – specifically marine biology where he was inspired by David
Attenborough and Marie Curie ('I am a science kind of nerd') suggesting a
comfortability with a 'geek' identity. It was his aim to attain a position at the
University of Adelaide, the most prestigious university in the state as, according to his understanding, it had the best program for what he wanted to do.

As Year 12 was concluding, how friendships would be maintained came up
quite frequently in conversations with the boys. Some of these friendships

would begin to fade as they all went along different pathways. When I asked Logan what he looked for in his friendships, he said:

> I look for people who, like me, always like to see the positives. I like people to have a good outlook on life even though the negatives are still happening and are present, I just prefer people who are always smiling, they attract me more than people who are always having a dull kind of expression. I also see humour as an attractive element of people because I think humour brings out the best in us, I think.

Logan elaborated that 'confidence, loyalty, trust' were both what he expected from his friends and what he 'treasured'. In a light-hearted tone, Logan said: 'my friendship group, they always say that I'm the happiest man alive, which I try to live to and I say to them that they inspire me to do that because without them, I can't do it'. This close connection to friends was a sentiment Logan expressed many times in our interviews and it was also tied to his perception of himself:

> I want people to see me as a happy and positive person. I don't even want people to – I don't really mind if people see me as an inspiration or as a guider, in a way, I just want people to know that I do try and live my life happily and so that's kind of what I want people to see me as – the happiest guy in the world.

I was always impressed with Logan's aspiration to maintain his happiness so that it could be of service to others who may be less fortunate. While the next few years would be filled with changes, I asked Logan if he felt unsettled this. He immediately framed his answer in terms of his longstanding friendships:

> It's something I'm quite questioning because I think some of my school friendships I think will become distant. They won't be there as much. Whereas my close personal friends I think are going to stay there because we've talked about what's going to happen in the future, where are we going to be, so we're kind of organising to already catch up and to see if we can arrange things about that to not lose contact.

This highlights that Logan had a high level of interpersonal intelligence, a commitment to those closest to him and also a willingness to openly discuss his feelings of vulnerability. Furthermore, compared to some of the other boys in the study, Logan expressed a strong disposition to preserve a work–life balance. He framed his future aspirations not in material terms or aligned with gaining prestige but in terms of his own personal sense of happiness and fulfillment:

> I think the one thing that I want from life is to be happy. I want to live my life knowing that I've done everything I could. I want to live life

knowing that I don't have any regrets, so I've studied what I want to study, I've been with the people I love and I've had fun while doing so. So I think that's the biggest thing I want from life is just to be happy.

These words reflect how Logan saw this moment in time. By his account, his experiences at secondary school had fostered this devotion to pursuing every opportunity available. He framed his experiences as rewarding, both socially and academically, and this contributed to his excitement about going to university. Another dimension of Logan's identity was his work ethic: he described himself 'as a student who does work really hard', explaining further: 'I do endeavour to complete every task to the best of my ability and I do strive to make sure that I've done my best with each task.' This devotion to happiness and a strong work ethic did not seem to be in tension for Logan and, based on his own words, his achievement seemed 'effortless' (Mac an Ghaill, 1994).

Research on boys and schooling has revealed that in many schools a narrow and often problematic version of masculinity is promoted, both explicitly and implicitly (Martino & Pallotta-Chiarolli, 2003), which influences how the transition from boyhood to manhood is navigated. When critically reflecting on his secondary school experience, Logan commented on an atmosphere where he could be himself:

I think the way – the main way that the school feels like you belong is they accept who you are, so they accept your subject choices, they accept what you want to do with life and they don't really judge you for it. So if you have a student who's doing all sciences and then doing music, they won't judge you. They won't say, oh, since you're doing all the sciences, we should push you into maths instead of music. They let you say that it's your choice so you can do that. So I think that's probably one of the best qualities of the school.

Logan also called attention to the supportive 'vibe' around learning, the spirit of camaraderie and commitment to one another's academic progress and well-being. Other boys in the *First-in-Family Males Project* who attended the same school as Logan voiced similar perspectives. Logan continued:

although we do have our differences at the school, we all follow a similar flow, we all follow a similar tone that we all work together. We all know that each person has their own struggles in their own subjects, so we all work together to try to help them. So I think that's kind of the atmosphere that I'm looking for is an atmosphere where people come together, they're willing to accept themselves, they're happy to express themselves without judgement and that there's always going to be that help if you need it.

While Logan expressed a commitment to science – his first choice to study at university – our conversations kept returning to his passion for theatre, where he had recently auditioned for *Peter Pan* ('I love science and I love drama'). Theatre, which is closely aligned with English, is often considered a traditionally feminine subject, but it seemed to resonate with Logan without infringing on his construction of masculinity. Skelton and Francis (2012) note that, for some high-achieving boys, choosing to engage with 'feminine' curriculum areas allows them to produce 'themselves as rational, liberal, multi-talented, expressive and autonomous, that is, as representative of Renaissance Masculinity' (p. 450). Linking back to the notion of a collective community around learning and skills, Logan mentioned:

> I just love the atmosphere of theatre, I think it's engaging and I love when you've done your play and you see – you look back on what you did and you think, woah, that was incredible. We all came together to make that.

Decision-making for working-class students is often pragmatic, rather than 'rational' where experiences – such as encountering a supportive teacher in primary or secondary school, having ambitious friends, or chance encounters – can lead to transformations, though these transformations can, as Lehmann (2009) notes, be 'confirming or contradictory, they can be evolutionary or dislocating' (p. 139). Logan described his drama teacher as one of his favourite people ('She makes the classroom feel like a home'). In calling attention to this positive atmosphere, Logan presented a sense of trepidation not just about leaving the comfort of his theatre class but about leaving what sounded like a supportive environment:

> I have mixed emotions [about the post-school year] because part of me is excited because once you finish school, you don't have this teacher, school support. You're out in the world now and so you have to – you get to kind of be yourself without that school support …

Throughout the *First-in-Family Males Project*, a common perception of university centred around it not being an inclusive environment but instead uncaring and unsupportive where there was a culture of high-stakes learning. Due to this perception, Logan, like the other boys I spoke with, highlighted that his time at university would involve a change to his learner identity and that he would need to adopt a more proactive approach to managing his time:

> I've been told that they won't hound you for a draft, that's up to you to submit a draft to them and to make sure that your assignments are definitely on time by the due dates. So I think it's going to be a lot more responsibility going to uni and just being more organised with my time management skills.

When Logan and I spoke about what he was anxious about, he further expressed some doubt around whether he has positioned himself well in applying to study science. A particular concern was his subject choice in Year 11 where he chose biology rather than topics considered more demanding like physics and chemistry:

> although I did achieve good grades across those sciences, I chose biology because I thought that in the biological sciences that biology would be the main subject but when I was looking at the course requirements [to get into university], it was more chemistry, and so I think that was one negative decision that I made for that area. But they are prerequisites for those courses, they only assume knowledge chemistry, so I think that it will be okay because I am a science kind of nerd … and I do know my chemistry, but I think that's probably the one negative thing that I've probably made towards my future was my subject selection.

Logan's deliberations here were not uncommon; however, this is where a more robust school counselling program could have assisted in positioning him advantageously or at least quelling some of these anxieties. Logan, who did not know many people currently attending university, largely relied on his attendance an Open Day at the university and internet searching to map out his future pathway.

Logan reflected on what had fuelled his aspirations throughout secondary school:

> when I got into Year 11 Biology and Year 11 Drama it was more my teachers who inspired me to keep going into those pathways because, although I did find an interest in the subjects and I began to grow a passion into the subjects, the teachers I think inspired me more to continue those pathways because they made the lesson so enthusiastic and it just made me more keen to go to those lessons and learn about that topic. So I think, yeah, it was mainly the teachers that sparked my interest –

This was a concern because, in Logan's mind, university will not have these same passionate educators. For whatever reason, he already envisioned his time at university as more transactional with less of a focus on inspiration. However, Logan did assert: 'I've always wanted to go to university through high school.'

As Logan stood on the verge of being the first in his family to go to university, we spoke about the ways in which his life may be different from his parents. Logan said:

> I think our lives going to be very different because my dad didn't go to university. He worked at [local chicken factory] for his first job and then stayed there the whole time. So he's worked at…from like store worker and he's a manager now.

While this shows Logan's acute awareness of a different trajectory, it does not capture how Logan felt about following a different course. His parents were supportive of whatever decision he made and, for the most part, he seemed to find comfort in this. In closing, Logan's plans for the summer included looking for a part-time job, spending time with his girlfriend and catching up with his friends.

Year 2: the post-school year

When I met up with Logan in the first few weeks of his course I found that his ATAR had been just enough for him to enroll at the University of Adelaide located in the city centre studying a Bachelor of Science, majoring in ecology and evolutionary biology, a traditionally masculine subject. This was about an hour commute from where he resided. While he had the necessary score to commit to his original plan to major in marine biology, he was concerned about the employment prospects and decided to play it safe and go a bit broader. Logan's girlfriend was attending TAFE and doing a Certificate III in Early Childhood Education and he was still struggling to find a part-time job that he felt he could fit around his demanding university schedule and substantial commute. We spoke casually and jokingly; Logan was speaking about cutting his very long hair but was reluctant to 'take the plunge'.

After a tumultuous first few weeks of adapting to more challenging subject matter ('little bit tricky trying to warm up to it, and find out this new information that we didn't quite learn in Year 12'), Logan appeared settled into the rhythm of university life:

> Emotionally I'd say I'm pretty stable, like I'm pretty happy with what's going on. I've got control of my emotions, not feeling too stressed, and if I am stressed, then I will just take it easy, take a few breaths. I'm not having any trouble with anything, so I'm pretty happy.

He also seemed to have established good procedures around time management and study habits, writing up his notes before the lectures and the tutorials. Given his schedule, when he had just one lecture in a day and no follow-up tutorial, Logan watched that lecture online. This saved him both time and money in what was a long commute to the city's CBD. Echoing a similar learner identity to the one he performed in high school, at university Logan said: 'I like to take pride in all the work that I do. I've given all my work 110% every single time.' Yet, the capacity to take pride in something was not without its barriers as previous areas of passion were no longer available to him:

> Yeah, so I'm trying to think, because I used to play basketball, and I would always take pride in that, but then I injured my knee so I haven't played basketball in over a year. And same with drama … I loved drama and … and took pride in that, even though I haven't been a part of any drama productions outside of school. But I do take a lot of pride in my relationships and friends and family, I'm very proud of all of them.

Adams and Coltrane (2005) write of the importance of boys and men incorporating 'the virtues of nurturing, caring, service, and emotional involvement' in family life and Logan held these in high regard (p. 243). In fact, Logan seemed proactive in expressing 'feminised' terms of nurturance and caring, often mentioning going out of his way to help his mother and his younger brother. Relationships have always been important to Logan and he talked about adjusting his schedule to catch the train with friends from his high school and local area: 'That's always one thing that we've always managed to keep together, it's just to keep in contact, because you've got to value those relationships.' Similar to many of the other participants in the study, Logan also voiced a commitment to his friends regardless of the pathways they were on in their post-school year:

> And then even with people who don't go to university, I've still kept in contact with. I've got two friends who didn't go to university, and I make sure that I see them regularly, because I don't really see them any other time.

When I asked Logan to draw some comparisons to where he was at the end of Year 12, Logan was clear that the experience of university had matured him and he consistently demonstrated ownership:

> Taking on a lot more responsibility for myself and for my actions. So, if I'm running late for something, I would say to myself you should have been on that, you know, that's your fault. So definitely becoming more of an adult now. Yeah, I think I've just gotten a lot more mature, a lot more responsible of my actions and consequences, and I think definitely more organised. Because in high school I wasn't doing any of this kind of pre-research and stuff like that, whereas I am now, because I want to get on top of things.

Logan here seems to embody the ideal university student who is diligent, self-motivated and proactive, absorbing every opportunity. Though, in charting his own maturity and his desire to 'get on top of things' and stay focused, Logan reaffirmed his commitment to his own happiness:

> I think the one thing I want most in life is just to be happy with what I'm doing, to be happy with how my life's going, to be happy with the friendships that I've made, to make sure that they're happy, the way I'm being a friend and how I'm treating them. Making my family happy, doing what's best and helpful for them. But I think, yeah, I don't really measure where I want to be on my money or what kind of house I've got or that kind of stuff. I just measure [things] on if I'm happy.

In focusing on how Logan conceptualised fulfilment we see how important maintaining good relationships was to him and how he resisted status symbols such as money and owning a house. This is interesting considering that science is frequently portrayed as a high-status profession and Logan was at a university that is high in symbolic capital. While Logan was certainly aware of these things, his motivation to be first-in-family was centred more on his passion for the subject matter than anything else. Perhaps more than other first-in-family males I spoke with, Logan talked about his excitement for the subject as integral to his aspiration. Interestingly, Logan did not speak about networking and, despite valuing close social connections, he had little desire and concern about making new friends at university, a phenomenon well documented in studies of working-class disadvantage (Rubin & Wright, 2015).

> I love studying and, at the end of the day, I don't get much money [Youth Allowance] for it. I'm not fussed about the money, it's the experience [of university] that I'm more into. It's just being there first hand, animals and plants and that kind of life, it's fascinating to me. So no money in the world could take away that experience.

Skelton and Francis (2012) construct an argument around the gendering of the all-rounder, emphasising that 'the production of "Renaissance Masculinity" is not either exclusively middle-class or, importantly, conceived of primarily in relation to social class', noting that boys from working-class backgrounds perform it as well (p. 450). However, Logan felt an internalised pressure that came from being an all-rounder that meant – as he progressed from schoolboy to university student – he began to feel somewhat unfulfilled and wandering. The narrowing of his scope to study science intensively left little room for all of Logan's other interests. Logan's passion for theatre remained very much part of who he was and he portrayed a drive and commitment to find opportunities to explore this side of himself:

> Yeah, they have got a Theatre Guild here [at the university] and I was going to join it for the first play, me and my friend Mitchell were going to, because we're both drama fanatics. But when we both applied for a role, we were too young for it, we were not old enough to act as the characters that were in the play, so it was like, oh. But we are still looking outside of university, like there's the Adelaide Youth Theatre which I'm thinking of joining, which would be an interesting experience.

When we discussed relationships – specifically spending time with family – Logan spoke about spending more time at home where sometimes his mother and him have the same afternoons off and therefore can catch up. Furthermore, Logan spoke about catching up regularly with his father and grandmother, just 'To know that I'm not dead or anything like that.' Though Logan did not describe his parents imposing any sort of pressure, he did describe his family feeling excited about his opportunity to attend university:

> Yeah, definitely, yeah, all excited for me in that I'm going to uni and that I'm being introduced to these new experiences. These are experiences that they'd never got introduced to, so they're hearing all these kinds of stories for the first time that I'm telling them. Yeah, they are excited. Pushing for me to get job – which I'm *still* trying to find.

A close connection with both his father and mother led us to speak about masculinity and the robust discussions in the media about #MeToo and toxic masculinity:

> Oh, my mother, my father always brought me up to be a man who's respect [ful] of everyone, is always helpful or wanting to help, isn't repulsive of anyone or hurtful to anyone. Yes, we have accidental movements where you might hurt someone, but not intentionally.

Interestingly, Logan framed this responsibility in terms of a commitment to freedom of expression:

> I think yeah, there are multiple societal pressures and stereotypes of what men should be and what men need to be. But I don't believe in stereotypes and that kind of pressure. I think you should be free to express who you are. If you're a man and you love more feminine things, it's okay. Like I don't personally think that pressure should shape who you are.

In considering masculinities and social change, around the time of our interview the gay plebiscite in Australia was present in the news cycle, a defining moment for sexual equality.

> I think that let's say if now a man wants to be gay or anything like that, I feel like he's allowed to be. I feel like we should be in a time now that that kind of stuff is acceptable and these stereotypes don't need to put that, or put those people under pressure. Because I don't agree with it, I don't agree with stereotypes – and that's for everyone, male or female, as children.

Year 3: new beginnings

When I met with Logan in his second year of university, he appeared to be a bit more unsettled, which he described as 'tossing and turning'. His first year of university had not gone the way he had thought it would based on his experiences at secondary school with science. The academic requirements were, according to him, quite gruelling. Logan noted: 'I have to admit though, recently I've drifted more towards my work life and my studies, and I've really neglected that social life.' This was compounded by him picking up work in the fast-food industry – mainly overnight shifts, meaning he could spend less time with friends and family. However, Logan was clear to assert he remained largely unchanged from his days as a secondary school student. He continued to speak of his efforts to do his best but also his humility:

> I still have that mindset of to work hard 100% of the time, and to not always … not be really … There's a better word for it. But not to be as big headed about myself, and to not have that idea of, 'I'm the most talented person here.' I want to be very humble about everything, and work hard, and prove that I've got the talent and the hard work through the result. Other than say, 'Ah, I'm so smart at this, I can deal with this.' I would rather be that person who is quietly working away, working hard at that work, and then to produce a result that blows everyone away.

Logan's words provide a glimpse into aspects integral to the continued maintenance of his aspiration. After all, Logan could leave university at any time and the social and familial consequences it appears would be minimal. While he was humble, he also framed his aspiration as something to be proven where he did not want to celebrate his achievements but rather quietly endeavour to fulfill his aspirations. This reaffirms research that suggests working-class men desire to be ordinary, to muddle along occupying a middling position, devoid of distinction (Stahl, 2013). Possibly part of what has informed Logan's aspiration has been his experience with science at university:

> what I thought I would be in the microbiology sciences and the molecular biological sciences. Didn't do as well as I thought I would, but I excelled in the animal sciences and the wildlife sciences. And so the … didn't do as well as I thought I would in the other sciences. So I did make the decision for this semester to drop those courses, to not stress myself out with them, to not stress myself out with those courses, and to just focus purely on these other sciences, which is give me a bunch of spare time to, yeah, do the other things.

Time allocation was particularly important here. Time to reflect and gain perspective is tremendously valuable when boys from non-traditional backgrounds struggle at university (Stahl, McDonald & Young, 2021). Furthermore, in Logan's case, this was a time when he could capitalise on his diverse interests. When asked to reflect back on his secondary school years and what he would tell his former self, Logan highlighted his cautious nature: 'I didn't really put myself out there as much as what I should have.' However, in his second year of university, Logan was in a different place where he hungered to express himself and try new things:

> And I think to myself, 'I want to live by putting myself out there, and doing things I wouldn't usually do.' And that's what I'd probably go back to myself [in secondary school], and say … I'd say, 'Don't worry

about the hard things in life. You'll get through them. Time will go on. Just make sure to keep yourself open to new experiences. There's a lot of world out there to try.'

It is important to note here that Logan rationalises 'putting myself out there' in contrast with his friends whom he perceives as not ascribing to the same belief. While Logan has gone against the grain, entering a competitive university program at an elite institution, his peer group have not had the same experiences. Logan asserted: 'And like a bunch of my friends who are unemployed at the moment, I believe if they ... they don't really put themselves out there. But I believe if they did, they could advance, they could experience more success.' For Logan, to construct himself as successful in the university context – which he is to a certain extent – involves constructing others in terms we would associate with failure.

Logan was clearly an all-rounder – a Renaissance man – who was capable and talented in many different curriculum areas. For the most part this served him well in a comprehensive schooling setting; but at university he had to proactively develop strategies to fulfill different aspects of himself. Recalling his unwavering commitment to his own happiness, he recently was able to see a traveling show of *The Book of Mormon* with a group of friends. Dropping the additional class in science had freed up time for himself, which led to him contemplating his next step:

> I've been planning a lot about my future at the moment, and what I'm going to do once I finish this degree. And I have been contemplating and talking to my other friends who were interested in theatre. And we've all been thinking maybe we might go back to uni, and do a degree in performing arts together. I've been speaking to one of my close friends [Mitchell], who did drama with me throughout high school. And he's really happy with the idea, because at the moment he's not doing a course he's really enjoying. So he wants to switch out of it, but doesn't really have the confidence to switch out by himself. And I said to him, 'Well, I'm thinking about it too. Let's do it together and we'll see how we go.' But I said to him, 'We'll have to wait till next year, once I finish this degree, because I want to have set foundations first.'

There were many things informing Logan's decision-making, from disillusionment to companionship to vacillating between multiple aspirational pathways. Always upbeat, Logan saw the world as filled with possibility. It was also clear he did not see a bachelor's degree as the end of his learning:

> At the moment, I'm really tossing and turning. When I was younger, I had a clear straight path as to what I wanted to do, what I wanted to be, and how to go about it. But as I've gotten older, I've just found where my interest truly lies, and what I truly want to do. And beyond this degree, I'm really not too sure if I want to continue doing an honours

program, and then major into a PhD, or if I want to maybe try something different like do a performing arts degree, or even the possibility of going to TAFE, do animal science, and go down that pathway – just to add some more certifications. So, really tossing and turning as to where I want to go in the future, because it's trying to find that line of, 'I enjoy science, but I also enjoy performing arts as well.' And I could always have the best of both worlds, and do one degree in science, and one degree in performing arts.

A key part of this narrative of 'tossing and turning' is Logan's search for inspiration as well as negotiating competing areas that interest him:

> And I've got friends at uni who are in their 50s, doing this degree. So it's pretty motivating to go back, because they tell you their stories, and how they've gotten two degrees, three degrees in the past, and they just keep coming back to learn more. And it's pretty motivating, pretty inspiring to make you want to come back, and be like, 'Well, you're never too young to, or never too old to stop studying, and learning more and more.'

Logan's commitment to exploring theatre and himself as an actor raises the tension between passion and pragmatism. On some level Logan knew that opportunities in the theatre scene in Adelaide remained limited, whereas science seemed a safer bet in terms of reliable employment. While he wrestled with his future, he mentioned that he had registered with acting agencies 'and had a few interviews and meetings with them', though he had yet to hear anything concrete. He did one audition to be an extra in a film, which he described as 'definitely out of my comfort zone'. Logan remained very close to his drama teacher and involved with his high school drama team, regularly attending rehearsals and performances.

The discussion of a second degree set Logan apart from the other boys in the study who generally saw university as a means to an end. For Logan learning and his passion are very much interwoven and he needs to feel fulfilled through his learning process. He is extremely inquisitive, 'if find something interesting, I'll always delve into it' and 'learn as much as I can', and he mentioned watching Netflix and YouTube documentaries extensively. Our conversation proceeded onto how many close friends are currently re-negotiating their pathways in and around higher education, TAFE or apprenticeships:

> So, yeah. I do know a few people who have dropped out. It has had an effect on me, because it makes me think about what I'm doing, and if it's something that I truly enjoy. And I've had moments and thoughts about that. But in saying that, I've also planned ahead what I'm going to do.

This prompted a discussion of the blind spots Logan felt he had encountered in the transition to university. These blind spots concerned not only what higher education entails but what higher education can offer: 'Like at first, I didn't actually really appreciate and understand how many courses there are [at university], and how diversified it gets once you finish school.' He recalled that his secondary school now offers courses in philosophy and psychology, which he found frustrating as he had missed the opportunity to study those things. Embedded in his love of learning is a passion to defend it. Logan spoke at length about the declining numbers of students choosing drama. As a result, his school had had to combine Year 11 and Year 12 drama, which he was concerned about.

All this 'tossing and turning' aside, Logan remained a fairly adept science student and committed to his current pathway. Returning to Logan's progress in the subject, he spoke about making some strategic moves to enhance his employability:

> And I think a lot of [employers] are looking for just your – I guess, professional experience – and your understanding of the science and commitment to that science. Because a lot of employers beyond uni are looking for that work experience you've done prior, or if you've actually done an internship, or something like that. And a lot of people do say that if you do an exchange study overseas, that's really good for your resume when you're getting employed in those positions.

Logan here called attention to what Ball and Vincent (1998) and Reay et al. (2005) call 'hot knowledge' where there can be an over-reliance on a few significant others or second-hand recommendations rather than direct experience, which can be, depending on the circumstance, problematic. Knowing employment will be competitive, Logan applied for internships as well as a study abroad opportunity and did not getting them, describing the experience as 'very pretty deflating'.

Altering his timetable to match the areas in science he has excelled in allowed Logan the necessary time to reflect. He intended to use this time to develop his hobbies but because the theatre opportunities did not come to fruition, Logan filled this time with extra shifts in a service-level position which he did not enjoy. Furthermore, as his hours were scaled back dramatically at Hungry Jacks, Logan told me he secured a second job working at Rebel Sport in 'a casual position, which is between about one to 17 hours a week. Which I can pretty much fit into my schedule if I work around it properly.' As he recounted this anecdote to me, there were echoes here of feeling stuck in place. Logan's story leads us to reflect on the opportunities made available to him as well as what could have made higher education a more enriching experience for him. At university, he flitted between social groups and did not establish more durable friendships, describing that it was 'hard to keep in contact'. Furthermore, his sense of belonging was also affected when he dropped a subject, because he was then only attending university two days a week – when there were practicals – and on the other days he watched the lecture at home, saving himself the commute.

Certainly, Logan's words suggest he is talented in many areas but he found university frustrating largely due to his lack of knowledge around what university could be. According to Logan:

> Back [in secondary school], I was pretty dead set with what I wanted to do, and how to get about it. I did all the research, and I was pretty confident with what I was going to do, and how to do it.

However, doing the research online did not transfer into the experience he hoped for. At his school students could opt into careers counselling if they wished. A more strategic approach to careers counselling would have probably assisted in Logan's journey – but, as we see below, Logan may not have taken advantage of it:

> I didn't really go to careers counselling. I did have friends who went, and they said it was okay, they didn't think it was the best. I have friends who go to careers counselling at university, and they say it's much better. But yeah, me personally, I didn't go to the careers counselling, and I guess it was just something I never really made time for. And it's one of those decisions I look back on and think, 'Maybe you should have just gone to them, and actually spoke to them for an hour or so. They might have opened up to what you were doing.'

Still, as Logan concluded his second year, the experience of university felt like a positive one. He spoke of wanting to make university work for him and his sense of achievement:

> I do feel a sense of pride because it makes me feel good that I am the first one to go into the university, and to not really … it's going to sound really bad, but to make myself out of something in uni. Not to say that my mom and dad haven't – that sounds horrible.

However, with this pride that Logan felt came expectations:

> But I also feel a sense of pressure as well with that – because I've been the only one to go, and everyone else is relying on me to finish this degree, and I guess to make something of myself, I guess.

Conclusion

Each of the previous five case studies presented has focused on questions of subjectivity and the discursive construction of masculinity. Logan's story is one of searching for a sense of belonging and a sense of fulfillment through his education. In terms of Logan's masculinity he is comfortable identifying strongly with traditionally feminine subjects such as drama, similar to Mac an Ghaill's (1994) 'Academic Achievers'. Given what we know about upwardly mobile working-class masculinities, Logan should be able to make university work for him and – for the most part – he does. However, while there are times he does find it an enjoyable experience, it largely appears to not fully integrate. Whereas he began as an all-rounder and very social, Logan's later words suggest a sense of isolation where, furthermore, he positioned himself at a disadvantage in terms of future employability. The perception of the all-rounder is that they are adaptable and resilient, but Logan's case suggests the level of adaptability has certain limits.

Thomsen et al. (2011) note that 'working-class students that venture into university studies are much more dependent on random "inspiration" by charismatic teachers, friends, student counselors, and youth organizations' (p. 470). In their research on prospective university students, Patfield et al. (2020) use the typology of 'opportunists' who 'saw their teachers as an important form of social capital – a key adult in their network of connections who has been to university' (p. 9). I did not get the sense from Logan's words that the drama teacher at secondary school fostered his aspirations to attend university but certainly this teacher was an important source of inspiration. Egeberg Holmgren (2013, p. 96) describes how we, as research-ers, want 'to remember successful interviews: rich narratives, rapport and disclosure'. With this in mind, what has stayed with me in regard to Logan is not necessarily the rich narratives but how much I felt he held back. I had a continual sense that Logan had burdens that remained undisclosed to me.

References

Adams, M., & Coltrane, S. (2005). Boys and men in families: The domestic produc-tion of gender, power, and privilege. In M. Kimmel, J. Hearn, & R. W. Connell (Eds.), *Handbook of studies on men and masculinities* (pp. 230–248). Sage.

Ball, S. J., & Vincent, C. (1998). 'I heard it on the grapevine': 'Hot' knowledge and school choice. *British Journal of Sociology of Education*, 27(1), 377–400.

Egeberg Holmgren, L. (2013). Gendered selves, gendered subjects: Interview per-formances and situational contexts in critical interview studies of men and mas-culinities. In B. Pini & B. Pease (Eds.), *Men, masculinities and methodologies* (pp. 90–103). Palgrave Macmillan.

Imms, W. (2007). Boys engaging masculinities. *Journal of Interdisciplinary Gender Studies*, 10(2), 30–45.

Lehmann, W. (2009). University as vocational education: Working-class students' expectations for university. *British Journal of Sociology of Education*, 30(2), 137–149.

Mac an Ghaill, M. (1994). *The making of men: Masculinities, sexualities and schooling.* Open University Press.

Martino, W., & Pallotta-Chiarolli, M. (2003). *So what's a boy?* Open University Press.

Patfield, S., Gore, J., & Fray, L. (2020). Degrees of 'being first': Toward a nuanced understanding of first-generation entrants to higher education. *Educational Review*, advance online publication. doi:10.1080/00131911.2020.1740172

Reay, D., David, M. E., & Ball, S. (2005). *Degrees of choice: Social class, race and gender in higher education.* Institute of Education.

Rubin, M., & Wright, C. L. (2015). Age differences explain social class differences in students' friendship at university: Implications for transition and retention. *Higher Education*, 70, 427–439.

Skelton, C., & Francis, B. (2012). The 'Renaissance child': High achievement and gender in late modernity. *International Journal of Inclusive Education, 16*(4), 441–459.

Stahl, G. (2013). Habitus disjunctures, reflexivity and white working-class boys' conceptions of status in learner and social identities. *Sociological Research Online, 18*(3), 1–12. http://www.socresonline.org.uk/18/3/2.html

Stahl, G., McDonald, S., & Young, J. (2021). Possible selves in a transforming economy: Upwardly mobile working- class masculinities, service work and negotiated aspirations in Australia. *Work, Employment and Society, 35*(1), 97–115.

Thomsen, J. P., Munk, M. D., Eiberg-Madsen, M., & Hansen, G. I. (2011). The educational strategies of Danish university students from professional and working-class backgrounds. *Comparative Education Review, 57*(3), 457–480.

Part 3

Changing masculine subjectivities and implications for policy

8 Masculine subjectivities in transition

In their research on 'matriculating masculinities' Harris and Harper (2015) call attention to how little is known about how lifeworlds inform the transition of young men from high school to post-secondary education. The biography of individuals – realised and interpreted through 'the critical moments' (Thomson et al., 2004) – offers us a glimpse into agency, the search for belonging and how struggles are negotiated. Longitudinal research foregrounds a study of the events in our lives which may provide us with resources to understand ourselves differently and lead to significant changes in our biography and aspirations (Holmegaard, 2020). And, within this, what we know to be research, data and analysis are 'produced through gendered power relations' (Hearn, 2013, p. 30) and, therefore, some discussion of researcher standpoint is warranted.

The *First-in-Family Males Project*, by its very design, foregrounded reflexive deliberations concerning changes in gender subjectivity. While Pease (2013) writes that male researchers 'generally do not think about how their structural and discursive positioning relates to their knowledge claims' (p. 43), the longitudinal nature of the project did contribute to thinking about these sorts of positionings in relation to power and privilege. Drawing on interactionist theory, Egeberg Holmgren (2013) focuses our attention on interactions as ways of *doing gender* and gendered performances. Class disparities structure all facets of the research process and perhaps become more pronounced in encounters where the researcher and participants are of the same gender. Here I draw on Swain's (2005, p. 219) contention that we, as researchers, 'need to be aware that lying behind these masculine identities is the powerful variable of social class'. With this in mind, the research presented in this book focuses on variations in upwardly mobile working-class masculinities and the discursive construction of masculinity. By addressing masculine subjectivities in transition I am interested in how boys, during a definitive time in their life, 'construct their identities as situated subjects within complex social and cultural networks' (Burke, 2009, p. 83).

Research continues to demonstrate that low-SES students have high aspirations but 'these aspirations cannot be realised with the lower school achievement levels and completion rates recorded for these students' (Harvey et al., 2016, p. 78). The six boys presented in these case studies have high aspirations and – in examining their identity work longitudinally – we see the labour they undertake to maintain these aspirations and, furthermore, how the opportunities that are presented to them reinforce these aspirations. The study of social mobility, albeit incremental in this case, concerns understanding how people separate themselves from normative aspects of their class background and gender identity. What informs one's aspirations is multifaceted, haphazard and fragmented. Overall, in presenting the case studies, the work seeks to complement scholarship which addresses intra-group differences and how these differences are deeply influenced by access to and operationalisation of capital (Gofen, 2009; Patfield et al., 2020). Adopting a comparative approach, I now focus on the following overlapping themes as important dimensions of upwardly mobile working-class masculinities: status identity (composed of narrative, social and future identity); how the participants became agentic; their sense of belonging; and their experiences with struggle and isolation.

Status identity

Discussions of social mobility often consider the inverse – class formation or what aspects contribute to people remaining in their class origin. In discussing class formation, Somers (1992) writes of the importance of ontological narratives and the 'stories that social actors use to make sense of – indeed, in order to act in – their lives', explaining that such narratives allow us to make sense of the 'multiple, ambiguous, ephemeral or conflicting' forms of identity we inhabit daily (p. 603). Somers (1992) calls for concepts that explore the ontology of the working-class experience and 'enable us to plot over time and space the ontological narratives' individuals actors both adopt and contend with as they come to identify with their class position which is, in turn, integral to their sense of social action (p. 608). After all, there is a 'complexity of class identities': as Lehmann (2009b) asserts, it cannot be assumed 'that working-class students have a single habitus, nor should we insist on a hegemonic middle-class culture at university and the unavoidable alienation of working-class students in it' (p. 146). While Bourdieu's habitus, as a form of socialised subjectivity, works to answer some of these questions, I draw on psychological constructs in an effort to explore the study of upward social mobility and identity.

Narrative identity, social identity and future identity – as concepts to think with – allow us to define some of the contours of the young men's changing habitus. Destin and Debrosse (2017) propose that a change in status identity is composed of three overlapping areas: narrative identity (cohesive sense of purpose, coherent themes); social identity (meaningful association to valued group); and future identity (what they want to be or not be). A narrative identity is one of coherence 'of certain distinct and coherent themes' built over time (Destin & Debrosse, 2017, p. 100). Social identities are grounded in validation, in feeling part of a group, and when people begin journeys of social mobility, they move into new social contexts, where a 'growing sense of uncertainty about their own SES can weaken the ability to form new social bonds' (Destin & Debrosse, 2017, p. 101). Finally, Destin and Debrosse (2017) note that future identities include the 'images of who people want to become in addition to who they want to avoid becoming' (p. 101).

In the first case study, Lucas's narrative identity, social identity and future identity all appeared to cohere over time, which places him as an outlier in relation to the rest of the boys. Through such a coherence his aspirations were reaffirmed. Campbell's future identity underwent significant change over the three-year period as he wrestled with his employment opportunities and was compelled to determine what education ultimately meant to his future trajectory. Working in the call centre allowed him access to a social identity which directly influenced his future identity. Rashid's social identity within his Islamic community primarily informed his aspiration to secure a place at a prestigious university and do well, though his future identity and narrative identity remain a more muddled picture. Similar to Rashid, Manny's aspirations were structured by the social identity of his Pacific Islander community. However, while Manny began to form close connections at university, his academic setbacks ultimately equated to significant social setbacks and he looked for validation elsewhere, specifically in his volunteer work. Therefore, Manny's story highlights the importance of a meaningful association with a valued group for a sense of well-being and purpose. Dominic did not seem to invest much in a social identity (he was distant from his family, and he did not identify strong with his Indigenous heritage). Instead, it was Dominic's future self that served to orient his daily actions. He had a very clear picture of what he wanted to achieve through his studies and how he would achieve this through a focus on academics and increasing his networks. Logan's narrative identity as an all-rounder with many interests did not necessarily translate well into the university space. He never became fully engaged with the social aspects of the university (social identity) and, as a result, his future identity fluctuated dramatically, and he even considered a second degree. While this is a psychologised interpretation of the young men's experiences over the three years, using these concepts highlights the importance of social validation. The alignment of narrative identity and future identity can be a powerful determiner of a sense of resilience.

Becoming agentic

The research addresses some aspects of the formation and generative capacity of the habitus over time through a consideration of aspirational trajectories where gender and class are inseparable and in a constant mutually informing interplay (see McLeod, 2000). As the participants came to interact with the institution of higher education, their subjectivities were worked upon through the everyday practices of navigating the institutional culture. Therefore, over the length of the study the participants were engaged in a process of meaning making both in terms of their own aspirational trajectories and in how they came to 'fit' within the institution. The young men worked on the agency incrementally through their enactment of gender and personhood. Agency is multifaceted, and I now briefly highlight several dimensions which seem relevant to the case studies of these young men.

As the six young men entered the post-school world – and become agentic within it – their experiences were both real and structured by a sense of the imaginary. The imaginary concerned what kind of the man they aspired to be but also what education may mean for their futures. Furthermore, their sense of their imagined future *informed their present* where, according to Connell (2005), 'imaginary masculinities are part of the routine enactment of gender' (p. 25). Therefore, arguably, these imaginaries perhaps for some of the young men work as a barometer or compass, supplying a sense of direction. After all, adolescence, according to Connell (2005), can 'be understood as a period in which the embodiment of masculinity takes new forms and moves towards adult patterns' (p. 15). Furthermore, these imaginaries are bound up in institutions – as institutions themselves are actively involved in promoting an idealised version of selfhood (e.g. the capable worker, the proficient student). One could argue, as institutions are encountered, preconceived imaginaries become fragmented – the visage slips, the myths recede as the weight of reality sets in. While this process occurs, the young men in this study are agentic in looking for spaces/places where they can feel a sense of value outside the university space (Alexander, 2019; Stahl, 2015). This can lead them to seek what Ramburuth and Härtel (2010) refer to as 'identity-safe' environments where they feel welcomed and supported. To varying extents, we see this agentic search for value in each one of the case studies. Lucas not only worked for an upper house Member of Parliament but also joined the fire brigade; Campbell found it in the call centre; Rashid at the mosque and in his local community; Manny in his volunteer work; Dominic in managing the pizza shop; while for Logan the search proved largely elusive.

Agency – and the capacity to be agentic – correlates with how aspirations are upheld. The experiences of the six young men enable a consideration of how their aspirations were 'cooling out, warming up, and holding steady' as they navigated the university space over the course of two years (Alexander et al., 2008, p. 375). Alexander et al. (2008) here extend the wording of Clark (1960) who documented how post-secondary experiences can dampen the unrealistic optimistic expectations of those from disadvantaged backgrounds. Agency and aspirations exist in tandem with opportunity. Clearly, looking across the case studies, not all of the young men were afforded the same opportunities. For Lucas and Campbell, arguably their experiences in the adult world prior to leaving secondary school as well as their experiences in white-collar employment while at university worked to increase their confidence and sense of agency. The concept of 'multiple masculinities' (Carrigan et al., 1985) has become one of the most influential ideas in Critical Studies of Men and Masculinities. Collinson and Hearn (2005) note that multiple masculinities 'are likely to interconnect with multiple sites such as the home, the shop floor, the office, and the outlet or branch' (p. 294). Lucas's and Campbell's experiences in their workplaces gave them a wider exposure to different enactments of middle-class masculinities, which influenced their capacity to adapt and feel a stronger sense of belonging. They were also well positioned to accrue the necessary social capital that will be integral to their upward trajectory (Patfield et al., 2020). Certainly, such experiences contrast greatly with Logan's and Manny's work in the fast-food industry and Dominic's work managing the pizza shop.

We have also seen how agency is realised through 'the critical moments' (Thomson et al., 2004) embedded in lived experiences within multiple areas of the young men's lives (Tomanović, 2018). These critical moments are closely tied to social class. In furthering the link between 'critical moments' and social class, we need to consider the first-in-family working-class experience and the desire for employability, income and mobility. Lehmann (2009b) writes:

> Rather than perceiving of university as an automatic transition path, a rite of passage, and insurance against social demotion, as is the case for many middle-class students, the working-class students in the study were urgently concerned with the employment value of their university education.
>
> (p. 144)

We see in the case studies that some of the young men were more active than others in positioning themselves advantageously, capitalising on 'critical moments' like job expos and university-based career services. However, others – like Rashid and Logan – seem to be either not as familiar with how to position themselves to be competitive in the job market or unlucky in their efforts.

I argue that the critical moments in the lives of upwardly mobile working-class men represent the psychic injuries of class. These moments bring to the fore feelings of inferiority, their own potential, and their sense of resilience and confidence (Mallman, 2017; Reay, 2005). Lucas's critical moment was quite clear – the ATAR breakfast where his aspiration was jeopardised. For some of the other boys these critical moments were more spaced out and, therefore, less intense. The low-stakes incremental nature is important to note. We see this in the case of Logan who appeared to experience several 'critical moments': his disappointment in his grades during his second year, his friends being out of work and his difficulty connecting with them, and his thwarted aspiration to be more involved in theatre. As a result, Logan felt less and less in control when the expectations of the people around him aligned with common conceptions of adulthood and concerned him becoming more 'independent' and 'autonomous' when, the data would suggest, he required strategic support.

A sense of belonging

Scholars of the first-in-family student experience have focused on the importance of a sense belonging (Mallman, 2017; Maras, 2007; O'Shea et al., 2017; Southgate et al., 2014). This sense of belonging is shaped by a normative ideal 'student experience', which has implications for how students come to see themselves as university students and belong to the institution (Pötschulat et al., 2021). More specifically, students enter into a negotiation with the norms and expectations attached to contemporary 'studenthood' and they judge their everyday practices in relation to such conceptualisations (Lehmann, 2009a; Pötschulat et al., 2021).

Christie (2009, p. 134) writes of the emotional labour that working-class students experience in defending their right to be at university (mainly to themselves), even though their achievements clearly entitle them to be there. Many consider fostering belonging to be an essential way to counteract the risk of students dropping out (Scevak et al., 2015). Belonging, while largely abstract and subject to debate, does seem to resonate with the equity and widening participation context (see Lumb et al., 2020) where considerable funding is directed at enhancing the student experience, specifically during Orientation Week. Increased exposure to institutional norms, we assume, brings with it a familiarity, a sense of belonging and increased confidence. According to sociologist C. Wright Mills (1959), 'Much of human life consists of playing … roles within specific institutions. To understand the biography of an individual, we must understand the significance and meaning of the roles he has played and does play' (p. 161). Therefore, a sense of belonging is performed by people playing roles and performing certain subjectivities depending on the institutional expectations and these performances may be comfortable or uncomfortable depending on the circumstances.

Furthermore, scholars writing on social mobility call attention to the importance of belonging as well as performing identities which could potentially foster a stronger sense of belonging. In Lehmann's (2009a) research on working-class and first-in-family students in a Canadian university, he notes how his participants constructed themselves relationally to their middle- and upper-class counterparts: their class habitus reflected 'their beliefs that they possessed a stronger work ethic, higher levels of maturity, responsibility, and independence, and first-hand experiences in the "real world of work"' (p. 639). Furthermore, Lehmann demonstrates how moral boundaries are intertwined with gaining recognition or justifying their right to be at university. In studies of boyhood, Badwan and Wilkinson (2019) argue that understanding young men's sense of belonging will assist institutions of higher education 'in creating spaces where young men can feel a sense of attachment, comfort, and belonging' (p. 30). In the *Life After School* study, Nichols and Stahl (2017, p. 179) argue that the transition from high school into university involves what they call a 'renovation of learner identity' in order to belong, as an 'easy-going' and 'laidback' masculinity becomes less salient in competitive university contexts which emphasise individual responsibility.

In considering how upwardly mobile working-class men negotiate belonging in a university context, it is first important to consider that they are in a small minority. Despite efforts to increase the participation of non-traditional students, many universities are still predominantly composed of the middle class, upper middle class and elites. This is important because masculinities come into existence through people's actions and 'are actively produced, using the resources and strategies available in a given social setting' (Connell, 2000, p. 12). These productions exist within constraints and various normalising regimes which – for upwardly mobile working-class young men – can lead to internal complexities and contradictions. Here I draw on the scholarship of Giazitzoglu (2014) and Giazitzoglu and Muzio (2020), who describe the ways in which upwardly mobile working-class men over-identify with 'embourgeoised masculinity' in an effort to actively find a sense of belonging in white-collar workplaces. Similar to Skeggs, they document the class pathologisation experienced but also the resourcefulness of the men who find ways to position themselves advantageously, whether it be through dress or adjusting their accent.

Each of the boys in the *First-in-Family Males Project* looked for acceptance and thus legitimacy. These searches could be either prolonged or fleeting. Clearly, Lucas and Campbell experienced substantial time in the white-collar world and it contributed to their personal development but also reaffirmed their aspirations and sense that they belonged to a world outside their working-class community. Rashid, Dominic, Manny and Logan did not have these experiences. Furthermore, Rashid and Dominic strongly desired these experiences and spoke of internships, while Manny seemed largely unaware, never alluding to such opportunities in his interviews. Dominic knew he needed access to the field of white-collar work but he saw university in transactional terms – as merely a stepping-stone to position himself advantageously for future employment. Therefore, he did not invest the necessary time into networking (though he did refer to 'networking' explicitly) and finding ways to use university activities to set himself apart, instead hoping his high marks would secure him interviews in his final year. The variations in how these young men come to belong echoes work by Patfield et al. (2020, p. 6) who argue that there is 'a continuum along which prospective first-generation students cluster in terms of their capacity to mobilise capital', that there are degrees of being first and such variations are linked to how social capital is operationalised.

Experiencing struggle and isolation

Working-class men experience multiple forms of disadvantage which can contribute to feelings of isolation and these can be more pronounced as they negotiate their education. While the boys in this study did not experience the extreme disadvantage of generational unemployment for the most part, they did live adjacent to areas enduring pervasive unemployment (ABS, 2015). Economic restructuring and post-industrialisation have significant implications for how young men in disadvantaged areas construct their personhood. In place of traditional, respectable working-class employment, we have seen the steady rise of service-level positions which require working-class men to 'learn to serve' (McDowell, 2003). If working-class boys are drawing upon employment as part of their identity construction, they are now more likely to draw upon the 'McJob' (Bottero, 2009, p. 9). These societal changes inform how upwardly mobile working-class men see their futures as they develop ways to distance themselves from normative patterns of working-class masculinity. This process can be a very isolating experience.

According to Moller (2007) research on masculinity should focus on men's weakness, vulnerability and disempowerment, thus challenging dominant models of masculinity. However, experiences of 'weakness', 'loneliness' and 'vulnerability' not only ebb and flow but are difficult to define. The study of Australian masculinity and serious episodes of loneliness (Franklin et al. 2018; Patulny, 2013) continues to be an important area of work. As men struggle to identify the causes of their suffering (see Franklin & Tranter, 2008), Franklin et al. (2018) call attention to the 'unmet belongingness needs' within the lifeworlds of Australian men (p. 137). Loneliness is formed over long periods of transition so 'biographical work offers a means of obtaining data on the shifting nature of belonging in time and space' (p. 138). Research from the United States has focused on an agenda in higher education to get men to problematise their understanding of gender where male bonding plays a pivotal role. Davis et al. (2011) propose that male bonding is essential as young men require spaces where they can feel vulnerable with each other.

We have only the words of the boys to draw upon and it is difficult to discern how isolation was experienced by the young men in the *First-in-Family Males Project*. Based on their accounts, some seemed to suffer more than others and, of course, some were more forthcoming about their vulnerabilities than others. In surveying the six case studies, the boys who seemed to suffer the most were Manny and Logan – though Dominic too had sustained moments of feeling isolated at university. This does not mean they were unable to establish and maintain friendships at university, but by their second year Manny and Logan seemed withdrawn from the social aspects and lacking direction. In considering their prolonged feelings of isolation, what is clear is that in their formal education both Manny and Logan lacked exposure to the close relationships with inspiring educators they relied heavily on in secondary school. Arguably, such a relationship opened up a space for them to feel valued. Thomsen et al. (2011) note a dominant pattern among working-class students where inspiration is structurally embedded and encounters with inspiring teachers, counsellors and friends serve to reaffirm aspirations. For boys, especially boys from low-SES backgrounds, these relationships can be critical to their success (Nelson, 2020; Reichert & Hawley, 2014). Within the wider data set, few of the participants spoke of powerful learning experiences at university and there was an implication in the interviews of 'going through the motions'. Therefore, the problem of isolation links back to my previous point about searching for spaces where they can feel valuable.

Reflections on fieldwork

There exists an adage among qualitative researchers that participants *hide behind their words*. Interview data is never complete, always fragmented and often contradictory; they are not reflections of true experience but instead 'partial and discursive constructions' (Burke, 2009, p. 84). McLeod (2003) writes of the importance of re-reading/listening to interviews to avoid 'flattening out the emotional and psychological dimensions of subjectivity', explaining that the 'interpretive challenge is actively and methodically to listen for both "immanent structures" and emotional investments, to play them back against each other' (p. 209). Over the course of the *First-in-Family Males Project* I re-listened to the interviews, which allowed for a 're-experiencing experience' where new things bubbled to the surface and became clearer though, simultaneously, I often picked up more of the contradictions as well.

Of course, these interviews function merely as snapshots in time and, while there was a certain level of trust, it is difficult to discern how much the boys actually came to trust me (though their continued willingness to meet up with me suggests some level of trust). Trust is often built through minor and major self-disclosures over a long period of time (Pitts & Miller-Day, 2007). Clearly, the methodological choices and the ethical decisions I made over the course of conducting the study significantly influenced the development of trust. Powell and Takayoshi (2003) draw our attention to the importance of researchers building 'truly reciprocal relationships' where 'we must be equally willing to share with them, to give them control over the spaces and forms in which they see us' (p. 406). While researchers always make an effort to keep a professional distance, multiple interviews over many years and shared experiences can make it challenging to keep this distance (Holmegaard, 2020, p. 119). Overall, I was not friends with the participants (cf. Dasgupta, 2013; Willis, 1977), though the interaction was always cordial and friendly. As my focus was largely on the transition to university life and the identity shifts that process required, I chose not to bring up more sensitive topics associated with the changes between boyhood and adulthood (e.g. sex/relationships, drugs, crime), though these did arise from time to time. Not being friends with the participants did perhaps restrict access to these more sensitive topics.

As is typical in longitudinal research, I made small but strategic efforts to engage the participants in the study and maintain their interest. Their schedules were crowded and I was grateful for the time they were able to provide. I was always clear with the participants on the data set I was trying to build and the questions I was trying to answer. I wanted the participants to feel a part of something and adopting some transparency around the methods and rationale I believe assisted in this. When approached from a longitudinal perspective, it is clear that the actions and identity practices of the young men were 'adjusted, reshaped, and recounted whenever the choice is challenged by new experiences and perceptions' (Holmegaard, 2020, p. 126). According to Schwalbe and Wolkomir (2001), the interview 'is both an opportunity for signifying masculinity and a particularly type of encounter in which masculinity is threatened'; as participants 'have a moral identity at stake' and may avoid certain topics or disclosing certain details (p. 98). In my view, the classed masculinities of the participants were not under threat despite speaking about topics such as educational failure. After all, the participants could also choose to not answer a question or to end the interview.

According to Dasgupta (2013) binaries foundational to fieldwork 'such as outsider/insider, researcher/informant and "objective" ethnography/"subjective" autobiography' are subject to change, what he calls 'the shifting sands of insider/outsider border zones' (p. 104). When interviewing some of the young men, there were times I felt more of an outsider than in other times. I have previously described how I could adopt insider knowledge to *understand what is valued* and this contributed to how I engaged with dialogues regarding practices of masculinity (Stahl, 2016). In his work with young men, Flood (2013) writes: 'People's accounts of their lives are contextual, interactional and dynamic – they change in different settings and to different audiences and over time' (p. 69) and people often recount stories which reflect societal and localised versions of gender. Given the longitudinal nature of the research *what was valued* by the participants changed over time, as they were exposed to new experiences and new social contacts. Therefore, with this in mind, in this research the longitudinal approach 'offer[ed] notably a view into the *complexity, negotiations,* and *processes* as they play[ed] out over time' (Holmegaard, 2020, p. 126).

The design of the *First-in-Family Males Project* allowed me to think critically about the changing subjectivities the boys presented. McLeod (2003, p. 205) writes:

> Issues of contingency and construction are significant and should not be ignored, but asking prospective and retrospective questions over time about 'the self' means that a body of 'evidence' from different perspectives is accumulated, and that responses can be 'checked', read and compared against each other.

Participants do contradict themselves and researchers have to be comfortable in deciphering their words as well as the subtext. Each interview was a negotiation of potential pitfalls and my positionality sometimes served as a barrier specifically in my lack of exposure to certain topics, for example. I knew little about Campbell's foray into working in a call centre and I only have a basic familiarity with the Muslim masculinity Rashid embodied. However, I was not a blank slate. Sometimes, my familiarity with the secondary school and university context worked to counteract the feelings of being an outsider. Therefore, as Dasgupta (2013) notes, during the research process I negotiated the insider/outsider border zones where 'the distinction between a seamless, bounded "self" as outside researcher "looking in" to the informant 'other' was more often than not ambiguous and slippery' (p. 108).

References

Alexander, K., Bozick, R., & Entwisle, D. (2008). Warming up, cooling out, or holding steady? Persistence and change in educational expectations after high school. *Sociology of Education, 81,* 371–396.

Alexander, P. (2019). Boys from the Bronx, men from Manhattan: Gender, aspiration and imagining a (neoliberal) future after high school in New York City. In C. Beverley & P. Michele (Eds.), *Interrogating the neoliberal lifecycle: The limits of success* (pp. 39–67). Springer Nature/Palgrave Macmillan.

Australian Bureau of Statistics (ABS). (2015). *Socio-economic indexes for areas*. ABS. http://www.abs.gov.au/websitedbs/censushome.nsf/home/seifa?opendocument&navpos=260

Badwan, K., & Wilkinson, S. (2019). 'Most of the people my age tend to move out': Young men talking about place, community, and belonging in Manchester. *Boyhood Studies*, 12(2), 29–50.

Bottero, W. (2009). Class in the 21st century. In K. P. Sveinsson (Ed.), *Who cares about the white working class?* (pp. 7–15). Runnymede Perspectives.

Burke, P. J. (2009). Men accessing higher education: Theorizing continuity and change in relation to masculine subjectivities. *Higher Education Policy*, 22, 81–100.

Carrigan, T., Connell, R. W., & Lee, J. (1985). Toward a new sociology of masculinity. *Theory and Society*, 14(5), 551–604.

Christie, H. (2009). Emotional journeys: Young people and transitions to university. *British Journal of Sociology of Education*, 30(2), 123–136.

Clark, B. R. (1960). The 'cooling out' function in higher education. *American Journal of Sociology*, 65, 569–576.

Collinson, D. L., & Hearn, J. (2005). Men and masculinities in work, organizations, and management. In M. Kimmel, J. Hearn, & R. W. Connell (Eds.), *Handbook of studies on men and masculinities* (pp. 289–310). Sage.

Connell, R. W. (2000). *The men and the boys*. Polity Press.

Connell, R. W. (2005). Growing up masculine: Rethinking the significance of adolescence in the making of masculinities. *Irish Journal of Sociology*, 14(2), 11–28.

Dasgupta, R. (2013). Conversations about otokorashisa (masculinity/'manliness'): Insider/outsider dynamics in masculinities research in Japan. In B. Pini & B. Pease (Eds.), *Men, masculinities and methodologies* (pp. 103–115). Palgrave Macmillan.

Davis, T., LaPrad, J., & Dixon, S. (2011). Masculinities reviewed and reinterpreted. In J. A. Laker & T. Davis (Eds.), *Masculinities in higher education: Theoretical and practical considerations* (pp. 147–160). Routledge.

Destin, M., & Debrosse, R. (2017). Upward social mobility and identity. *Current Opinion in Psychology*, 18, 99–104.

Egeberg Holmgren, L. (2013). Gendered selves, gendered subjects: Interview performances and situational contexts in critical interview studies of men and masculinities. In B. Pini & B. Pease (Eds.), *Men, masculinities and methodologies* (pp. 90–103). Palgrave Macmillan.

Flood, M. (2013). Negotiating gender in men's research among men. In B. Pini & B. Pease (Eds.), *Men, masculinities and methodologies* (pp. 64–76). Palgrave Macmillan.

Franklin, A., Barbosa Neves, B., Hookway, N., Patulny, R., Tranter, B., & Jaworski, K. (2018). Towards an understanding of loneliness among Australian men: Gender cultures, embodied expression and the social bases of belonging. *Journal of Sociology*, 55(1), 124–142.

Franklin, A. S., & Tranter, B. (2008). *Loneliness in Australia* (Occasional Paper 13). Housing and Community Research Unit, University of Tasmania.

Giazitzoglu, A. (2014). Qualitative upward mobility, the mass-media and 'posh' masculinity in contemporary north-east Britain: A micro sociological case-study. *Sociological Research Online*, 19(2), 1–11.

Giazitzoglu, A., & Muzio, D. (2020). Learning the rules of the game: How is corporate masculinity learned and enacted by male professionals from nonprivileged backgrounds? *Gender, Work and Organization*, advance online publication. doi:10.1111/gwao.12561

Gofen, A. (2009). Family capital: How first-generation higher education students break the inter-generational cycle. *Family Relations*, *58*(1), 104–120.

Harris, F., & Harper, S. R. (2015). Matriculating masculinity: Understanding undergraduate men's precollege gender socialization. *Journal of the First-Year Experience & Students in Transition*, *27*(2), 49–65.

Harvey, A., Andrewartha, L., & Burnheim, C. (2016). Out of reach? University for people from low socio-economic status backgrounds. In A. Harvey, C. Burnheim, & M. Brett (Eds.), *Student equity in Australian higher education: Twenty-five years of A Fair Chance for All* (pp. 69–87). Springer.

Hearn, J. (2013). Methods and methodologies in critical studies on men and masculinities. In B. Pini & B. Pease (Eds.), *Men, masculinities and methodologies* (pp. 26–39). Palgrave Macmillan.

Holmegaard, H. T. (2020). Complexity, negotiations, and processes: A longitudinal qualitative, narrative approach to young people's transition to and from university. In N. E. Fenton & W. Ross (Eds.), *Critical reflection on research in teaching and learning* (pp. 107–130). Brill.

Lehmann, W. (2009a). Becoming middle class: How working-class university students draw and transgress moral class boundaries. *Sociology*, *43*(4), 631–647.

Lehmann, W. (2009b). University as vocational education: Working-class students' expectations for university. *British Journal of Sociology of Education*, *30*(2), 137–149.

Lumb, M., Burke, P. J., & Bennett, A. (2020). Obscenity and fabrication in equity and widening participation methodologies. *British Educational Research Journal*, advance online publication. doi:10.1002/berj.3663

Mallman, M. (2017). The perceived inherent vice of working-class university students. *Sociological Review*, *65*(2), 235–250.

Maras, P. (2007). 'But no one in my family has been to university': Aiming higher: School students' attitudes to higher education. *Australian Educational Researcher*, *34*(3), 69–90.

McDowell, L. (2003) *Redundant masculinities? Employment change and white working class youth*. Blackwell.

McLeod, J. (2000). Subjectivity and schooling in a longitudinal study of secondary students. *British Journal of Sociology of Education*, *21*(4), 501–521.

McLeod, J. (2003). Why we interview now – Reflexivity and perspective in longitudinal studies. *International Journal of Research Methodology*, *6*(3), 201–211.

Mills, C. W. (1959). *The sociological imagination*. Oxford University Press.

Moller, M. (2007). Exploiting patterns: A critique of hegemonic masculinity. *Journal of Gender Studies*, *16*, 263–276.

Nelson, J. (2020). Relationships of (re)imagining: Black boyhood, the race–gender discipline gap, and early-childhood teacher education. *The New Educator*, *16*(2), 122–130.

Nichols, S., & Stahl, G. (2017). 'Gotta get that laziness out of me': Negotiating masculine aspirational subjectivities in the transition from school to university in Australia. In G. Stahl, J. Nelson, & D. O. Wallace (Eds.), *Masculinity and aspiration in the era of neoliberal education: International perspectives* (pp. 166–184). Routledge.

O'Shea, S., May, J., Stone, C., & Delahunty, J. (2017). *First-in-family students, university experience and family life motivations, transitions and participation*. Palgrave Macmillan.

Patfield, S., Gore, J., & Fray, L. (2020). Degrees of 'being first': Toward a nuanced understanding of first-generation entrants to higher education. *Educational Review*, advance online publication. doi:10.1080/00131911.2020.1740172

Patulny, R. (2013, July 11). Don't be fooled, loneliness affects men too. *The Conversation*.

Pease, B. (2013). Epistemology, methodology and accountability in researching men's subjectivities and practices. In B. Pini & B. Pease (Eds.), *Men, masculinities and methodologies* (pp. 39–53). Palgrave Macmillan.

Pitts, M. J., & Miller-Day, M. (2007). Upward turning points and positive rapport development across time in researcher–participant relationships. *Qualitative Research*, *7*(2), 177–201.

Pötschulat, M., Moran, M., & Jones, P. (2021). 'The student experience' and the remaking of contemporary studenthood: A critical intervention. *Sociological Review*, *69*(1), 3–20. doi:10.1177/0038026120946677

Powell, K. M., & Takayoshi, P. (2003). Accepting roles created for us: The ethics of reciprocity. *College Composition and Communication*, *54*(3), 394–422.

Ramburuth, P., & Härtel, C. (2010). Understanding and meeting the needs of students from low socioeconomic status backgrounds. *Multicultural Education and Technology Journal*, *4*(3), 153–162.

Reay, D. (2005). Beyond consciousness? The psychic landscape of social class. *Sociology*, *39*(5), 911–928.

Reichert, M., & Hawley, R. (2014). *I can learn from you: Boys as relational learners*. Harvard Education Press.

Scevak, J., Southgate, E., Rubin, M., Macqueen, S., Douglas, H., & Williams, P. (2015). *Equity groups and predictors of academic success in higher education: A 2014 Student Equity in Higher Education Research Grants project*. National Centre for Student Equity in Higher Education, Curtin University. http://bit.ly/1FU4pgj

Schwalbe, M., & Wolkomir, M. (2001). The masculine self as a problem and resource in interview studies of men. *Men and Masculinities*, *4*, 90–103.

Somers, M. (1992). Narrativity, narrative identity, and social action: Rethinking English working-class formation. *Social Science History*, *16*(4), 591–630.

Southgate, E., Douglas, H., Scevak, J., Macqueen, S., Rubin, M., & Lindell, C. (2014). The academic outcomes of first-in-family in an Australian university: An exploratory study. *International Studies in Widening Participation*, *1*(2), 31–35.

Stahl, G. (2015). *Aspiration, identity and neoliberalism: Educating white working-class boys*. Routledge.

Stahl, G. (2016). Relationship-building in research: Gendered identity construction in researcher–participant interaction. In M. R. M. Ward (Ed.), *Gendered identity construction in researcher–participant interaction* (pp. 145–164). Emerald.

Swain, J. (2005). Masculinities in education. In M. Kimmel, J. Hearn, & R. W. Connell (Eds.), *Handbook of studies on men and masculinities* (pp. 213–229). Sage.

Thomsen, J. P., Munk, M. D., Eiberg-Madsen, M., & Hansen, G. I. (2011). The educational strategies of Danish university students from professional and working-class backgrounds. *Comparative Education Review*, *57*(3), 457–480.

Thomson, R., Holland, J., McGrellis, S., Bell, R., Henderson, S., & Sharpe, S. (2004). Inventing adulthoods: A biographical approach to understanding youth citizenship. *Sociological Review*, *52*(2), 218–239.

Tomanović, S. (2018). Reconstructing changes in agency in the young people's social biographies through longitudinal qualitative research. *Young*, *27*(4), 355–372.

Willis, P. (1977). *Learning to labour: How working class kids get working class jobs*. Columbia University Press.

9 Improving the transition to university experience through policy

In Australia today, more people attend university than ever before and, furthermore, there is evidence of an increase in students from non-traditional backgrounds. Given the policy remit to widen participation, there now exist multiple pathways into university which demonstrates substantial progress; furthermore, an 'extensive body of evidence has since been built around university aspiration, awareness, access and achievement' (Harvey, Andrewartha, & Burnheim, 2016a, p. 81). However, the body of evidence reveals that access to higher education for students from low-SES backgrounds is still compounded by an array of disadvantages. Furthermore, in terms of social mobility it is important to note 'the payoffs to mass higher education are unclear, and empirical evidence for human capital style decision-making, such as the use of rates of return data, is weak' (Marginson, 2016, p. 418). Rising participation rates also do not necessarily translate into labour market advantage, producing what Brown (2013) calls 'social congestion'. The case studies presented in this book are, after all, narratives of incremental social mobility and we do not know if the experiences of these young men will lead to the employment they seek.

Clearly, university has come to mean something different within Australian society than it did a generation ago. However, it is also undeniable that universities have struggled to find the best ways to support a more diverse intake. The experiences of the young men who participated in the *First-in-Family Males Project* exist in tandem with neoliberal restructuring of university life, with what Blackmore (1997, p. 92) calls 'lean-and-mean' pedagogies of fewer contact hours, large class sizes, the rise in online learning, as well as increases in accountability and performativity measures for staff. With this in mind, scholars have called for an increase in research which will improve both the student experience and academic outcomes. Naylor et al. (2016) present an agenda for a careful consideration of 'hyper-intersectionality' in widening participation, contending that Australia needs more 'evidence-based typologies based on … needs, behaviours, or cognitive or motivational factors' (p. 269). Creating better evidence through a consideration of the different identity vectors could improve equitable outcomes through more strategic targeted support.

In this concluding chapter, I seek to make connections between the empirical data from the six case studies and policies in higher education. The application of case study inquiry requires finding connections between empirical data from the research sites and theoretical analysis drawing upon scholarly concepts which ultimately help the reader 'make sense of the case in more complex ways' (Tracy, 2013, p. 265). Embedded in the case study approach is 'the intent of developing or modifying theory' (Eidlin, 2010, p. 64) as well as influencing policy and practice. Cases, albeit unique and limited, can be used as a basis for subsequent further exploration and theorising.

Drawing on aspects of the widening participation literature, I propose some practical strategies for those working in policy and in university-based pathway programs which would make the experience of transitioning to university life easier and more rewarding for young working-class men. These are not exhaustive by any means. Those who work in positions of power are not always aware of the ways in which the working-class experience can be, and often is, shaped by poverty. Echoing the words of Rubin et al. (2019), the 'onus is on universities to adapt to working-class students rather than vice versa' (p. 96). Close attention over time to the participants' changing lifeworlds has not only problematised the rhetoric of a 'poverty of aspirations' or 'lack of aspiration', it foregrounded how class and gender work to structure the present and the future for these young men. There exists considerable work on masculinities in higher education focused on fixing men through problematising masculinities (Laker & Davis, 2011). In their research from the United States, Harris and Barone (2011) write:

> What new and important lessons might we learn from men who excel academically; consume alcohol legally and responsibly; never express and always challenge homophobia, sexism, and racism; refrain from aggression and violence when resolving conflicts; enjoy relationships with peers that are grounded in authenticity, love, and respect; and invest their time selflessly in campus activities and community service? Surely these men are present on every college campus. However, rarely are their experiences and perspectives the exclusive focus on studies of college men.
>
> (p. 60)

The six young men described in this book are exactly these men. Despite their separate challenges, they do make university work for them and they do not require fixing. What they require are effective and strategic policies to ensure that not only is the university experience enriching but they are well positioned to access gainful employment when the degree concludes. This, after all, is what determines social mobility. I will now explore how their transition to university could have been positively influenced through more effective policy implementation in five policy areas: career and subject selection counselling; employment; going together; the over-emphasis on the first year; targeted support and mentorship; and institutions working together.

Career counselling

For the most part, in Australian secondary schools, career counselling remains limited. At all stages of schooling, the abilities and interests of the students should inform how educators adapt their craft to meet their needs, but this does not always happen. Working-class young men and women need forms of schooling which broaden their views of what is possible. We are reminded here of Logan's words: 'Like at first, I didn't actually really appreciate and understand how many courses there are …' It is clear young people need strategic career as well as subject selection counselling by trained professionals. In contrast to many upper-middle-class students who, equipped with greater support networks, pursue academic pathways to university with relative ease, institutional guidance for their working-class counterparts is crucial. We see across the six case studies parents advocating for their children's choice of education, but sometimes they lack knowledge of both how admittance to higher education works and what the experience will entail, similar to other studies on first-in-family students (see Thomsen et al., 2011). Each of the boys, to varying degrees, had misunderstandings regarding university, despite their internet searches and proactively attending university open days. In figuring out university, there was an overreliance on university websites and brochures, what is considered 'cold knowledge' (Ball & Vincent, 1998; Smith, 2011). Of the six secondary schools represented in the *First-in-Family Males Project*, the school with the most resources devoted 20-minute one-to-one sessions to career counselling and an information booklet to accompany the university admissions centre guidebook. It is unclear what was offered in these 20 minutes.

Employment

Many students from working-class backgrounds spend very little time actually at university; instead their 'student experience' is framed by a rigid attention to scheduling as they often hold down multiple jobs. Obviously, these young men would have radically different university experiences if they could reduce the hours they work. There are widening participation programs that adopt a more multifaceted approach and provide financial, academic and social support simultaneously (see Hoare & Lightfoot, 2015). For example, research by Denny et al. (2014) focused on an access/pathway program aimed at first-in-family students who came from households below a certain income threshold and attended secondary schools labelled as disadvantaged. The findings of this study indicate that, with a blend of financial, academic and social support, students were able to perform academically at the same level as students entering through the standard admissions system.

In analysing the experiences with employment of these six boys, there are three things I wish to emphasise. First, most university students in Australia regardless of class background engage in some form of part-time work so the participants are not exceptional in this regard. It is normal practice within Australian society so the young men do not see it as unusual. Second, it remains unclear whether the participants in the study had to work as much as they did. Manny was the only participant who voiced a need to work when his mother lost her job. Rashid was unable to pick up casual employment during the three years and was surviving on Youth Allowance and, I assume, money his parents gave him. Third, and perhaps most important, what work itself can offer is highly variable. Lucas and Campbell have work experiences which will not only bolster their CVs but also provide them with the necessary skills and social capital to navigate the white-collar world effortlessly or, in Bourdieusian terms, *with ease* (Bourdieu, 1984). Bourdieu and Passeron (1979) write of those individuals whose capital resources foster a sense of self-assurance. Jack (2016) notes that middle-class students are much more likely to build personal relationships with authority figures and the work experiences of Lucas and Campbell suggest these opportunities afford them a chance to do the same. Furthermore, these work experiences reaffirm their aspirations and sense they are in the 'right place' and one step closer to where they want to be.

In contrast, Manny, Dominic and Logan do not accrue much in terms of capital from their service sector positions; they get very little sense of fulfillment and, while it serves as a means to an end, it also exhausts them physically. As the boys contend with fatigue, this has a knock-on effect and they invest less time in studying, maintaining past friendships or establishing new ones at university. Given the significant empirical and theoretical work on masculinities and the importance of employment as well as constant calls from government for university graduates with 'work-ready skills', it is bewildering that there is not more attention to the benefits for boys from working-class backgrounds – statistically the least likely to end up at university – of employment-related training schemes.[1]

Going together

One widening participation initiative that remains largely untapped in Australia is counteracting social isolation before it occurs by sending non-traditional students in small groups. One of the most celebrated examples of this approach is the Posse Scholars program in the United States, a non-profit organisation that aims to increase the pool of qualified, diverse students in selective universities (Contreras, 2011; Oguntoyinbo, 2014). This is a multifaceted program that adopts an array of strategies, though its signature feature is an eight-week intensive exercise to foster team building with the aim of strengthening the group – or posse. The intention is the posse will journey through university life together over the duration of the program and that peer accountability will strengthen a strong sense of purpose, self-identity and community. Evidence suggests that such an approach guards against drop-out and, by promoting a collective spirit, it can serve as a buffer for students from non-traditional backgrounds who may struggle to feel like they belong.[2]

While the Posse Scholars recruit from disadvantaged backgrounds, they do not purposefully select for gender. Based on recent scholarship concerning masculinities in higher education, it does seem that a version of the program that foregrounds gender could be useful. Davis et al. (2011) describe how male bonding 'can become congruent with inclusive, pro-social, and healthy masculinities' because young men 'need a place where they can feel vulnerable, honest, and open with each other' (pp. 150, 159). Given what we know about the discursive construction of masculinities and how masculinities are enacted and performed during the transition to university, the intentional fostering of relational connections between young men who are first-in-family could prove fruitful. After all, an integral aspect of belonging is the opportunity to care for others. Drawing on theories of masculinities and 'affective sociality', young men value spaces where there is 'active engagement with the care of the self at the same time as caring for others' (Loeser, 2014, p. 194). The approach of the posse program, which promotes the importance of a close-knit social group of peers, could have counteracted feelings of isolation for Manny and Logan. In fact, in examining these six case studies it seems like elements of the posse program seem to develop naturally, for example Rashid relied heavily on his friends from secondary school who supported him at university.

The over-emphasis on the first year

The six case studies presented provide a glimpse into the experiences of the participants who had various struggles but ultimately did make university work for them, though often more in an academic sense than a social sense. In Australia, the social integration of students primarily takes place in and around the Orientation Week, although, depending on the program, there will be events throughout the first year with the aim of building a sense of belonging in the cohort. Orientation Week itself often serves more as a promotion of the university through branding than as a way to foster bonds amongst students. However, Orientation Week, while a crucial point in the participants' journeys as learners, was not the only crucial point. Part of this over-emphasis on the first few weeks is to make university as enjoyable as possible so students will not drop out before the census date, reflecting an agenda founded on what Lynch et al. (2015) call a 'bums-on-seats' approach to widening participation. Even within this small subset of data it is clear that support structures need to go far beyond the transition into the first year (Harvey, Burnheim, & Brett, 2016b; Stahl et al., 2020). The journeys of each of the young men presented here suggest a variety of support structures need to be available prior to the transition to university life and throughout academic careers.

An over-emphasis on the first year also ignores the chopping and changing of trajectories over the course of study. When students falter academically – through reducing timetables or retaking courses they have failed (e.g. Manny and Logan) – they become out of sync with their cohort. As a result, they have to renegotiate the social aspect of university and failure to do so successfully could mean they experience a fragmentation in their sense of belonging. Furthermore, while this process can occur at any stage in a student's time at university, it often happens during the first year during a time when the new shine of university has begun to wear off. An obvious improvement here would be multiple points where there are 'opportunities to integrate' throughout the first semester as vulnerability occurs at multiple points in the journey of the learner.

Targeted support and mentorship

The institutions these young men attend have substantial support efforts in place, though these are mainly in the core literacy and numeracy skills. However, while each participant was aware of these services, they did not use them and their words suggest they did not necessarily see the need. Research continues to document that young men at university often are reluctant to seek out forms of support (Harper & Harris, 2010). Within the six case studies, it was mainly Manny and Logan who required academic support though it seems that work in maths and literacy was not what was needed but instead intensive tutoring in chemistry in Manny's case and molecular biological sciences for Logan.

Australia has a robust funding agenda to promote mentorship programs that respond to the under-representation in higher education of people from low-SES backgrounds, specifically through the Higher Education Participation and Partnerships Program (HEPPP) (see Geagea & MacCallum, 2020; Lynch et al., 2015; for full listing see Beltman et al., 2017). Typically, within the higher education context 'support' is considered primarily in academic terms and a wider conception of support is needed focused on the lifeworlds of the participants where future aspirations and current experiences are considered in tandem with one another. Rashid, Manny, Logan – and even to a certain extent Dominic – would have benefited from such a form of targeted support. There exists robust research on various forms of mentoring for students from low-SES backgrounds and, within this, the most salient seem to be mentorship from those current working in industry (typically alumni from the university) and peer mentorship. Such forms of mentorship facilitate access to social and cultural capital (Geagea & MacCallum, 2020) as well as 'hot knowledge' which students from low-SES backgrounds find essential for navigating university life. When 'hot knowledge' is conveyed affectively, through a trusted source, this can be a powerful determiner of success at university (see Smith, 2011). Furthermore, in considering the salience of a gender dimension to mentorship, Morales' (2009) work on Dominican American first-generation male college students draws attention to mentors' critical role as 'approvers', where they are 'legitimizing, encouraging, and facilitating the participants' educational plans' as a figurative 'stamp of approval' (pp. 395–396). Smith et al. (2019) note that mentoring programs for men – specifically men of colour – can foster a more seamless transition to university life through bolstering confidence and resilience.

The importance of targeted support is made clear through the case study of Manny, who attended a university without a program targeting the Pacific Islander community, perhaps due to not having a sizeable enough population. In contrast, two other universities in the study had very well-funded and strategic initiatives to recruit, engage and support Pacific Islander students throughout their studies. Many other boys in the *First-in-Family Males Project* benefited from such a culture-based approach and, if Manny had attended a university with a similar support structure in place, it may have assisted him greatly when he struggled. Though, it should be noted, Manny could have accessed other forms of support present at his working-class university but either did not allow himself enough time to do so or did not feel comfortable accessing the different types of support available.

Institutions working together

Bolstered by HEPPP funding, there is evidence of universities and secondary schools working together to increase students' access to university (see Geagea & MacCallum, 2020; Lynch et al., 2015). Research has noted that first-in-family students can often be enrolled in access courses prior to their entry into university, which 'seems to have trained them with an educationally oriented habitus, cultural capital, and dispositions to interpret university-level work and assessments' (Wong, 2018, p. 5). Manny and Dominic were part of a specialist higher-level maths course in their final years of compulsory schooling, which involved spending one afternoon a week at the university they eventually both attended. Though participating in an advanced maths program should have assisted Manny to familiarise himself with the university space and perhaps bolstered his confidence, this did not seem the case.

By his own admission, Manny was way out of his depth in the engineering program, having never completed chemistry in high school. Bolstering his ATAR with bonus points – to compensate for educational disadvantage – did not necessarily set him up for success although evidence suggests that low-SES students are successful even with low scores (Denny et al., 2014; Harvey & Burnheim 2013) and school attributes (i.e. school type and student population) are responsible for almost 20% of the ATAR variation between students (Gemici et al. 2013). At the end of the day, these are simply numbers on a piece of paper and not interchangeable with authentic learning experiences. Lecturers rarely check student ATARs, or consider where they attended school or what courses students have taken in Year 12. Furthermore, in large first-year courses it would be very difficult to create a class profile and tailor the pedagogy to fit the needs of the students. As most universities now offer special entry access schemes such as enabling programs (Pitman et al. 2016; Vernon et al. 2019) and remedial enabling programs which are undertaken concurrently with university study to compensate for different types of disadvantage (Harvey, Andrewartha, & Burnheim, 2016a), it is worth considering that Manny may have benefited from an enabling program.

Concluding thoughts

Despite a substantial policy agenda to widen participation for students from non-traditional backgrounds, these students still remain severely under-represented in the Australian higher education system. The six in-depth longitudinal case studies from the *First-in-Family Males Project* highlight how they engage with the complex social inequalities. The boys in this study are embedded in social practices which are grounded in a working-class context and they are in search of ways to adopt subjectivities which will help them move beyond their working-class roots. As the young men enter higher education we see that they are agentic within the institutional constraints as they balance family, service work, peer groups and academic study. Such a delicate balance determines how their aspirations are realised. With this in mind, these case studies speak to the relationship between masculinities and social class – they illuminate some of the ways social class is etched on masculinity and vice versa as masculinities are performed in relation to class as an affective and lived experience. As they experience *being* and *becoming* university students, the young men enter into universities as future-oriented spaces where there is an in-built expectation that they will self-craft in order to become employment ready. Such is the production of the university student where aspects of the self are shifted and realigned. In reflecting back on the research, I am left with, to borrow from Denny et al. (2014), the importance of 'money, mentoring and making friends' in widening participation. For upwardly mobile working-class men to find some fulfillment in higher education it appears they need to have all three.

I would like to thank the Australian Research Council for funding this research.

Notes

1 To be clear, work-integrated learning (Universities Australia, 2019) does exist in Australia, stemming from the 2015 National Strategy on Work Integrated Learning in University Education, but only one student in the First-in-Family Males Project participated to my knowledge.
2 This program is not without its critiques and it can differ depending on the locale. Students undergo a rigid and competitive selection process and entry into the program does usually come with a generous scholarship.

References

Ball, S.J., & Vincent, C. (1998). 'I heard it on the grapevine': 'Hot' knowledge and school choice. *British Journal of Sociology of Education, 27*(1), 377–400.
Beltman, S., Samani, S., & Ala'i, K. (2017). *Mentoring programs and equity groups: The Australian story*. National Centre for Student Equity in Higher Education, Curtin University.
Blackmore, J. (1997). Disciplining feminism: A look at gender-equity struggles in Australian higher education. In L. G. Romand & L. Eyre (Eds.), *Dangerous territories: Struggles for difference and equality in education* (pp. 75–96). Routledge.
Bourdieu, P. (1984). *Distinction: A social critique of the judgement of taste*. Routledge.

Bourdieu, P., & Passeron, J.-C. (1979). *The inheritors: French students and their relation to culture*. University of Chicago Press.

Brown, P. (2013). Education, opportunity, and the prospects for social mobility. *British Journal of Sociology of Education*, 34(5–6), 678–700.

Contreras, F. (2011). Strengthening the bridge to higher education for academically promising underrepresented students. *Journal of Advanced Academics, 22*(3), 500–526.

Davis, T., LaPrad, J., & Dixon, S. (2011). Masculinities reviewed and reinterpreted. In J. A. Laker & T. Davis (Eds.), *Masculinities in higher education: Theoretical and practical considerations* (pp. 147–160). Routledge.

Denny, K., Doyle, O., McMullin, P., & O'Sullivan, V. (2014). Money, mentoring and making friends: The impact of a multidimensional access program on student performance. *Economics of Education Review, 40*, 167–182.

Eidlin, F. (2010) Case study and theoretical science. In A. J. Mills, G. Durepos, & E. Wiebe (Eds.), *Encyclopedia of case study research* (pp. 65–66). Sage.

Geagea, A., & MacCallum, J. (2020). Murdoch's Aspirations and Pathways for University (MAP4U) Project: Developing and supporting low SES students' aspirations for higher education participation using school-based university outreach programs. In G. Crimmins (Ed.), *Strategies for supporting inclusion and diversity in the academy: Higher education, aspiration and inequality* (pp. 287–306). Palgrave Macmillan.

Gemici, S., Lim, P., & Karmel, T. (2013). *The impact of schools on young people's transition to university*. NCVER.

Harper, S. R., & Harris, F., III. (2010). Beyond the model gender majority myth: Responding equitably to the developmental needs and challenges of college men. In S. R. Harper & F. Harris III (Eds.), *College men and masculinities: Theory, research, and implications for practice* (pp. 1–16). Jossey-Bass.

Harris, F., III. & Barone, R. (2011). The situation of men, and situating men in higher education: A conversation about crisis, myth, and reality about college students who are men. In T. Davis & J. A. Laker (Eds.), *Masculinities in higher education: Theoretical and practical considerations* (pp. 50–78). Routledge.

Harvey, A., Andrewartha, L., & Burnheim, C. (2016a). Out of reach? University for people from low socio-economic status backgrounds. In A. Harvey, C. Burnheim, & M. Brett (Eds.), *Student equity in Australian higher education: Twenty-five years of A Fair Chance for All* (pp. 69–87). Springer.

Harvey, A., & Burnheim, C. (2013). Loosening old school ties: Understanding university achievement and attrition by school type. *Professional Voice, 9*(2), 29–36.

Harvey, A., Burnheim, C., & Brett, M. (Eds.). (2016b). *Student equity in Australian higher education: Twenty-five years of A Fair Chance for All*. Springer.

Hoare, T., & Lightfoot, J. (2015). Student funding, student retention and student experiences: Perspectives from Bristol. *Widening Participation and Lifelong Learning, 17*(3), 110–125.

Jack, A. A. (2016). (No) harm in asking: Class, acquired cultural capital, and academic engagement at an elite university. *Sociology of Education, 89*(1), 1–19.

Laker, J. A., & Davis, T. (Eds.). (2011). *Masculinities in higher education: Theoretical and practical considerations*. Routledge.

Loeser, C. (2014). The potentialities of post-essentialism for hearing (dis)abled masculinities in friendship. In F. G. Karioris & C. Loeser (Eds.), *Reimagining masculinities: Beyond masculinist epistemology* (pp. 193–219). Inter-Disciplinary Press.

Lynch, J., Walker-Gibbs, B., & Herbert, S. (2015). Moving beyond a 'bums-on-seats' analysis of progress towards widening participation: Reflections on the context, design and evaluation of an Australian government-funded mentoring programme. *Journal of Higher Education Policy and Management*, *37*(2), 144–158.

Marginson, S. (2016). The worldwide trend to high participation higher education: Dynamics of social stratification in inclusive systems. *Higher Education*, *72*, 413–434.

Morales, E. E. (2009). Legitimizing hope: An exploration of effective mentoring for Dominican American male college students. *Journal of College Student Retention: Research, Theory & Practice*, *11*(3), 385–406.

Naylor, R., Coates, H., & Kelly, P. (2016). From equity to excellence: Reforming Australia's national framework to create new forms of success. In A. Harvey, C. Burnheim, & M. Brett (Eds.), *Student equity in Australian higher education: Twenty-five years of A Fair Chance for All* (pp. 257–275). Springer.

Oguntoyinbo, L. (2014). Posse program. *Diverse Issues in Higher Education*, *31*(6), 14.

Pitman, T., Trinidad, S., Devlin, M., Harvey, A., Brett, M., & McKay, J. (2016). *Pathways to higher education: The efficacy of enabling and sub-bachelor pathways for disadvantaged students*. National Centre for Student Equity in Higher Education, Curtin University.

Rubin, M., Evans, O., & McGuffog, R. (2019). Social class differences in social integration at university: Implications for academic outcomes and mental health. In J. Jetten & K. Peters (Eds.), *The social psychology of inequality* (pp. 87–102). Springer.

Smith, L. (2011). Experiential 'hot' knowledge and its influence on low-SES students' capacities to aspire to higher education. *Critical Studies in Education*, *52*(2), 165–177.

Smith, T., Klobassa, V., & Salinas Jr, C. (2019). Men's peer education and mentoring programs. In D. Tillapaugh & B. L. McGowan (Eds.), *Men and masculinities: Theoretical foundations and promising practices for supporting college men's development* (pp. 147–165). Stylus Publishing.

Stahl, G., McDonald, S., & Stokes, J. (2020). 'I see myself as undeveloped': Supporting Indigenous first-in-family males in the transition to higher education. *Higher Education Research & Development*, *39*(7), 1488–1501.

Thomsen, J. P., Munk, M. D., Eiberg-Madsen, M., & Hansen, G. I. (2011). The educational strategies of Danish university students from professional and working-class backgrounds. *Comparative Education Review*, *57*(3), 457–480.

Tracy, S. J. (2013). *Qualitative research methods: Collecting evidence, crafting analysis, communicating impact*. Wiley-Blackwell.

Universities Australia. (2019). *Work-integrated learning in universities: Final report*. https://apo.org.au/sites/default/files/resource-files/2019-04/apo-nid242371.pdf

Vernon, L., Watson, S. J., Moore, W., & Seddon, S. (2019). University enabling programs while still at school: Supporting the transition of low-SES students from high school to university. *Australian Educational Researcher*, *46*, 498–509.

Wong, B. (2018). By chance or by plan? The academic success of nontraditional students in higher education. *AERA Open*, *4*(2), 1–14.

Index